AFTER SPUTNIK

On October 4, 1957 in the midst of the Cold War, the Soviet Union launched Sputnik I, the first artificial earth satellite. For the West, and especially the United States, it was a shattering blow to national morale and pride. It led to a deep-seated fear that the Soviet Union would surpass the United States in both technology and power and that even nuclear war might be near.

After Sputnik shows that the late 1950s were not an era of complacency and smugness, but were some of the most anxious years in American history. The Cold War was by no means a time of peace. It was an era of a different kind of battle—one that took place in negotiations and in the internal affairs of many countries, but not always on the battlefield. While many choose to remember President Eisenhower as a near-pacifist, his actions in Lebanon, the Taiwan Straits crisis, Berlin, and elsewhere proved otherwise. Seconded by his able secretary of state, John Foster Dulles, he steered America through some of the most difficult parts of the Cold War, not always succeeding, but preventing disaster. The Middle East and Berlin crises, the Indonesian Civil War, Fidel Castro's rise to power, and other events are all bluntly discussed in the light of Western, and other, illusions and delusions.

In this engaging history, Alan J. Levine delves deeply into this often misrepresented period of history, and provides new insight into one of the most formative decades in American history.

Alan J. Levine is a historian and adjunct assistant professor of history at Borough of Manhattan Community College. He specializes in twentieth-century international relations and the history of World War II and the Cold War, and has written eleven books.

AFTER SPUTNIK

America, the World, and Cold War Conflicts

Alan J. Levine

Routledge
Taylor & Francis Group

NEW YORK AND LONDON

First published 2018
by Routledge
711 Third Avenue, New York, NY 10017

and by Routledge
2 Park Square, Milton Park, Abingdon, Oxon, OX14 4RN

Routledge is an imprint of the Taylor & Francis Group, an informa business

Library of Congress Cataloging-in-Publication Data
A catalog record for this book has been requested

ISBN: 978-1-412-86512-8 (hbk)
ISBN: 978-1-412-86548-7 (pbk)
ISBN: 978-1-351-29512-3 (ebk)

Typeset in Bembo
by Swales & Willis Ltd, Exeter, Devon, UK

MIX
Paper from
responsible sources
FSC
www.fsc.org   FSC™ C013985

Printed in the United Kingdom
by Henry Ling Limited

CONTENTS

Introduction   1

1 Eisenhower's Paradise? America in the Late 1950s   4

2 Cold War Policy and Military Strategy to 1958   24

3 The Enemy: Khrushchev's USSR   46

4 The Sputnik Shock   57

5 The "Missile Gap" and Space Race   75

6 The Muddled East: The Middle East Crisis of 1958 and
   the Lebanon Landing   90

7 Battle in the Taiwan Strait: The Second
   "Quemoy–Matsu Crisis"   117

8 The Berlin Crisis   140

9 The Last Domino: American Intervention in the
   Indonesian Civil War   159

10 The Rise of the "Maximum Leader": The Cuban
    Revolution, Castro, and Latin America   177

Epilogue   209
Index   210

INTRODUCTION

This book recounts the story of the United States and the Cold War in a very special period that has not been adequately dealt with, the late 1950s, after the orbiting of the first earth satellite, Sputnik I. It is perhaps now the hardest part of the Cold War to understand, for it was the part of the conflict that seems the strangest following the collapse of the USSR. It was the sole period of the Cold War in which the Western world feared an imminent Soviet military superiority, even, fantastic as it now seems, that the Soviet Union was overtaking it on a broad front, and even surpassing it economically! At best, the Cold War then looked like an interminable conflict. As President Eisenhower remarked, it might well go on for another forty or fifty years. There was no expectation, and less hope, that it would soon end.

For the only way it could end soon, people thought, was by a horrible war that could end everything, or a Western collapse before Soviet blackmail. And, while a rapid and overt collapse was not a real danger, in one or two cases, notably Berlin, and the Taiwan Straits, the Communist great powers may have come dangerously close to wearing down or splitting the Western powers sufficiently to get agreements that would have enabled them to gradually undermine the Western positions in both places. But, miscalculating, they just overreached themselves sufficiently to miss their chances.

That era saw no less than three major international crises, and several smaller ones, in which, apart from the apparent growth in Soviet power, the Western powers and their allies faced not only Soviet power but also adverse trends in the underdeveloped countries. I have tried to describe these crises and their background, which often proves an interesting if complex story, for most Cold War crises were a mixture of local conflicts, often revolving around issues of immediate interest, originally, only to the often bewildered local peoples involved, but in which the big powers were entangled. In discussing these local issues I have sometimes been a bit more blunt than has been fashionable. But I hope that I have been just as blunt in discussing Western delusions and illusions.

The facts of this era may often be surprising. Many myths are punctured, most notably, the common picture of the 1950s as a period of complacency and smugness. The late 1950s in particular were some of the least complacent, most anxious years in American history. Another myth is that the Cold War was just a Soviet–American duel in which others were bystanders or pawns. That idea, to be sure was always incompatible with the once well-known role of the British in the early stages of the Cold War, during and right after World War II, but, along with the related idea that the United States was always "harder" or more "trigger-happy" than its allies is no truer of the later period. There were often sharp differences between the leading Western power and its allies, but they do not conform to this stereotype. One of the Americans' problems, in fact, was that they believed that the Chinese Nationalists were deliberately trying to drag them into war! Other allies—not only the Nationalists but the British, French, Turks, and Israelis all turn out to have taken a harder line in this or that crisis than the Eisenhower Administration—the French over Indochina and Berlin, and the British and Turks over the Middle East.

On the other hand, President Eisenhower was basically a hard-liner, not a near-pacifist as has sometimes recently been pictured. As we shall see, in the Taiwan Straits crisis he took an exceedingly hard line, going far beyond American (much less Allied) popular opinion. This should be yet another nail in the coffin of the once-popular idea that he was a passive, complacent president. Instead, teamed with Secretary of State Dulles, he closely supervised foreign policy, and energetically pushed new military programs and even new modes of management and drastic reorganizations of the military and space research.

Some of the other myths that are disposed of are the centrality of the Arab–Israeli conflict in the Middle East, and the supposed uselessness of the intermediate-range ballistic missiles installed in Britain in the late 1950s. Some matters have simply been forgotten or disregarded—notably the CIA's aid to Castro, and the latter's strange plans for conflict with the United States. Another surprise is John Foster Dulles' private pessimistic view of the West's chances in the Cold War.

Contrary to a widely held view, the Eisenhower Administration was well aware that many of the problems in the underdeveloped world were not created by the Soviets or other Communists, however much they were exploited by them. Some things ought not be a surprise, but have often been forgotten—notably the American public's enthusiasm for Castro and some elements of the fashionable contemporary liberal critique of the Eisenhower Administration. As we shall see, Eisenhower and Dulles were more able and interesting than has been thought. And they dealt with a remarkable rogue's galley—outright enemies like Khrushchev, Mao, Nasser, Sukarno, and Castro, but also dubious allies like Chiang Kai-shek. Some of these men prove interesting, if different from the way they have often been perceived. Khrushchev was hardly the "almost fondly remembered uncle-like character actor" as Peter Wyden sarcastically described later American perceptions of him, while Castro was an extraordinary man as brilliant in his rise to power as his later rule over Cuba was disastrous. Others of the West's foes turn out to be fools or clowns—but nevertheless dangerous fools and clowns.

My evaluations of what happened may be different from that of many others who have dealt with the Cold War. That is because I, as many others do not, take the Cold War seriously. It *was* a war, short of all-out war, but a war nevertheless, and very different from "peacetime."

And that is the way most Americans thought of it at the time; a time in which the happy conclusion to the struggle that we take for granted now, was far off. It will be observed that the United States, and the other Western powers, during this period, were not always exactly punctilious in their observation of international norms—notably in plotting the overthrow of hostile governments, usually through covert means, but sometimes considering outright armed intervention. That is often considered shocking or outrageous nowadays, but against the background of a deadly struggle with what was perceived, and rightly, as an evil enemy, which itself had engaged in the overthrow of governments and had famously broken vital agreements, the moralistic criticisms of such behavior often uttered are not very convincing. That is not to say that covert operations were beyond criticism—in fact, as we shall see, they usually failed. But the attitudes often taken toward such things are all too often one-sided and unrealistic.

1

EISENHOWER'S PARADISE?

America in the Late 1950s

A bit over half a century ago, conditions obtained in the United States that may seem rather strange today. Americans enjoyed a high degree of national unity and morale, proud of the successes of American society, which they expected to continue, and confident in the justice of their cause in the deadly struggle against Communist totalitarianism.

A well-distributed prosperity, low unemployment and inflation, conditions of greater social equality than ever before or after, coincided with high income taxes and huge defense costs, which consumed well over half the budget of a federal government rather smaller than the one we are used to. Prosperity for private enterprise coincided with a union movement stronger than ever before or after. Working men could usually support families reasonably well without another family member working, although an increasing number of married as well as single women did work. The middle class grew rather than shrank, indeed it seemed to many that the middle class, and suburbs, would devour the rest of society, and some people professed to see this as a bad thing. Divorce rates were stable or declining, after a rash of dissolutions of hasty wartime marriages contracted during World War II. "Single-parent families" were rare, often the product of death rather than divorce or a failure to marry. (There was a slight increase in illegitimate births during the 1950s.) Drug use was rare, and crime rates stable or declining.

Homelessness was almost unheard of. People, who, in later decades would have roamed city streets were in mental hospitals, or housed, if very badly, in distinct "Skid Rows."

On the other hand, people smoked like chimneys—half of American men, and 30 percent of women, smoked. Diets, by later standards, were rather unhealthy, heavy in red meat and eggs, although people were far less apt to be

grossly obese than Americans of the twenty-first century. The disenfranchise-
ment and segregation of blacks in the South was only beginning to crack. There
was still much poverty, but it was rapidly declining, and not a few people saw
other problems, but by every material measure life was incomparably better
than it had been before World War II. People saw problems, but they expected
them to be resolved, one way or another, sooner or later, and they had a high
degree of confidence in most institutions. More important, perhaps, they had
confidence in themselves, and their ability to determine their lives and the way
society would go. The idea that social and political elites could get away with
the high-handed, stupid, and anti-social actions they would carry out in the
1960s and after would have met general disbelief in the 1950s.

Americans' main fears were oriented outside, toward the Cold War enemy,
the apparently still solid Soviet–Chinese alliance, and the fear, not just of an
"ordinary" war—"another Korea" as most people conceived of it in the 1950s
and early 1960s (most Americans would have thought that they would be lucky
to avoid even that)—but of a nuclear war that could end just about everything. This, of course, was hardly an American peculiarity. As Bertrand Russell
remarked, "The world in which we are now living would have seemed, before
1945, too horrible to be endured. But we have gotten used to it."[1] Fear of
nuclear war alone insured that, contrary to a widely accepted but absurd stereotype, the 1950s—and especially the last two years of that decade—were
one of the most anxious, least complacent periods in American history.[2] But in
the last resort, most people did think, most of the time, that they would avoid
nuclear destruction, and even most of those most critical of the existing state
of things, saw the arrow of change flying upward, toward a future of greater
prosperity, freedom, and happiness. That corresponded, in fact, to their current
experience.

The greatest fears of the 1950s would not be fulfilled, but neither would
most of the hopes.

Population and Economy

The American population, just under 175 million in 1958 (it had been just 150
million in 1950) was growing rapidly. This was not due to immigration, which
remained low despite many exceptions made to the old national origins system
but by an extraordinarily high birth rate, which—like most aspects of the postwar era—had not been expected by earlier forecasters.[3] The baby boom began
to drop off after 1957 but continued through 1964.

The American population was overwhelmingly composed of native-born
whites; the offspring of the "new immigration" of 1880–1920 seemed to have
been largely assimilated, and the old foreign-language enclaves in the great cities
were dying out. Indeed, to the surprise of many, the descendants of some later
groups were outdoing old stock white Protestants economically. There had

been a serious problem of illegal immigration from Mexico in the late 1940s and early 1950s. But that unwanted influx, in another vivid contrast with the way things were handled, or not handled, later, was expeditiously reversed by the Eisenhower Administration. Its bluntly named "Operation Wetback" unceremoniously hustled over a million Mexicans home in 1954 with little difficulty and no public protest, or indeed much attention, outside the Southwest.

High domestic population growth in the postwar era may have had negative aspects in the long run, but was one factor in the postwar economic boom. Other elements accounting for the long postwar prosperity were the pent-up demand for consumer goods dating back to the Depression and increased purchasing power accumulated by high wartime wages and savings, the expansion of plants and tool capacity, and new technological developments fostered by World War II and continuing advances in productivity, easy credit, and the generally wise policies of the Truman and Eisenhower Administrations. A stream of novelties appeared: television, air conditioning, jet travel, tape recorders and hi-fi, credit cards, antibiotics, antihistamines, washers and driers, synthetics, ball-point pens, Polaroid quick-developing cameras, computers, and Xerox machines. From 1948–1973, the economy grew at an average of 3.7 percent per annum. Even in the most serious postwar recession, that of 1957–1958, it would continue to grow, the Gross National Product increasing from $442.7 billion in 1957 to $444.5 billion in the following year. In contrast to later periods, that growth was well distributed. Real wages and median family income both grew 30 percent in the decade of the 1950s, and stock ownership almost tripled.

The postwar economy was dominated by the domestic production of durable consumer goods—most of all, cars and housing. Although Western Europe and Japan had fully recovered from the war by the latter half of the 1950s, the low level of imports of 1929 would not be reached again until 1969. Industry was still concentrated in its traditional strongholds of the Northeast and Middle West. Although, starting in World War II, the domination of those regions had begun to be diluted by the development of the West and South, no one, in the 1950s, would have understood the expression "rust belt." Detroit and Pittsburgh were still bywords for heavy industry. One change that was expected, and caused some worry, was automation, which was expected to displace many workers but assure shorter hours and greater leisure. That, sixty years later, the typical working week was hardly shorter than in the 1950s, would have amazed everyone.

Most big American industries were "oligopolies," neither monopolies nor examples of traditional competition. The car industry was the greatest of all, overwhelmingly dominated by GM, Ford, and Chrysler, with American Motors and Studebaker the last holdouts among the small producers. American prospered for a time, when efficient small cars came into fashion in the late 1950s.

The "Big Three" carmakers were so strong that the second biggest, Ford, was no more than staggered by the most notorious business flop of the era, the failure of its new Edsel line, which generated more jokes than any other event of the late 1950s. The automobile manufacturers were not only the biggest of big businesses, but the most influential, sparking the reorganization of many great corporations along new lines—the decentralized, multi-divisional organization pioneered by Du Pont and GM between the World Wars, and popularized by Peter Drucker's famous book *The Concept of the Corporation*, which rested on a study of GM during World War II. It proved vastly more effective than the traditional "functional" organizations for big business, and seemed to be one of the factors guaranteeing the supposed near immortality of America's biggest companies. Although in the long run the new form of corporation had more problematic results, fostering the domination of accountants and lawyers unfamiliar with, or even hostile to, the basic tasks of production and product development, it and the basic forms of mass production, spread into all forms of business, even housing and "fast food."

In contrast to the period after the 1970s, the United States had a lively consumer electronics industry—in fact, it had created the consumer electronics industry. Electronic computers were rare, huge mainframes operated by government agencies, universities, and a few big businesses. Solid-state devices were just beginning to eliminate the old vacuum tube. Long-distance phone calls were costly, and people still communicated by telegram. They flew, mostly, in propeller-driven planes—when they flew; only the last generation of prop-driven airliners could make non-stop flights from the Eastern seaboard to London or Paris. Some cities were still served by streetcars and trolley buses. Coal-fired boilers and horse-driven "junk" wagons, while not common, could still be seen in cities. Air conditioning, while becoming common, was not yet universal; summer in a big city could be purgatory. Containerization had not yet started; freighters were still tediously loaded and unloaded by big gangs of often gangster-dominated longshoremen. New York was still a dominant port, as well as an industrial center.

Regional distinctions, while shrinking, were still strong. The South was still alien territory to most outsiders, even though many elderly Northerners were starting to retire to Florida. Even Northern whites not especially worked up about racial matters tended to think of the South as a sort of giant-sized Dogpatch, the setting of Al Capp's immensely popular comic strip *Lil' Abner* (adapted very successfully as a Broadway musical and movie in that era), while some Southerners were not done with refighting the Civil War.

Northern cities were still overwhelmingly white. New York, while it contained chunks of almost every ethnic group, was still overwhelmingly a Jewish, Irish, and Italian town, just as it had been when the twentieth century began. Its popular mayor, Robert Wagner, son of the great New Deal Senator, was regarded as a fit successor to the great LaGuardia. Puerto Ricans were becoming an important part of the mix, but otherwise Spanish-speakers were limited to the Southwest.

The government had long since picked off the last important Jewish mobs, and organized crime was tightly controlled by the Sicilian Mafia. It behaved more circumspectly than in the Capone era, and suffered neither serious competition from newer groups nor much government harassment. But a long series of exposes and Congressional investigations were producing growing public anger against organized crime, although crime rates in general were low. Late in the decade, President Eisenhower, fed up with J. Edgar Hoover's excuses, finally made the FBI begin to seriously tackle the problem.

Balancing the power of big business and government, it seemed, was a strong union movement. People often spoke of Big Government, Big Business, and Big Labor in the same breath. The union movement, reunited in the AFL-CIO in 1955, was at the peak of its strength, mobilizing 35 percent of non-farm workers. In contrast to later eras, unions organized overwhelmingly workers in private enterprise, not government. Public worker unions were weak numerically and even less influential than their numbers might have suggested. Strong unions seemed perfectly compatible with business success and a vibrant economy. It was not obvious, however, that the labor movement had hit its ceiling. It had basically finished the job of organizing heavy industries during World War II, but had failed to penetrate the South, and had lost morale and public support. The utterly irresponsible behavior of some major unions during and right after the war, and growing recognition of organized crime penetration of some others, had rather tarnished the labor mystique, and cost labor much public sympathy, while many liberals were getting a bit bored with labor and its problems. Still, unions secured major gains for their members, to the point that some working-class people were better off than some in traditional middle-class occupations.

The composition of the work force was changing. In 1956, for the first time, white-collar workers outnumbered blue collars. There was slow but steady growth in female employment. By the mid-1950s, women formed just under one-third of the work force and by the end of the decade 35 percent of adult women worked outside the home compared with 29 percent in 1950. Blacks, moving north, were a substantial component of the work force in the "smoke-stack industries" of the Midwest and Northeast. The male black labor force participation rate—the proportion of black men employed—actually slightly exceeded that of white men. Unions, the general economic advance, and the growth of higher education—access to which was fostered by the GI Bill, and that showed a higher "return on investment" than it did later, enabled many to rise in society, and with the general post-New Deal egalitarian ethos, further blurred boundaries between social classes in the United States.[4]

To be sure, many people remained poor, but one reason that poverty remained an issue of relatively slight political interest in the 1950s was that the poor were a rapidly diminishing minority whose own standard of living was rising. There are different standards for just what constituted poverty, but most estimates cluster about those of Herman Miller, suggesting that the percentage of the population who were poor declined from about 27 percent in 1950 to 21 percent by 1960. More pessimistic observers, like Michael Harrington, regarded about 25 percent as poor in 1960.[5] Even the pessimistic estimates suggest that, had the rate at which poverty was being diminished in the 1950s only been maintained, poverty in the United States should have vanished entirely in the 1980s, if not before.

The era saw a huge redistribution of population, much of what took the form of what is still usually called "suburbanization" but really constituted a general decentralization of business and industry as well as residences from the older central cities. Of the 13 million houses built from 1947–1958, 11 million were in the suburbs. By the 1960 Census, suburbs contained at least one-third of the population, and by some estimates less restrictive in classifying just what constituted a suburb, much more. Businesses increasingly migrated there. "Suburbanization" was accompanied by the enormous growth of the "car culture" of malls, motels, drive-ins, and "fast food" restaurants that had been only incipient before World War II. The traditional rural population also declined. Many farmers abandoned their occupations. In some years during the 1950s nearly a million people left the farms.

Suburbs, however, were widely disliked by intellectuals and the opinion-forming media. With more reason, many criticized overdependence on the excessively large, overpowered, over-decorated, and unsafe cars of the period. Few, however, offered sensible alternatives to either suburbia or the car. (New public housing and the few new mass-transit operations were poorly designed.) Despite decentralization, the wheezing commuter rail lines blundered on, and overall railroad passenger traffic dropped 30 percent from 1947–1958; even for freight, railroads were being beaten out by other forms of transportation. So were ships; for the first time, in 1958, more people crossed the Atlantic by plane than ocean liner.[6]

Mood and Politics

The great advance had already lasted so long that it had begun to seem normal, even tiresome to some. To most older people, with vivid recollections of the Depression and war—many of working age could recall the first of the World Wars—it still seemed magical, a life better than anyone had ever expected, while by 1958, people were entering adult life who had no memory at all of the Great Depression and only faint childhood memories of wartime. The strange combination of prosperity and stability at home, and the Cold War struggle abroad seemed more or less normal to them, even, sometimes, boring. Some of the older generation were starting to decide that the Cold War bored them, a key, perhaps, to some attitudes that became common later.[7] Unfortunately, as we shall see, the Communist powers failed to share this mood.

The domestic politics of the late 1950s would not have startled anyone twenty years earlier. They represented the continuation of the approximate deadlock that had developed in 1938 between conservatives and liberals. The traditional two-party division and organization, or lack of it, was still intact. The Democrats remained the majority party. The Republicans had ridden Eisenhower's coat tails into control of Congress in 1952, but had promptly lost both houses in 1954. Eisenhower's triumphant reelection was a personal victory, not a party one. The major parties had not yet reformed along ideological lines. Both still contained significant liberal and conservative wings. The Republicans were not the "conservative" party, just the "more conservative" party, the Democrats merely the "more liberal" party. Many Republicans were liberals, while many Southern Democrats were to the right of almost any Republican. The Democrats still overwhelmingly dominated the South, although, thanks to Eisenhower, the Republicans had begun to crack the "Solid South." (Actually, a return to the situation of the late 1920s, before the Great Depression caused many Southerners to flee back to their traditional allegiance.) Thanks to their long careers, resulting seniority, and the traditional rules and customs of Congress, conservative Southerners dominated Congress when there was a Democratic majority, and Southern Committee Chairmen were in a position to block liberal and civil rights legislation. Conservative Southerners were loosely allied with conservative Republicans, although the latter almost always disagreed with them on civil rights and some other matters. Conservative rural areas, both Democratic and Republican, were overrepresented in Congress. For all these reasons, in the 1950s the legislative branch was more conservative than most Americans. While the latter might have liked a somewhat more liberal course, they were not, however, deeply stirred in that direction. Unless liberal Democrats not only secured the presidency but a huge majority in Congress, there was little prospect for massive change. This worked both ways, however, for there was no prospect of undoing the New Deal or reducing government to its pre-Depression dimensions—not that President Eisenhower wanted such an effort. Liberals and blacks were also sufficiently strong, that, while not yet able to secure strong civil rights legislation, they could strongly influence government policies, and rule out the presidential candidacy of any segregationist Southerner. The balance between branches of government changed little. Congress and the states slightly regained some power from the Presidency and Federal Government, but not very much. The Supreme Court's arrogance and incompetence were growing, but its liberal majority was bitterly split between the more extreme "Black-Douglas" wing and the "Frankfurter-Jackson" faction, which, while strongly liberal, believed in judicial restraint.

In contrast to most other Western nations, the United States lacked a far left, or for that matter, a far right. Democratic Socialists were few in number, although had an influence out of proportion to their numbers in the intellectual world. Truly antidemocratic movements were violently unpopular and had no influence at all. The cranky right was well represented in the John Birch Society, founded in 1958, but its claims that all the presidents since 1933, including Eisenhower, were Communists excited general ridicule. The pro-Soviet left had almost, but not quite, ceased to exist well before Eisenhower became president, not because of the much overstated impact of "McCarthyism" but because of universal contempt, and its inability, even before the Korean War, to say anything that sounded convincing even to itself. Its members did not all convert to good sense, of course, but sulked until the political climates changed. In retrospect, it is clear that this had begun to occur in the late 1950s, but that change did not proceed very far. It became visible in the year after Sputnik.

Eisenhower

President Eisenhower was, and remained, enormously popular, and in a way unlike any of his successors. For he was not just popular, but almost universally trusted. In fact, the boundaries of extremism in the 1950s could almost be defined by the tiny minorities—Communists, Klansmen, and Birchers—who questioned his integrity. To be sure, a substantial minority of Americans—by no means solely left of center—did not like, or even respect him, regarding him as a senile old fool who hardly ever did anything right. But even they did not doubt that Eisenhower was a completely decent man trying to do his best according to his dim lights. Such critics—not a few of whom would repent later, after seeing some of Eisenhower's successors in action—thought of "Ike" as a weak leader, a reversion to the despised Republican presidents of the 1920s (whose reputations were far worse in the 1950s than today). But such people, while well represented among intellectuals and the opinion-makers of the time, did not reflect public opinion. If not for the Republicans' self-destructive folly in passing the 22nd Amendment in the 1940s, Eisenhower could unquestionably have gotten a third term.

The critics were guilty of a fantastic misjudgment of an extremely able individual, who was one of the best men ever to occupy the White House, and vastly superior to any of his successors. He was hardly a weak president. Focusing, necessarily, on foreign and defense policies and an indirect style of management that made his role seem less than it was. He also relied, heavily, on the elaborate machinery of the National Security Council (which would largely be wrecked, with disastrous results, by Kennedy). Contrary to his critics, he was an experienced Washington insider and able administrator. Dissatisfied with the administrative system he inherited from Truman, he reformed it, defining clear channels of authority and thrashing out major policies in detail, drawing on a broad range of advisers. He relied especially heavily on his closest brother, Milton, an experienced civil administrator who he would have liked to see succeed him. Unlike his recent predecessors and successors, he held frequent Cabinet meetings and encouraged open exchanges of views both in the Cabinet and National Security Council meetings. While basically a leader rather than a driver, he had learned to make much use of seemingly harsher characters as chiefs of staff—Walter Bedell Smith during World War II and Governor Sherman Adams when he was president—as shields and tools to carry out unpleasant tasks, one trick he apparently picked up while working for Douglas MacArthur, under whom, he liked to say, he had studied dramatics. Eisenhower was sometimes regarded as a moderate middle of the roader, or even as a liberal, when he ran in 1952, but basically he was a conservative, although not an ideologue, whose opinions on particular issues could be quite liberal, as on environmental matters (then usually referred to as "conservation") and transportation. He opposed building more dams in the west, and the extension of the Interstate Highway System into the cities—indeed, he favored a tax on taking cars into downtown areas. On other matters, he could be more conservative than his supposedly more conservative ally, Senator Robert Taft. Overall, Eisenhower was far more conservative than any of his successors, including Ronald Reagan, whose career he would promote. While he once described himself as "socially liberal but fiscally conservative," this must be understood in terms of the language of the time. His "social liberalism" referred to his acceptance of, and willingness to extend, New Deal programs like Social Security, not at all to the social issues prominent later. He had less than no use for most of the social changes and issues that developed after he left office (for example, he favored sterilizing any woman who had a second illegitimate child while on welfare). Contrary to legend, as we shall see, he had no problems with the Supreme Court's unanimous 1954 decision in favor of school desegregation, but was disgusted by the Warren Court's later decisions, to the point that he vocally regretted making Earl Warren Chief Justice. Earlier, he had once contemplated Warren as a good successor if he was unable to run again in 1956, or as a substitute for Richard Nixon as Vice President.

Eisenhower's relations with the "Old Guard" of right-wing Republicans, however, were bad—they, not he, still wished to undo the New Deal. He got along surprisingly well with Robert Taft, the Senate majority leader, but poorly with Taft's successor, William Knowland. Even before the Republican rout in 1954, he placed more reliance on the Democratic leaders, Lyndon Johnson in the Senate and Sam Rayburn in the House.

On economic matters, Eisenhower was unmistakably conservative, more so than any successor. He was of course, pro-business, in the sense that he believed that private enterprise was, usually, vastly superior to any government operation, although he was no free-market fanatic and did not suppose that the former could always substitute for the latter. Government should do what private enterprise could not do, or not do well. Like Franklin Roosevelt, he liked to quote Lincoln's formulation of the issue. A true fiscal conservative, not a nominal one, he feared the effect of deficits and inflation. (If he was, perhaps, somewhat over-cautious about the threat of inflation, this did far less harm than the insouciance of his successors.) This, along with defense costs, was the key to his policies. So he opposed not only non-vital expenditures but also the drive of many Republicans for premature tax reductions and cutting necessary expenditures for defense in his first administration. He even deferred implementing already passed tax reductions; the nominal upper limit of the income tax rate during his presidency was 91 percent for the highest income bracket, although in practice loopholes prevented almost anyone actually paying that rate. He carefully pared expenditures. He reduced public investment in such matters as dams (which he farsightedly suspected were unneeded and undesirable anyhow) and public housing. The scandal-ridden Reconstruction Finance Corporation was terminated after one of its functions, aiding small enterprises, was shifted to the new Small Business Administration. Korean War price and wage controls were lifted and regulations reduced. Defense expenditures were cut to what Eisenhower considered a safe minimum, but necessarily a high minimum, one that could be maintained as long as the Cold War lasted. In April 1958, in countering calls for a tax cut, he bluntly remarked, "defense is expensive and is growing more expensive, and we have got to be ready to pay those defense costs for the next 40–50 years, possibly."[8]

Nevertheless, he was ready to carry on, even expand, reforms of proven value, such as Social Security, but not undertake costly new domestic programs. He held the line against "the spenders" well enough so that, while unable to eliminate deficits in most of his budgets, he kept them at relatively low levels. If anything, he was perhaps too rigid in not reducing taxes and altering monetary policies in "countercyclical" efforts against the serious recession that began in September 1957. Typically, he wisely and successfully opposed proposals for huge public works programs, involving some projects he suspected were downright idiotic, and that in any case could not be implemented until the recession was past. On the whole, his economic policies were successful, although growth rates were not quite as good as in the Truman years. Apart from the handling of the 1957 recession, not all of his polices worked well, of course. His farm policies, and Secretary of Agriculture Ezra Taft Benson, were not very successful, and quite unpopular, costing the Republicans much of the farm vote. Despite fiscal pressures, however, Eisenhower broadened Social Security, formed NASA and the Department of Health, Education, and Welfare, began federal aid to higher education and the Interstate Highway System, and built the St. Lawrence Seaway. He revised the tax code and got anticorruption measures passed.

Like anyone, Eisenhower had faults, and made mistakes. The oldest man to enter the White House up to Reagan, he inevitably lacked some energy, and suffered three serious illnesses—although, in each case, making a remarkably quick recovery, at least once surprising doctors, many of whom did not expect him to come back at all after his ileitis attack in 1956. He was inclined to be overawed, at least at first, by successful businessmen. His first cabinet was wittily described as "eight millionaires and a plumber" and inspired Robert Taft to wryly remark, "I don't know any reason why success in business should mean success in public service. They're very different fields." Eisenhower was not always a good judge of men. Apart from his bitterly regretted admiration for Earl Warren, he held an exaggerated opinion of others, notably Richard Nixon. Although he did not really like Nixon, and would have liked to dump him in 1956, he did not realize just how bad the man was, either. He was rather overimpressed by Treasury Secretary Robert Anderson, who he did like and regarded as one of the few men fit to succeed him. (Interestingly, he preferred a woman, his first Secretary of Health, Education, and Welfare, Oveta Culp Hobby, to Nixon as a successor!) Occasionally, his moral compass slipped, notably in his reluctance to promptly squash Joe McCarthy, as he could easily have done, although his course was dictated neither by political cowardice or calculation, but the estimate that McCarthy loved attention and would fade without it, and a reluctance, as he put it, to "get down in the gutter with that guy."[9] That might be a more important criticism if McCarthyism's power and importance were not wildly overestimated. But, despite the arguments of some of Eisenhower's more enthusiastic apologists, it cannot be said that he destroyed Joe McCarthy. It was McCarthy who forced the issue, and caused his own ruin.

Civil Rights

One particular feature of Eisenhower's policies has often been misunderstood, even deliberately misrepresented. The reality, as Oscar Barck, an early chronicler of the postwar era put it, was that the "record of the Eisenhower Administration in the civil rights field far surpassed that of previous ones."[10] Yet, for some decades, it was widely believed (largely, it appears, on the dubious authority of Earl Warren) that Ike, and even his administration as a whole, was hostile to civil rights.

In 1952, Eisenhower referred to racial discrimination as "criminally stupid," arguably a crisper and more to the point assessment than that made by any other president. In his first Inaugural address he condemned ideas of racial superiority and inferiority. His first administration desegregated Washington DC and federal installations in the South, and secured anti-discrimination clauses in all federal contracts. Attorney General Brownell filed a brief in favor of desegregation in support of the Brown suit in Brown v. Board of Education. Nevertheless, the rather astonishing idea arose later that Eisenhower did not support school desegregation. His journal and a letter to his closest friend, Everett Hazlett, show this claim to be quite false.

Eisenhower did not publicly endorse the Brown decision, but he did not consider it proper to endorse or criticize Supreme Court decisions. (He nevertheless seemed to endorse it at a press conference on September 3, 1957, during the Little Rock crisis, as well as unequivocally condemning the riots there as "disgraceful." Later, in October 1958, he spoke of the universality of civil rights.) His own inclination would have been to strike at segregation differently, tackling public accommodations and segregation at colleges and universities first before going on to lower schools, which, he thought, would rouse less opposition among Southern whites (psychologically, he was almost certainly right). But he did not question the justice of the Brown decision.

He was indeed cautious about implementing it, as was the Supreme Court, for that matter. He believed that such a drastic social change—drastic, at least, from the point of view of white Southerners—could not take place overnight, and was cautious for a more concrete reason—the danger, that, if pushed too hard, Southern states would simply shut their public schools, connive at establishing private or pseudo-private school systems for white children only, and leave black children flat, with no education at all. That was a chance he could not take, so rather than trying to force things by threatening states over the Brown decision, he preferred to praise those Southern locales that obeyed it, like Louisville. So school desegregation, perhaps unavoidably, remained very slow, encountering, in most places, passive resistance, and in some savage opposition. Most Southerners, though, even in the 1950s, seemed to believe that desegregation was, as Harry Ashmore put it, only a matter of time, and were prepared to go along with it, however little they liked it.

It is possible, even probable, that Eisenhower underestimated the moral influence that he might have exerted and the effectiveness of a more active campaign of persuasion. But he was perhaps the only president who could have exerted such influence; the idea of most of his successors trying such moral persuasion seems ludicrous, if not disgusting. On matters such as voting rights, Eisenhower was unequivocal. The Civil Rights Acts of 1957 and 1960, overwhelmingly backed by Republicans, were weakened by the Southern Democrats (possibly with some Northern liberal Democrat connivance), not by the Administration. Throughout the 1950s and far into the 1960s, it should be remembered, almost all Republicans supported civil rights legislation; it was the Democrats who were split. Despite the sluggishness of school desegregation, the 1950s saw considerable progress in reducing discrimination and bettering the lives of black Americans. It also saw the rapid decline of discrimination against other groups, to the point of vanishing in the subsequent decade, so that the very meaning of "minority group," which had once encompassed Catholics, Jews, and people descended from immigrants from Eastern and Southern Europe, was abruptly redefined to mean only "nonwhite" minorities.[11]

One rather belated attempt to intimidate some nonblacks misfired spectacularly in 1958, giving most Americans a badly needed laugh. When the Ku Klux Klan tried to bully Lumbee Indians in North Carolina (this was one of the places in the South where there was "tri-racial" segregation), the Klansmen found themselves greatly outnumbered by several hundred well armed and angry Amerinds. They showed some rare running before the County Sheriff warned the Lumbees that if they continued pursuing their foes they would miss that evening's episode of *Gunsmoke*.[12]

Culture and Entertainment

In cultural terms the late 1950s did not differ much from the period immediately preceding or following, although there was a slow erosion of the boundaries of censorship and/or good taste in the depiction of sex, and less noted, of violence in both serious literature and the mass media. This did not pass without resistance; Vladimir Nabokov's *Lolita* was bitterly attacked in liberal magazines of the time, such as the *New Republic*.

The ten best-selling novels of 1958—some were holdovers from the previous year—were a mix of the good and the ephemeral: Boris Paternak's *Doctor Zhivago*, Robert Travers's *Anatomy of a Murder*, Vladimir Nabokov's *Lolita*, Patrick Dennis' *Around the World with Auntie Mame*, John O'Hara's *From the Terrace*, Kay Thompson's *Eloise at Christmas*, Edna Ferber's *Ice Palace*, Anya Seton's *The Winthrop Women*, Jerome Weidman's *Enemy*, and Francis Parkinson Key's *Victorine*. Curiously, only the two works by Russians have lasted, although *Anatomy of a Murder* was quite good. A disproportionate number of these works seem to have been aimed at a female audience, some were not very distinguished examples of the fad for historical novels that had started with *Anthony Adverse* in the 1930s. The top nonfiction bestsellers of 1958 were even more ephemeral; the only serious work was John Gunther's *Inside Russia*. The rest were typically humor or non-serious commentary such as Art Linkletter's *Kids Say the Darndest Things*, Harry Golden's *Only in America*, and Jean Kerr's *Please Don't Eat the Daisies*.

Magazines by this time had ceased to be serious venues for fiction, except for science fiction, for which the late 1950s was not a particularly good period. Newspapers and magazines, especially the traditional "slicks" like the *Saturday Evening Post*, were in terminal decline. However, Henry Luce's Time-Life empire was still strong, and exerted considerable influence in this era. It sometimes actually reported the news accurately, although not overdoing that. Despite Luce's generally Republican orientation, it turned sharply critical of Eisenhower in 1958.

1958 was not a particularly good year for plays, although Broadway produced Richard Rodgers' and Oscar Hammerstein II's penultimate collaboration, *Flower Drum Song*; not one of their best or most popular works, it represented a recovery from the nasty and unfair reception of their 1957 television special, *Cinderella*, which had shaken both men.

The top ten grossing movies of 1958 were led by the film version of one of their earlier works, *South Pacific*—perhaps surprisingly, since most people who had seen the original Broadway production did not think that Hollywood did it justice. The other leading moneymakers were *Auntie Mame*, *Cat on a Hot Tin Roof*, *No Time for Sergeants*, *Gigi*, *The Seventh Voyage of Sinbad*, *The Vikings*, *Vertigo*, *The Young Lions*, and *Some Came Running*. If not all were great, a list of the best movies of 1958 and the most successful might coincide more than usual. A notable number of the movies made were adaptations of major novels and plays—notably by William Faulkner (*The Long Hot Summer*), Ernest Hemingway (*The Old Man and the Sea*), Irwin Shaw (*The Young Lions*), James Jones (*Some Came Running*), John O'Hara (*Ten North Frederick*), Tennessee Williams (*Cat on a Hot Tin Roof*), and Terence Rattigan (*Separate Tables*). Some literary adaptations were rather unusual, e.g. Richard Brooks' version of *The Brothers Karamazov*. There was an odd fad for the disillusioned romantic works of Françoise Sagan (*Bonjour Tristesse* and *A Certain Smile*). One truly unusual film of the era was *The Goddess*, an attack on the Marilyn Monroe cult written by Paddy Chayefsky.

Although only one war film, *The Young Lions*, made it into the top ten, films about World War II were quite common in 1958, and generally of high quality, notably *Run Silent, Run Deep* and *Kings Go Forth*. They certainly compared well with the bloated and often downright phony all-star "epics" of the 1960s that attempted to imitate *The Longest Day*. The brief vogue for movies about the Korean War was drawing to an end; the undistinguished adaptation of James Salter's *The Hunters* was the only major movie about Korea to come out in 1958. 1958 also saw the near end of movies made about the other side in World War II (a brief fad that had started in 1951 with *The Desert Fox* and *Decision Before Dawn*), notable examples in 1958 being the film version of Erich Maria Remarque's *A Time to Love and a Time to Die* and *Fraulein*.

Race-conscious movies were fairly common in 1958, notable examples being *The Defiant Ones* and *Kings Go Forth*. Westerns were still immensely popular, notably *The Big Country* (a particular favorite of Eisenhower), and *Man of the West*. Gary Cooper, in the last movie, typified a feature of the late 1950s; it marked the last phase of the reign of many older stars—Clark Gable, Cary Grant, James Stewart, Spencer Tracy, and Tyrone Power—who had been well established before World War II.

Oddly, no Western was among the most profitable movies. This was a vivid contrast to television, which was practically overrun by Western hordes. In the 1958–1959 season, seven of the ten most popular shows—according to the Nielsen ratings—were Westerns: *Gunsmoke*, *Have Gun Will Travel*, *Maverick*, *Wyatt Earp*, *Tales of Wells Fargo*, *The Rifleman*, and *Wagon Train* (*Maverick* and *Have Gun, Will Travel* were the two best products of the genre). The remaining three were two not very distinguished comedies—*Danny Thomas* and the *Real McCoys*—and a game show, *I've Got a Secret*, one of the few never tainted by scandal.

After a short breathing space in the mid-1950s, television was again crowding the movies; to save themselves, some of the movie studios were entering television. This was true, although, by today's standards, there was, relatively speaking, little television. Some 80 percent of American homes had TVs, but they only received broadcasts on a small number of VHF channels. Instead of serving a vast number of specialized niche markets, TV was dominated by three networks and a conformist mass culture, supervised by people who were, generally speaking, socially responsible and influenced by considerations of good taste as well as the restraints of censorship. Although many people even then complained about violence on television, the depiction of violence, as well as sex, was incredibly restrained by later standards.

Curiously the later stereotyped "family comedies"—*Father Knows Best, Ozzie and Harriet, Donna Reed*, and *Leave It to Beaver* (the last really a kids' show) did not make it into the top ten. Apart from Westerns, comedies and game shows—the last only just beginning to come under suspicion as fixed—television was characterized by variety shows (*Ed Sullivan* and *Garry Moore*) and a new fad for private eyes (*Peter Gunn, 77 Sunset Strip*, and *The Thin Man*). Although reduced in number and on the way out, there were still some significant original drama shows, including some of the very best—*Playhouse 90* and the *United States Steel Hour*. Such late staples as shows about lawyers, doctors, and cops were rare or unknown. Lawyers were represented only by the interminable and ridiculous *Perry Mason* series. Television news, although possibly already the main source of news, was rather small in scale—until 1963 the evening national news shows were just fifteen minutes long, but they were run by able men trained as print reporters and by later standards were singularly unbiased. If people were not well informed by television, they were, at least, not misinformed either. The news divisions of the networks, notably CBS, occasionally produced outstanding documentaries.[13]

Television was a unifying influence, rock and roll, still fairly new in the late 1950s, was not. It was hated by almost everyone born before the early 1930s (even those who made money from it). Many older people could barely hide their delight when Elvis Presley was drafted into the Army in 1958, and even that threw much of the younger generation into mourning, and inspired the popular musical *Bye Bye Birdie*. Many adults hoped that, by the time Elvis finished his two-year hitch, the horrible fad for rock and roll would be finished, and they would not have to hear it, or Elvis, ever again.

If President Eisenhower noticed the Elvis Presley crisis, it might have given him some badly needed amusement, for, as he later remarked, 1958 was the worst year of his life.[14]

From his point of view, little went well in domestic affairs, leaving him full of foreboding for the future of the United States. His oldest friend, Everett Hazlett, died. But it was his main preoccupation, foreign affairs, which made 1958 particularly unpleasant. Other years of the Cold War may have seen more dangerous crises, but none so many difficult and continuous crises in far-flung parts of the world. The democracies and their allies faced relentless pressures amid a particularly demoralizing situation, for the Soviets had scored a technological triumph over the West, one that seemed to presage actual Communist strategic superiority, possibly even a general superiority. Ike had good reason to regard 1958 as the worst year of his life. But, difficult as it was, he never shone better than in that supremely difficult year.

The Faults of American Society in the 1950s

The country Eisenhower led was hardly without faults, although, for practically everybody, life was better than ever before. Some of these faults were not without later results, but it has not always been fashionable to discuss them, while others have been played up with no sense of proportion, e.g. racial discrimination, which was actually being rapidly dealt with in this period. Some of these problems include:

1. An overemphasis, perhaps, on the development of suburbs and cars—something not uncriticized at the time (suburbs never got a good press from fashionable opinion). It should be noted, however, that suburban development and a preference for private cars over public transportation was strongly desired by the public at the time, and the competence of those promoting and designing public housing for the poor and mass transit was so low that greater emphasis on those things, perhaps otherwise desirable, might have been worst than wasted.[15]
2. The almost unrecognized corruption of the political system, implicit in the rise of figures like Richard Nixon and the Kennedys.
3. The failure, until nearly the end of Eisenhower's presidency, to attack organized crime.
4. Many false or mistaken ideas, usually associated with the intellectual currents of the 1960s, actually had their origins in the Eisenhower era, and sometimes before, notably the concepts associated with Theodor Adorno and the Frankfurt School, the beatniks, and the highly falsified research of Alfred Kinsey.
5. The related spread of "Millsian" or absolutist concepts of civil liberties. Their consequences would wind up shocking even their advocates, like the distinguished attorney Morris Ernst, and many innocent people would pay with their lives for their impact on the justice system.
6. An overestimation of the potentialities of government, the social sciences, and, probably, education to effect positive social transformation. This was accentuated by naïve assumptions about the quality of political leadership that could normally be expected in democratic (or any) countries. Liberals praised, rightly, the unique qualities of great men like Franklin D. Roosevelt and Fiorello LaGuardia, but failed to appreciate the consequences of the point—if they even recognized it—that political leaders of such quality were bound to be rare. They exhibited great confidence in "planning" and "social engineering" although the sheer complexity and unpredictability of modern society made true planning supremely difficult;

and so little was really known by social scientists that it would make more sense to talk of planned social change as "social alchemy" than "social engineering." In general, as the following era would show all too clearly, Americans, and not just intellectuals and opinion makers, reposed far too much confidence in the probity, much less competence, of lawyers (and especially judges), psychiatrists, social scientists, and business managers.

Some of the things go far to explain some of the changes of the following half-century:

1. Erratic and generally lower economic growth with a redistribution of income from the middle class to the wealthiest fraction of the population, an alarming proportion of whom were idle or largely idle rentiers. To be sure, the composition of the work force changed somewhat with the relative decline of traditional heavy industries and manufacturing in general. While public employee unions rose in strength, unions in the private sector sharply declined.

2. The decline of and politicization of education even while huge sums were lavished on it. (Typically, while college freshmen were worse and worse prepared, the number of teaching days in a college year declined from 191 in 1964 to 156 by the early 1990s.) Much of the investment in education, of course, went not to actually educating but administering education.

3. An almost reciprocal rise of superstition and irrationalism, often of a quite traditional nature, but often disguised as "New Age" beliefs—in astrology, psychic powers, mediums, tarot cards, etc. as well as creationism.

4. A huge increase in crime and drug addiction, along with changes in the law that virtually disregarded the ongoing crisis in the pursuit of ever more bizarre protections for those accused of crimes. In a curious counterpoint was a process that might be described as "shysterization." American society, already amazingly litigious and lawyer-ridden compared to other democracies, became more so, with enormous powers and financial rewards being usurped by the legal profession.

5. A grotesque failure of most attempted social reforms; most notably the War on Poverty, which was such a misfire that the Apollo Moon project, although hardly intended for the purpose, proved more successful in generating employment than all the jobs efforts of the Great Society program.

6. Reopening of mass immigration of a very different ethnic background from earlier arrivals, accompanied by massive illegal immigration.

7. "Balkanization"—an obsession with race and ethnicity, usually positively disguised as anti-discrimination and "multi-culturalism."

8. A vast change in attitudes toward sexuality and the position of women; while the latter gained access to jobs and positions from which they had

earlier been excluded (or more often just been uncommon) there was an unmistakable coarsening of, and greater hostility in, relations between the sexes. Marriage declined, with people marrying later and less often, divorcing more, with marriage virtually disappearing in the "underclass." Eroticism became strongly public, and homosexuality and, though less discussed, other phenomena traditionally regarded as perversions became increasingly accepted or at least public.

9. Spectacular increases in the depiction of violence as well as sexuality in the mass media and entertainment, also a clear decline of originality. This was most obvious in the movies, which depended on sensational exploitation of sex and violence to compete with TV, and increasingly depended on recycled material—remakes of older movies, almost all incredibly worse than the originals, sequels and series (often disguised remakes) and rip-offs of old television shows and comic books.

10. The growth of medicine and its increasing absorption of a greater and greater part of society's resources. Of course, this was accompanied by a great increase in lifespan, and, for lucky people, greater well-being.

11. The decline of traditional religions, i.e. the mainline Protestant churches and the Roman Catholic Church, partly (but only partly) counterbalanced by the rise of evangelical Protestantism.

12. An enormous change in attitudes to the history of the United States, and Western civilization in general, with a remarkable emphasis on their negative aspects, indeed the cultivation of elaborate guilt complexes revolving around matters that, usually, pertained to racial and ethnic matters.

    a. The history of slavery and racism against blacks.
    b. The treatment of Amerinds and the Mexican War.
    c. Western imperialism in Asia and Africa.
    d. The destruction of the European Jews—the blame for which was extended from the Nazis, or even Germans in general, to other non-Jewish Westerners.
    e. The use of the A-bomb against Japan in 1945.
    f. The mistreatment of Japanese-Americans during World War II.
    g. American intervention in Latin America.
    h. The real and supposed misdeeds of the CIA.
    i. McCarthyism.
    j. The medieval crusades against Islam (not, curiously, the crusades against Eastern European pagans!).

Attitudes associated with these things were not unknown in the 1950s, but they were exceedingly rare. Unpleasant as most Americans in the 1950s would have found many of the changes described above, they might have found the collective guilt complex the most bewildering of all.

But all the developments of the subsequent half-century we have noted were far from the main worries of Americans in the late 1950s. So was victory in the Cold War. A happy end to that struggle never seemed farther away than in 1958. The greatest problem then was avoiding defeat and surviving the Cold War, not winning it. How Americans handled that problem is the chief subject of the rest of this book.

Notes

1 Peter Lewis, *The Fifties* (New York: Lippincott, 1978), p. 31.
2 For typically inane descriptions of the 1950s, cf. Randall Woods, *Quest for Identity* (New York: Cambridge University Press, 2005), p. 106; Douglas T. Miller and Marion Nowak, *The Fifties: The Way We Really Were* (Garden City, KS: Doubleday, 1977), esp. pp. 3–7, 14, 131, 253; George Herring, *From Colony to Superpower* (Oxford: Oxford University Press, 2008), p. 637; Stephen Ambrose, *Eisenhower: The President* (New York: Simon & Schuster, 1984), p. 424. A curious case of a repetition of the usual stereotypes of the period, in an otherwise arresting and outstanding work, is Klaus P. Fischer, *America in White, Black, and Gray* (New York: Continuum, 2006), p. 4.
3 Most pundits and "experts," during the 1930s and World War II, did not foresee the baby boom, postwar prosperity, the Cold War, rapid decolonization, or the success of West German and Japanese democracy. It is perhaps worth noting that the vast majority of economists failed to predict the Great Depression, the postwar boom, or the end of the postwar boom. This has strangely failed to impair the prestige of economics, or its status as a "science." If astronomy was at the level of economics, we would not know what year it is, or perhaps, how long a year is.
4 Wyatt Wells, *American Capitalism 1945–2000* (Chicago, IL: Ivan Dee, 2003), pp. 19–22, 34, 36, 38, 41–42; Michael French, *US Economic History Since 1945* (Manchester, UK: Manchester University Press, 1997), pp. 5, 26, 38–41; Thomas McGraw, *American Business 1920–2000* (Wheeling, IL: Harlan Davidson, 2000), pp. 73–74, 110–113, 161; Landon Y. Jones, *Great Expectations* (New York: Coward McCann & Geoghegan, 1980), p. 165; James Patterson, *Grand Expectations* (New York: Oxford University Press, 1998), p. 311; Ronald Oakley, *God's Country: America in the Fifties* (New York: Dembner Books, 1990), pp. 7, 111, 228–231, 245.
5 Alan J. Levine, *Bad Old Days* (New Brunswick, NJ: Transaction, 2008), pp. 10–11, 55–56, 58–60; James Patterson, *America's Struggle Against Poverty in the Twentieth Century* (Cambridge, MA: Cambridge University Press, 2000), pp. 13, 40–41, 77–80, 91–96, 112–113, 157–162; Charles Murray, *Losing Ground* (New York: Basic Books, 1984), pp. 27, 57–65.
6 Oakley, *God's Country*, pp. 111–122; John Brooks, *The Great Leap* (New York: Vintage, 1968), pp. 104, 108–111, 130–136, 138, 157; Kenneth Jackson, *Crabgrass Frontier* (New York: Oxford University Press, 1985); Levine, *Bad Old Days*, pp. 123–138.
7 For an extended discussion of the mood of the late 1950s, see Levine, *Bad Old Days*, pp. 71–111.

8 Levine, *Bad Old Days*, pp. 71–111.
9 Peter Boyle, *Eisenhower* (Harlow, UK: Longman, 2005), esp. pp. 15, 19–20, 24–25, 33–34, 56, 69; Eric Goldman, *The Crucial Decade and After* (New York: Vintage, 1960), esp. pp. 269, 280–297; Oscar Barck, *A History of the United States Since 1945* (New York: Dell, 1965), pp. 201–203, 211, 226–229, 250–256; Wells, *American Capitalism*, pp. 48–50; Raymond Saulnier, *Constructive Years* (Lanham, MD: University Press of America, 1991), pp. 9, 23, 39–42, 47, 56, 97–99, 109–113, 222–230; Levine, *Bad Old Days*, pp. 18–20; Sherman Adams, *First Hand Report* (New York: Harper, 1961), pp. 4–6, 9, 25–27, 29, 135–137, 202–203; Oakley, *God's Country*, pp. 148–166, 225, 410–411; Ambrose, *Eisenhower: The President*, pp. 510, 547–548, 606–616. Like other Ambrose works, his Eisenhower biography is inaccurate, and must be used with care. Notably, he unduly downplayed Eisenhower's anti-Communism and toughness in foreign policy, as did Robert Divine, otherwise a far better historian, in his *Eisenhower and the Cold War* (New York: Oxford University Press, 1981).
10 Barck, *A History of the United States Since 1945*, p. 285.
11 Goldman, *The Crucial Decade*, pp. 298–299; Barck, *A History of the United States Since 1945*, pp. 275–279, 285; Levine, *Bad Old Days*, pp. 32–34, 37–38; Boyle, *Eisenhower*, p. 30; Adams, *First Hand Report*, pp. 331–335, 339, 341–348; Dwight D. Eisenhower, *Waging Peace* (New York: Doubleday, 1965), pp. 311–315; Dwight D. Eisenhower, *The Eisenhower Diaries*, ed. Robert Ferrell (New York: Norton, 1981), p. 313; Dwight D. Eisenhower, *Ike's Letters to a Friend*, ed. Robert Griffith (Lawrence, KS: University Press of Kansas, 1984), pp. 10, 133, 135, 186–187. Cf. Ambrose, *Eisenhower: The President*, pp. 124–126, 191; Oakley, *God's Country*, pp. 193–195 for the conventional critical picture. The myths about Eisenhower's civil rights record have been finally exploded by David Nicols' fine book *A Matter of Justice* (New York: Simon & Schuster, 2007). Nicols is nasty enough to compare Eisenhower's record with the real, and highly unattractive, record of his successor!
12 Oakley, *God's Country*, pp. 335–336.
13 Leo Bogart, *The Age of Television* (New York: F. Ungar, 1972).
14 Ambrose, *Eisenhower: The President*, p. 486.
15 I have treated these issues at greater length in *Bad Old Days*.

2

COLD WAR POLICY AND MILITARY STRATEGY TO 1958

Eisenhower took office when the basic strategy of the Cold War had already been set. Two great alliances, the Soviet–Chinese axis and the loosely grouped Western democratic powers, and their friends—real, pretended, and bought— faced each other across the world, and were at war in Korea, a war later usually called a "limited" or local war but more accurately described by an early observer as "not so much a local war as a localized general war," and that nearly became World War III.[1] That struggle had long since reached a stalemate. Arguably, the Cold War in general had become stalemated. No great crisis had developed in Europe since the end of the Berlin Blockade and the Greek Civil War in 1949, and no great Communist successes had taken place elsewhere since the Communist victory in China. But this was not apparent at the time, as aside from Korea, half a dozen local struggles raged in Southeast Asia between local governments and Western rulers and Communist guerrillas. In 1950–1951, those wars—except in Indochina—had turned in favor of the anti-Communists, but that was not clear at the time. Behind the Cold War front, Western Europe had recovered from World War II, and was moving, slowly, toward unity. Japan, the last major country to recover from the war, had not yet finished doing so, but its political and social development had gone well. Its economy seemed, to most contemporaries, to be desperately fragile and likely to remain so. (Japan's emergence as an economic powerhouse was yet another development unexpected by professional economists.) The remnants of the Chinese Nationalists sheltered on Taiwan under American protection. The rest of Asia and Africa faced grim problems of decolonization and underdevelopment.

It was widely thought that a situation of "atomic plenty," in which both the West and Communist blocs would have large nuclear stockpiles, and the ability to deliver them, and "atomic stalemate" would develop in the near future, in which there might be a more or less stable state of mutual deterrence. Some, however, feared that such a situation would lead to a Soviet victory, while others doubted that it was quite accurate. A July 1953 report representing a consensus of opinion of the State Department, CIA, and military intelligence held that the West would probably retain a "substantial absolute advantage in capabilities for atomic warfare" for the next fifteen years, but admitted that this might be radically altered by some accident or unexpected technological development. Although judging that trends in the underdeveloped world were against the West, it refused to say whether, over all, time favored the West or the Communist world. The Joint Chiefs of Staff were not so optimistic.

Actually, the Soviets' stockpile of nuclear weapons was smaller than supposed, and their ability to deliver it to the United States, due to their unexpected delay in developing long-range bombers, was far less than was believed at the time. (The Soviets probably did not attain true "nuclear parity" in the strict sense until about 1975.)[2] Even in 1953, however, appraisals of the maximum possible attack estimated that it could not defeat the United States, although many people were troubled by the weakness of American air defenses.

Eisenhower's Foreign Policy

The central foreign policies, alliances, and programs, and the first great military buildup of the Cold War, had been put in place by the Truman Administration. Under the circumstances there was little room for comparable innovation by its successor. (John Foster Dulles' alleged, and much criticized "pactomania" added—in some cases only formalizing earlier arrangements—only the Republic of Korea, the Chinese Nationalists, Thailand, and Pakistan to American alliances.) After considering alternatives, notably in the "Solarium" studies of 1953, aimed at "liberation" or rollback of Communist power—short of war, for Eisenhower, like his predecessor and successors, essentially rejected considering preventive war out of hand—the Administration continued the policy of containment of Communism, a policy more accurately described by Dean Acheson, and occasionally in Eisenhower Administration documents, as building "situations of strength." The fear of imminent world war, which had shaped policies early in the Korean War, had already ebbed, and a military buildup aimed at achieving a high level of readiness by a critical year was discarded in favor of "long-haul" policies, which Eisenhower estimated could be economically and politically sustained for many years.

To develop and execute those policies, Eisenhower relied on a closely working team—Secretary of State John Foster Dulles, Secretary of Defense Charles E. Wilson, and the Chairman of the Joint Chiefs of Staff, Admiral Arthur D. Radford. The first two would often be caricatured by contemporaries, and later writers, even more than Eisenhower himself. Dulles' image, in particular, was distorted, although he had been the Republican expert on foreign policy for years and had long been expected to become Secretary of State in the next Republican administration. Dulles, then and later, was widely pictured as a rigid, humorless, fanatical Calvinist moralist, opposed to negotiations, hostile to neutrals, unable to comprehend non-Westerners; his policies parodied by constant references to his supposed predilection for "pactomania" and "brinkmanship" and his phrases "massive retaliation" and "agonizing reappraisal"—usually yanked out of context or misinterpreted. Many saw him as dominating a naïve Eisenhower, and some as "double-tagging" the President in cahoots with his brother Allen, head of the CIA.[3]

All this had little relation to the reality of a man who the Communist rulers regarded as one of their outstanding foes. As Nikita Khrushchev wrote in his memoirs, "Dulles was a worthy adversary. It always kept us on our toes to match wits with him." The Chinese leaders appear to have held a similar view.[4]

The nephew of Woodrow Wilson's Secretary of State, Robert Lansing, and grandson of another, he was an extremely able lawyer and negotiator, and was well prepared for his role. He had been a member of the American delegation at Versailles in 1919, and had skillfully handled the peace treaty with Japan in 1951.

Dulles drew great strength from his Presbyterian faith, and bitterly criticized Communist atheism, but he was hardly a religious fanatic. Nor, although a stroke had pulled down one side of his mouth, making it hard for him to smile, was he humorless or anti-social. Those close to him appreciated the sense of humor of a man who once described Khrushchev's laugh as sounding like a horse having an orgasm, and who was delighted by Carol Burnett's song, "I Lost My Heart to John Foster Dulles." (He asked that it be shown again on TV.) Although he considered it proper to appear solemn in public, his humor occasionally surfaced under pressure; in a news conference, when one reporter interrupted a rival giving Dulles a hard time, the Secretary of State rebuked him, remarking, tongue in cheek, "You're interrupting. Schoenbrun hasn't finished working me over yet."

The diplomat and Soviet expert Charles Bohlen, who did not like Dulles, reflected in his memoirs, that Dulles "had many more virtues than defects. He had character and was capable of firmness of purpose and steadiness in execution." Even some of his British critics, angry at Eisenhower and Dulles, with some justice, over the Suez crisis of 1956, respected the Secretary's tenacity and skill; one British magazine joked that his middle name was really an acronym for "Fear of Soviet Territorial Expansion Reactor." Foreign Secretary Selwyn Lloyd later remarked that, while dealing with Dulles "One had to be on the watch for the escape clause, the double meaning, often inserted from habit rather than intention" but nevertheless had a high opinion of him. It was Dulles' tendencies toward legalism and lawyerly wiliness, not his religiosity that struck those who dealt with him.[5] The documents of the era hardly leave anything of the hostile stereotype of Dulles, revealing a clever, flexible man surprisingly friendly toward non-Western neutralists, despite his oft-cited remark that neutrality was usually immoral. As he remarked on television in March 1956,

Let us remember that while we think first of the danger that stems from international Communism, many of them think first of possible encroachments from the West, for that is the rule that they have actually known at first hand.[6]

Dulles hardly dominated Eisenhower, an idea showing a total misunderstanding of the President; nor did he necessarily agree with his brother. The brothers often disagreed and do not seem to have been all that close. (Nor, as has sometimes been suggested, does Allen Dulles seem to have been either wiser or more liberal than his elder brother.) Rather, Ike and Foster Dulles formed a true team, and agreed on most matters. The two became good friends; Dulles was one of only two Cabinet members with whom the Eisenhowers socialized.

Dulles, and the basic policy formulations of the Administration, accepted the desirability, indeed necessity, of negotiating with the Communist powers, including China, but these were not expected to bear fruit for a long time. Arms control was a conceivable objective, but would be attained piecemeal after lengthy efforts.

Dulles was perhaps more anxious than Eisenhower about both general war or further local defeats at the hands of the other side, remarking, "Communist nibbling has already reached the point that we can't see much more territory go to the Communists without real danger to ourselves." At least in Eisenhower's first term, he was inclined to take a tougher line than the President. He favored reopening some issues already settled in the Korean armistice talks, and a drive to the "waist" of Korea (the Pyongyang-Wonsan line) to end the war, commenting to Emmett John Hughes, "I don't think we can get much out of a Korean settlement until we have shown—before all of Asia—our clear superiority by giving the Chinese one hell of a licking."[7] But Eisenhower was far less willing to do this, unless the Communists were so stubborn as to give him no other way to end the fighting. Dulles was also, perhaps, more inclined to intervene in Indochina in 1954 and certainly more favorable to the Allies in the Suez crisis. Dulles early confessed to his British and French counterparts that the Americans had made a dreadful mistake in stopping Britain, France, and Israel, a view Eisenhower would reluctantly accept only in 1967.[8]

Secretary of Defense Wilson ("Engine Charlie" to distinguish him from the head of GE, who had the same initials), who had been an extremely successful head of General Motors, played a less important role in the Administration. Eisenhower did not expect him to formulate strategy, but to administer the armed forces and military procurement in a businesslike manner. Strategy and major decisions on weapons systems were the province of Eisenhower and the Joint Chiefs. Nor did Wilson, or Eisenhower's subsequent Defense secretaries, unlike some of their successors, confuse themselves with field marshals. Wilson was basically able, and generally respected by those who worked with him, and apparently even by newsmen, although the latter could not resist the temptation to exploit the

Secretary's frequent verbal gaffes (often expressing politically unwelcome truths), which caused the Administration some embarrassment and led to the joke that while at GM Wilson had had the automatic transmission developed so that he could drive with one foot in his mouth. He was often caricatured as a stereotyped narrow Republican big businessman, although he was one of the most enlightened industrial managers of his time and had excellent relations with organized labor. But he disappointed Eisenhower, who thought that Wilson came to him with decisions Wilson should have made himself. Nevertheless he did a reasonably good job. Although he made no pretense of being a Cold War strategist, Wilson exhibited one bit of foresight. He was the highest official in any administration up to 1965 to argue that holding Indochina against the Communists was a hopeless cause, and it should be written off.[9]

Eisenhower's chief partner in formulating national strategy was Admiral Radford, who had commanded a carrier task force in the Pacific War and the Pacific theater in the Korean War. Eisenhower appreciated his knowledge of Asian matters, which also pleased the Republican right, and he seemed to Eisenhower the only senior officer who appreciated the economic constraints facing the country and was able to overcome service loyalties. Radford was the toughest of Eisenhower's advisers toward the Communist powers—tougher than Ike was prepared to be; alone of the Joint Chiefs, he strongly favored intervening in Indochina in 1954. He enjoyed good relations with Secretary Wilson.[10]

Avoiding Nuclear War

The overwhelming issue facing the Eisenhower Administration was, of course, the threat of nuclear war. On entering office, Eisenhower and Dulles accepted the view of the CIA and other agencies that the Soviets were nowhere near ready for such a war, or at least deliberately initiating it, in the next few years. Dulles expressed the general view at the National Security Council meeting of March 31, 1953, remarking that global war was "not inevitable" but remained a real possibility. The greatest danger was from Soviet miscalculation of American intentions and unintentionally precipitating war, but in the long run the only real safety was, somehow, to secure the disintegration of Soviet power by causing it to collapse or forcing it to transform itself. This general assessment that deliberate enemy initiation of war was unlikely for the next few years would be repeated in major estimates and policy statements for the rest of the 1950s. Eisenhower may have been marginally more optimistic than Dulles and others about the Soviet ever deliberately starting a nuclear war, believing that they were too cautious to do so even if the odds ever seemed to favor them. At any rate, he did not consider a deliberate Soviet resort to war likely, as he told his press secretary, James Hagerty, in 1954, for a long, long time. But he was hardly dogmatic about this, and preventing a nuclear Pearl Harbor was a major preoccupation of the Administration. He might not think it likely, but it was the worst possible development, and he could not ignore those who rated it rather more likely than he did.[11]

Nor did he, or Dulles, adhere to their views unswervingly. In 1955, during the part of the first Taiwan Strait crisis, both men suspected, almost certainly wrongly, that the Soviets might be egging on the Chinese in the hopes of starting a war in East Asia that would tie down the United States and split it from its Allies. (Radford, and the Ambassador to the USSR, were highly skeptical of this idea, which, incidentally shows that Ike and Dulles did not regard the Soviet–Chinese axis as a band of brothers.)[12]

Later in the 1950s, Dulles worried that Khrushchev might be reckless, characterizing him, in September 1957, as an "extremely dangerous man," "crude and impulsive rather than calculating and careful as previous Soviet leaders have been." In December 1958, during the Berlin crisis, he told a NATO meeting that Khrushchev was more of a gambler than Stalin or Molotov, and, for that reason, must not be encouraged by being given even a partial success. (The British Ambassador in Moscow, and Prime Minister Macmillan thought along similar lines, and Khrushchev's associates would probably have agreed; and later events justified Dulles' concern.)[13]

While Dulles tended to deprecate the likelihood of all-out war, this was not necessarily because he was optimistic. At a National Security Council meeting in January 1957, he suggested that it was quite unlikely that the United States would ever get involved in an all-out nuclear war of the sort described in a report submitted in December 1956, which estimated that 40 percent of the American population would be killed in such a struggle. "If the United States were ever to get into a military posture inferior" to that of the USSR, it would suffer defeat without war, comparing it to a checkmate in chess.

> Now, if the Soviet Union should ever get itself into a position where it would checkmate the United States, the Soviet Union would never have to resort to war in order to destroy the United States. We would be obliged to give in.

He made these remarks in the context of emphasizing how essential it was to keep up missile development, "We simply cannot afford to be inferior to the USSR." Some remarks he dropped, here and there, suggest that he was not all that confident that such a situation would be avoided in the end, although he probably would have died under torture rather than admit that in public. In public, Dulles sounded optimistic, but in fact, he was not sure that the West would prevail in the end.[14]

The real, or at least most likely danger was not a surprise nuclear attack, but defeat by gradual erosion of our position, an estimate carried over from the Truman Administration. Trends for the West were especially adverse in the underdeveloped countries, especially the remaining colonial ones. As one study noted, "The US finds itself in the anomalous position of being identified in Asia as imperialist and the supporter of Western European colonialism and in Europe as hastening the breakup of colonial relationships." The latter idea, of course, was closer to reality. Policy papers of the time typically commented that the United States must "refrain, so far as feasible, from taking or supporting actions which run counter to the forces of anti-colonialism and legitimate nationalism." The Basic National Security Policy adopted in 1955 was that "As far as possible the US should attempt to work with, rather than against, those forces, such as constructive nationalist and reform movements, which are likely to remain powerful over a long period." Both Dulles and Eisenhower commented with some feeling on the penalties exacted elsewhere by being tied up with the Western Europeans, Dulles remarking in 1957 that "we have not only our own sins to bear, but also the sins attributed to us by association."[15]

In a heated exchange in 1954 he told the British Foreign Secretary that the United States was eager to beat the Communists at their own game and sponsor nationalism in the colonial areas, which was in accordance with our national traditions, but that we were restrained from doing so by a desire to cooperate with Britain and France. The fear—indeed even a bugaboo—about associating with European "colonialism" was a major factor in Eisenhower's decision not to intervene in Indochina in 1954 and in American actions in the Sinai-Suez war of 1956.

Curiously, on matters of relations with the underdeveloped world, the Eisenhower Administration was sometimes to the left of a fair number of American liberals, some of whom held opinions far from those fashionable later. The later well-developed guilt complex toward the so-called "Third World" (a term not used in America in the 1950s) was far from universal in this period. Eleanor Roosevelt and some others supported the Anglo-French attack on Suez (putting them on the same side as the Joint Chiefs of Staff!). Not a few liberals were disgusted by the need to compete with Communist tyranny by flattering and cajoling Asian and African "neutralists." The well informed resented criticism of American racial discrimination from peoples notorious for caste, ethnic, and religious hostilities and brutal customs. As Adlai Stevenson angrily remarked in April 1956,

> we, whose position is fundamentally decent and honorable, we must now try to prove that we love peace as much as the Russians and are as much concerned with the problems of economic development and national independence as they are. It is fantastic, but true.

(Stevenson was satisfied with the pace of decolonization—if anything, he suspected that it might be going too fast.)[16]

But there was a worse danger than Communist advances in the underdeveloped countries—the unraveling of existing alliances due to the West's growing vulnerability to nuclear attack and distrust of the Americans as either too trigger-happy or unreliable. As early as 1954 the growth of Soviet strength was expected to adversely influence the cohesion of Western alliances. The CIA judged that the growing vulnerability of America's allies had already reduced their willingness to run any risk of war to prevent any Soviet successes outside Europe, and they would become still more reluctant. A National Intelligence Estimate of June 1955 concluded that our allies would stay with us "as long as general war does not appear imminent." But, in a crisis when war seemed imminent, "If events developed in such a way as to confront governments with a clear and immediate choice between nuclear devastation and neutrality, we believe that practically all would choose neutrality." In May 1958, as the Berlin crisis loomed, Dulles remarked that within a few years the Europeans would doubt that we would resort to nuclear war or would dissociate themselves from us if they thought we would do so. Commenting on his planned visit to Berlin, when he would repeat that an attack there would be considered to be an attack on the United States, he wryly noted that "he did not know whether he himself quite believed this, or indeed whether his audience would believe it." When the President remarked that if we did not defend Berlin, we would lose it, and soon after, all Western Europe, Dulles said that he hoped that Ike would indeed order nuclear war if need be, he doubted very much that Eisenhower's successors would issue such an order.[17] Although Eisenhower seemed to be more confident in the solidity of alliances, the prospect of their collapsing, especially in a situation where we were entangled in a local war, was enough to cause him, in 1953–1954, to qualify his normal rejection of "preventive war." He remarked, several times, that in such a case, he might have to initiate a world war against the Soviets, as he once put it, it might be "our duty to future generations." Of course all his day-to-day policies were aimed at preventing his ever being forced to make such a terrible decision.[18]

The Administration intended rather to split the enemy alliance, reviving, in a different way, the objective of the Truman Administration before China entered the Korean War—promoting "Chinese Titoism." But the "wedge strategy," trying to attract the Chinese leaders by showing that the United States was basically friendlier to them than the Soviets, had become bankrupt when the Chinese intervened. Already, in 1952, Dulles envisaged a very different strategy— breaking the enemy alliance by bringing the maximum possible pressure on the weaker partner, making things as hard as possible for the Chinese as long as they stuck by the Soviets. Tito had not broken with the Soviets, he noted, because the West had been especially nice to him.

He did not expect this strategy to work fast, but thanks to Mao Zedong's mentality, it did work and more quickly than expected. The objective of splitting China from the USSR was frequently referred to in policy papers from 1953, although as a very long-range objective—Dulles, in a National Security Council meeting in August 1954, opined that it might take twenty-five years, and, Eisenhower emphasized, we could not count on such a development. The American government, throughout the 1950s, prudently assumed that the enemy axis would remain solid for the next few years, and that, in any crisis, the Soviets and the Chinese would, in the end, stick together. By March 1955, however, during the first Taiwan Strait crisis, Dulles began to suspect that the Soviets might already be having difficulties with China. By March 1959, as Dulles was on his deathbed, the NSC would be discussing what to do if there was a war with the Soviets in which China was *not* involved. American leaders were usually cautious about referring to their hopes for a Soviet–Chinese clash in public, but Eisenhower did so in June 1958, remarking that he would give almost anything to divide the Communist countries.[19]

The "New Look" Strategy

The basic defense policies of the Eisenhower Administration, formulated as NSC 162/2 became known as the "New Look." It was based on maintaining "long-haul" policies geared to a Cold War of indefinite duration, and the need to avoid dissipating American power in indecisive local struggles and maintain that power in way that would not erode American security or turn the country into a "garrison state." The New Look involved greater reliance on airpower and nuclear weapons, primarily tactical nuclear weapons. The Air Force would be built up further, with more effort aimed at continental air defense, while the Army would be reduced (although not to the pre-Korea level); the Navy would also be cut, although not by much. Heavy reliance would be placed on tactical nuclear weapons and a willingness to expand local conflicts, not into a general war, but beyond the boundaries imposed or desired by the Communist side. (It should be noted that tactical nuclear weapons, some of which had variable and adjustable yields, could range from a power of 60 kilotons, several times that of the bomb dropped on Hiroshima, down to a tenth of a kiloton.) Eisenhower and Dulles thought, we now know mistakenly, that the threat to expand the war outside Korea and use tactical nuclear weapons had been responsible for the Communist powers' decision to end the Korean War. This policy was the heart of Dulles' doctrine of "massive retaliation," expressed in a famous, if often misunderstood, speech in early 1954. Eisenhower and Dulles were hardly committed to use atomic weapons in *any* clash with the Communists, as the President wryly noted in a press conference in March 1955, "you don't send for an A-bomb when a riot occurs." He did expect to use tactical atomic weapons in any conflict of Korean dimensions, and in response to questions at another news conference in 1955, indicated that the United States would probably use them in any general war in Asia, although, he emphasized, against "strictly military targets." A local conflict might be expanded as convenient; Dulles once spoke of a "three-front doctrine" for Asia, in which any Communist move in Korea, Taiwan, or Southeast Asia might be countered by action on another of those fronts. Eisenhower was convinced that using tactical nuclear weapons in a "limited war"—a local, Korean-type conflict, would not touch off a general nuclear war, a point he made several times, both publicly and privately. He described the idea that any use of nuclear bombs would touch off all-out war as "silly" as late as 1957. However, the geographical extent in which a limited war could take place was, for him, itself strictly limited. He, and everyone else at the time, accepted that there was no possibility of a limited war in the NATO area. A Soviet attack in Europe was always expected, as in the Truman years, to quickly if not instantly lead to general nuclear war, and Soviet–Western fighting in the Middle East would probably do so. And a general war with China would probably lead to one with the Soviets. Although American intelligence believed that the Soviets would try to limit such hostilities, they would, in the end, go to all-out war if the Chinese regime's survival seemed in question.[20]

Early in his presidency, Eisenhower and Dulles had spoken of breaking the "taboo" on the use of nuclear weapons and regarding tactical ones as "conventional." But, during the first Taiwan Strait crisis, Eisenhower became more cautious when it seemed likely to lead to an actual military clash, stressing that, to defend the offshore islands at issue, conventional weapons would be tried first. Both, especially Dulles, became more and more worried about world reaction to the use of nuclear weapons, a problem Eisenhower noted even in 1955. Dulles remarked, in 1956, on the "terrible repercussions which we would experience if we had recourse to the use of nuclear weapons against the colored people of Asia." In mid-1957, the Secretary speculated that atomic weapons were identified with "white supremacy" to many Asians and Africans and stressed the danger of adverse reactions. In 1958, he deplored the lack of a non-nuclear limited war capability in the Far East as a weakness. There was an argument in the National Security Council over this, the Secretary of Defense maintaining that we did have such a capability. In the late 1950s, the Eisenhower Administration increasingly recognized the weaknesses and dangers of a policy of over reliance on tactical nuclear weapons and revived interest in conventional weapons. It bent toward something like the "flexible response" policy later accepted.[21]

Nuclear War Strategy

Should general war occur, Eisenhower expected nothing but disaster, in which both sides would go all out, using every available weapon. Early in his first administration, he referred to the possibility of victory, but in 1956 and after, he generally expected that in the event of a war, North America would become a desert. Initially, it was assumed that after a nuclear exchange, a lengthy war would follow, in which a conventional ground campaign might be waged in Europe and perhaps also in the Middle East. After an initial defensive phase, a main advance would be launched in Northern Europe through the Polish plain, with, perhaps a secondary advance in Southeast Europe. Fighting in the Middle East would be left to British and local forces, which would stand on the defensive. Eisenhower and Dulles, in 1954, supposed that such a war might last ten years or more! But this seemed unlikely to many in the Administration at the time, and increasingly so as the years passed. Rather, as the Air Force had long expected, a nuclear exchange would probably be the end of a war, not just decide it. Eisenhower himself had always tended to think that any use of ground forces, and "mobilization" would be at home to clean up after the nuclear attack, not for operations overseas. And, by 1957, the planners were increasingly skeptical of the importance of the Middle East in a general war, however critical it was in "cold war" terms. The Air Force Chief of Staff, General White, noted that the Soviets need deliver only a small number of nuclear weapons to destroy those elements of Western power in the region of significance in a general war and deny the Allies oil resources and base facilities.[22]

"Hot Negotiations?"

The Eisenhower–Dulles policies did not go unchallenged within Eisenhower's first administration. There was significant pressure, not for softer, but harder policies, with which some political leaders, notably William Knowland, the Republican leader in the Senate, vocally sympathized. There was hardly any open advocacy of "preventive war" by this time, but some favored what were called, in the 1950s, "hot negotiations," taking an aggressive stance toward the Soviets and Chinese to make them come to terms while the United States still enjoyed strategic superiority. That never-implemented policy was something of a mirror image of what Khrushchev, albeit largely on a basis of bluff, rather than real strength, would try to do after Sputnik. This episode is of interest as the last attempt to change American Cold War policy from "containment" to something stronger.

"Project Control," a set of studies made by the Air Force from mid-1953 to June 1954, was based on the premise that the United States would enjoy nuclear superiority up to at least July 1957. It suggested using this interval to induce or compel the Soviets to change their policies—freeing the satellites, agreeing to German unity, and dissolving their control of the world Communist apparatus, and their alliance with China. "Control" envisaged using pressures up to and including a surprise attack on Soviet nuclear delivery facilities, although the latter idea tended to drop out of discussion. Admiral Radford openly sympathized. Looming reviews of the basic national policy formulated with NSC 162/2 in 1953 crystallized the Joint Chiefs in favor of a tougher position. In a paper submitted to Secretary Wilson in late June 1954, pointing to the growth of Soviet power and unfavorable developments in the underdeveloped countries, they opposed further attempts to negotiate with the Soviets, stressing the Soviet violation of earlier agreements, until they clearly changed their attitude. They warned that U.S. atomic superiority would be neutralized by 1959. We should demand, *now*, that the Soviets free the satellites and undertake other actions demonstrating such a change of attitude. At a National Security Council meeting, Secretary Dulles remarked that, because of fear of atomic war, our "tough policy," as he viewed it, was becoming unpopular. He conceded that there was much to be said for the JCS view, but none of our allies, except for Syngman Rhee, Chiang Kai-shek, and perhaps the Greeks and Turks, would go along with the course proposed.

During reviews of U.S. policy in the Far East, in August, the Joint Chiefs, especially Chairman Radford, advocated policy alternatives aimed at reducing Communist Chinese power even at the risk of war. Radford remarked that "there would be no way of preventing all of Asia from going Communist if Communist China's power continued to expand." Later, in November 1954, the Joint Chiefs, influenced by a paper by Brigadier General Charles Bonesteel, the Defense Department representative on the NSC's Planning Board, which argued that Communist power was growing, that a "creeping advance" was eroding the free world's position in Asia, and we were losing the overall propaganda war, again expressed their concern to Wilson. They argued that the next few years would probably be decisive. The Communists were getting stronger militarily while neutralism and the fear of war weakened our side. We could be forced to "accommodate" the Soviets or fight them under unfavorable circumstances. They advocated taking the initiative with a harder line, although not making clear just what, one taking greater risks, but avoiding preventive war. The Army Chief of Staff, Matthew Ridgway, who never loved the "New Look" strategy, added his own recommendations, which his colleagues declined to support, for essentially reversing the "New Look," and rejecting restrictions on the military budget in favor of an all-out buildup of a "balanced" flexible military establishment capable of countering the Communist threat at any level.

Dulles, commenting on these ideas in a paper on November 1954, clearly disagreed. He commented that while the Soviets were basically hostile, they were anxious to avoid general war, "as of now," and might really want an extended period of lesser tension; remarks that rather ignored the point that the real issue was what might happen later on. He concluded that while the adverse trends in the underdeveloped countries were real enough, it was impractical to refuse to negotiate while the United States must forego acts generally regarded as provocative.

At the National Security Council meeting on November 24, the issues were clearly fought out. The way things were going, Radford remarked, once "atomic plenty" was achieved by both sides, the relative power position would have so changed that we could no longer count on the Soviets fearing starting all-out war. Assuming Soviet objectives were unchanged, the Joint Chiefs thought "some time or other the Soviets would elect to force the issue. Accordingly, the Joint Chiefs had concluded that the United States has only a limited period of time with which to reach an accommodation with the Communists." They could not suggest specific courses of action because they could not be exclusively military, although they did guarantee that if harder policies resulted in either limited or full-scale war, the outcome for the United States, prior to the Soviets achieving "atomic plenty" would be successful. Radford held that Soviet policy had, on the whole, been successful; if we went on reacting, instead of forestalling Communist action, "we cannot hope for anything but a showdown" . . . by 1959 or 1960.

Robert Cutler suggested that Secretary Dulles was less pessimistic than the Admiral. Dulles, surprisingly, said that this was not the case. He remarked that the difference between them was that the JCS favored taking greater risks for bigger goals. Implying that the military really favored some sort of ultimatum, he argued that, on the whole, save in Indochina, our policy had had good results; and the setback there had not been preventable. The Joint Chiefs, he said, did not suggest any way of stopping the Soviets from achieving a nuclear balance with the United States, which was the real issue. If Dulles intended to smoke out an intention to advocate actual preventive war, the Joint Chiefs did not rise to the bait. Curiously, he did not raise the point that a nuclear standoff might be fairly stable, although this idea was not new in 1954. (It was recognized in the Basic National Security policy adopted in January 1955.)

At about this time, a few leaks in the press alluded to the policy debate, and Senator Knowland, possibly not coincidentally, made a widely publicized speech arguing that an atomic stalemate would result in ultimate Communist victory.

Drafting of the new Basic National Security Policy went on, but not on terms favorable to the Joint Chiefs. On December 21, the issue was settled at another NSC meeting. Radford did not attend. Dulles took the initiative. He admitted that he had some sympathy for the Joint Chiefs' desire for "greater dynamism." But experience suggested that it was not easy to go beyond existing policies. Noting that preventive war had been ruled out, he dealt with the view that while we still had atomic superiority we should apply forceful means to change the basic characteristics of the Soviet system. He assumed that this meant an effort to overthrow the Communist regimes in China and the satellites and detach those countries from the USSR. He warned that an effort to implement such a course of action would involve us in a general war. Even if it did not, and detached China and the satellites from the Soviets, this would not touch the heart of the problem: Soviet atomic plenty. We would still face an unimpaired Soviet nuclear capability. He did not think that this more dynamic and aggressive policy would achieve the desired goal unless it eventuated in a general war we could win. And such aggressive policies would almost certainly cause the disintegration of the free world bloc, for our allies would never go along. He suggested, rather in contrast to his earlier and more typical views, that the areas in which the Soviets could expand would not notably increase the actual power of the Soviet bloc. Later,

Dulles suggested there was hope for change in the Soviet bloc, and pointed to the possibility of a Chinese break from the Soviet connection. The Joint Chiefs had no answer to these points, although, ever lawyer-like, Dulles had made a "case" in which he himself could not have entirely believed, one vulnerable to counterattack on several points. He seemed, after all, to be suggesting that the preservation of our alliances was more important than the reason for the alliances in the first place, i.e. sustaining American security, to omit the possibility that even if our allies were panicky enough to threaten to break with us we might be able to coerce them into going along, and ignore the possibility that the Soviets might *not* reform, and that the Soviets and the Chinese *might* stick together or at least quarrel too late to benefit us, and, a point he himself was usually well aware of, that trends in the underdeveloped world did not favor us. But Eisenhower and Wilson, who had remained passive earlier in the discussion, made clear that they agreed with the Secretary, as did the next National Security Basic Policy, NSC 5501, on January 7, 1955.

Radford, and some others, probably continued to hope that circumstances and Communist actions would force a change in policy. He took a hard line during the first Taiwan Strait crisis, remarking, in March 1955, that he did not think the situation in the Far East could be stabilized in the Far East without hostilities and without giving the Chinese Communists a "bloody nose." Unlike Eisenhower and Dulles, he pooh-poohed the idea that a war with China would either benefit the Soviets, or lead to all-out war with the USSR.

This is not to say that Radford, or others, "conspired" to bring about a clash with China, much less all-out war. His views were always openly expressed, and in executing policy exactly followed Eisenhower's direction. It seems doubtful that Radford, or other Joint Chiefs, ever wanted an all-out war with the Communist powers, even if they, or some of them, may have considered such an eventuality, in the next few years, a lesser evil than the disasters they feared would result if current policies continued, and failed. In March 1954, Radford, Admiral Carney and General Ridgway all concurred that in the event of nuclear war, "it was impossible to visualize how the United States could cope with the victory it might achieve over the Soviets, or how it might hope to establish a workable occupation regime."

The views of the military hard-liners, and Knowland, were by no means completely isolated, or, even, totally different from those of the liberal Democratic opposition of the time, much less Eisenhower and Dulles. They were hardly alone in thinking that the Cold War was going badly. Indeed Adlai Stevenson, and many others, then and later—in the election campaign of 1956, and not just that of 1960—argued that the Cold War was being lost. And this was their real belief, not just political posturing, however cynically they liked to pretend that everything that was going wrong was the fault of the Eisenhower Administration. To be sure, Stevenson, and probably most liberals (there were exceptions) rejected the emphasis on military power, the idea of "hot negotiations," or the rejection of other attempts at negotiation, but they were at least as worried about the political aspects of the Cold War and especially developments in the underdeveloped countries.[23]

It should be noted that the fears of the time, both within and outside the Administration, were by no means irrational, nor the proposals for a tougher policy as irresponsible or reckless, as they might be made to seem, at first sight, sixty years later. Had the arms race gone just a little bit differently (as we shall shortly see) or had either Khrushchev or Mao handled certain matters a bit more cleverly, the Cold War might have taken a turn just as ominous as the "alarmists" of the time feared. Had some of Khrushchev's reforms, notably in agriculture, been just a bit better designed, the Soviet Union would have been immensely strengthened. Had Mao been even slightly less of a megalomaniac, or had been gracious enough to die in the late 1950s (or had his colleagues been far-sighted and patriotic enough to murder him, which, incidentally, would have saved some of their own lives) the Soviet–Chinese alliance might have survived considerably longer, and China would have avoided the disasters of the Great Leap Forward. The political orientation of some important underdeveloped countries, notably Indonesia, might have turned out very differently. To those who survived the resultant disasters, Admiral Radford and his allies might well have been vindicated, and prophets as wise as Winston Churchill.

The Missile Race

The Eisenhower Administration may not have regarded nuclear war as likely; nevertheless, it expended great thought and effort at averting the most fearful danger of all, a task complicated by an ongoing technological revolution—the development of long-range ballistic missiles. (There was, for a time in 1955–1956, a brief flap over a "bomber gap," when the Soviets were wrongly thought to be building an unexpectedly large number of the overrated Mya-4 bombers, but this had little effect on national policy.) The dangers and difficulties involved would later be obscured by the often-made point that the "missile gap," which many feared in the late 1950s, never existed. But the fact that it did not develop was a near thing, and one of the Administration's greatest achievements. Had things fallen just a little differently, the Joint Chiefs' fears of the Soviets forcing a "showdown" on their terms might well have come to pass, although it was not the orthodox military policies favored by the military that averted such a danger. In contrast to the Soviets, who followed a steady path of developing larger and larger missiles that led directly to an intercontinental ballistic missile (ICBM), American missile development in the immediate postwar era was sluggish and erratic. Early interest in both ICBM's and satellites, by the Air Force and Navy respectively, proved abortive. The first, small ICBM program was canceled in May 1947. Insofar as it was interested in anything but manned bombers, the Air Force focused mainly on air-breathing cruise missiles. The development of large rocket engines proceeded, not to power ballistic missiles, but to provide boosters for the ramjet-powered Navaho cruise missile. Up to 1950, the German missile team brought to America by the Army (a most unpopular move) did little but launch captured V-2 rockets for high-altitude research; the Navy developed the specialized Viking and Aerobee rockets for the same sort of work. Only in July 1950 did the Army team start work on the Redstone missile, really an improved V-2 capable of hauling a nuclear warhead only 250 miles.

The Air Force revived ICBM development, sluggishly, in 1951, but made little progress before Eisenhower became President. It expected to get an operational Atlas missile by 1963. Had American missile development continued at this pace, the West would probably have been hopelessly outmatched well before that date. By late 1952, however, the Americans were getting reports, accurate as it happened, that the Soviets were developing far bigger rocket engines than anything in the West, engines that could hardly power anything less than an ICBM.[24]

In the nick of time, the Eisenhower Administration turned a sluggish missile effort into a crash program.

A review of missile projects in mid-1953, ordered by the Secretary of Defense to eliminate duplication and waste, was used by Trevor Gardner, the Special Assistant to Secretary of the Air Force Talbott, to push for a new approach to ICBM development. The "Strategic Missiles Evaluation Group," or "Teapot Committee," loaded by Gardner with advocates of the ICBM and chaired by the great mathematician John von Neumann, first met in November. It rejected the Air Force's concentration on cruise weapons. Its report, in February 1954, urged an accelerated, radically reorganized ICBM program to get an operational weapon in six to eight years, cutting the accuracy requirements and warhead weight earlier specified. A separate ICBM development group, with overall technical direction by unusually capable scientists and engineers, from outside of the aircraft industry, and free of excessive control by existing agencies, was needed.

The test of the first deliverable H-bomb in March 1954 showed that warhead weights could be safely reduced. Pressured by Secretary Talbott, the Air Force, reluctantly, got behind the Teapot Committee recommendations and gave them its highest priority. A member of the Committee, General Bernard Schriever, an exceptionally able officer and engineer, became head of a special office, the "Western Development Division" of the Air Research and Development Command. Thanks to Gardner, the start of a major ICBM effort was advanced by one or two years. He, von Neumann, and Schriever provided the correct organizational recipe for success. In September 1954, the Teapot Committee, reorganized as the Atlas Scientific Advisory Committee, secured more authority for Schriever and the job of supplying technical direction and responsibility for systems engineering for the Ramo-Wooldridge Company (later the nucleus of the computer firm TRW). It would oversee the work of the prime contractor, Convair (now General Dynamics). It has been estimated that the combination of the Western Development Division, Schriever's leadership, and Ramo-Wooldridge advanced the Atlas by more than another year.

In December 1954, the Atlas was scaled down in size, something permitted by advances in nuclear weapons development. A decision was made, also, to use dual source development—two major sources for each major subsystem of the missile, lest one supplier fail. This led to a further decision, to build a more advanced ICBM, Titan, using the backup subsystems for Atlas, and designed from the start to be put in underground silos.[25]

Other developments further sped up the ICBM effort, and led to other important developments. In March 1954, Eisenhower had established a Technological Capabilities Panel under James Killian of MIT to investigate the danger of surprise attack. Even before it submitted its "Surprise Attack Study" (usually just called the "Killian Report") in February 1955, it greatly influenced the Cold War. In November 1954, its preliminary appreciation, and the efforts of Trevor Gardner, and CIA officials disappointed with the quality of intelligence, and especially the CIA's inability to get agents into the Communist world—efforts to do so had failed at a horrendous cost in lives—led the President to approve the development of a very high-altitude reconnaissance plane to overfly the Soviet Union—the U-2. Lockheed launched a super-secret operation, the "Skunk Works," which got the U-2 into the air with remarkable speed. First flying in August 1955, it entered the Soviet Union in July 1956. Gardner also pushed efforts to build a radar station in Turkey to monitor Soviet missile tests. (A Royal Air Force Canberra had overflown the Soviet test range in 1953, but was badly damaged by MIGs and was lucky to return at all.) Even before the Killian Report, NSC 5501 had suggested that the Soviets might have ICBMs by 1963, or even 1960.

The Killian Report warned that, unless the United States worked harder, the Soviets might get a decisive lead in missiles by 1960. It recommended a higher priority for the ICBM, and developing a 1,500-mile range intermediate-range ballistic missile (IRBM) as an interim and supporting weapon, as well as reducing the vulnerability of the Strategic Air Command's bombers, then concentrated on a few ill-defended bases. The report envisaged the development of the nuclear arms race, in the forseeable future, as unfolding in four phases. In Period I, up to 1956, the United States would have immensely superior offensive strength but because of an inadequate warning system and air defense would be vulnerable to surprise attack. In Period II, from 1956 to 1958 or 1960, the United States would still be immensely superior in nuclear strength, but far less vulnerable to surprise. It would win any war, although at heavy cost. Afterward, there would be a transitional phase in which things might be fluid. The United States could still be stronger, but the Soviets might gain a dangerous superiority if Americans were careless or neglected critical programs.

In Period IV, whose length would be indefinite, but that might begin in a decade, an attack by either side would result in the destruction of both. The

Killian Report regarded this as very dangerous. It thus envisaged what was later called "mutual assured destruction" but had no confidence that it would be stable. The United States should stay in Period II as long as possible, avert Soviet superiority in Period III, and escape from Period IV as fast as possible, if it could. The report warned that it was impossible to say if the stalemate of Period IV would be permanent.

There were further worrisome reports of Soviet efforts. In July 1955, the CIA suggested that the Soviets might have a two-year lead in missile development. On September 8, the President gave the ICBM effort a "DX" priority, the highest possible, and five days later approved work on an IRBM, which, he then thought, "for the time being" might be practically as militarily valuable as the ICBM. The view of the ICBM's importance was widely shared in the Administration and by key Democratic Senators such as Clinton Anderson and Henry Jackson. Undersecretary of State Hoover, at an NSC meeting on September 8, warned that if the Soviets got an ICBM before us, the political results would be devastating, "neutralism would advance tremendously through the free world." In November, in a final step at acceleration, time-consuming normal administrative procedures were eliminated for the Western Development Division. In that month, the Administration also approved a joint USAF-Atomic Energy Commission project, separate from the WDD, to develop a nuclear reactor rocket as a possible power plant for ICBMs, although that was a far less likely use for such engines than space exploration, a point recognized in 1956. (Alleged military needs were already a stalking horse for space exploration.)

It is likely that the decisions made in 1954–1955 were the military turning point of the Cold War. They ensured that the United States would overtake an initial Soviet lead in rocket development and that the West retained strategic superiority until the Soviet collapse. That was fortunate, and not inevitable, for the Truman Administration, whatever its many other praiseworthy achievements, had dangerously neglected rockets and ballistic missiles. Only the lucky decision to boost the Navaho ramjet intercontinental cruise missile with rocket engines had ensured that a large rocket engine would be under development when the belated decision to launch a serious ICBM program was made. Without that, an American ICBM would have been hopelessly delayed. Without Gardner and von Neumann, a major effort might not have started until 1956. Without the special organizational framework and innovations of the Western Development Division, and Schriever's outstanding leadership, the ICBM project would have been run on traditional lines by the Air Force and aircraft industry. The example of other missile projects suggest that, even with a DX priority and maximum appropriations, an operational ICBM would not have been ready until the mid-1960s. Without any one of these things, a very dangerous situation might have developed even earlier, without all three—as easily might have happened—catastrophe would have resulted.

Things would have been even worse had the Soviet program been any more efficient than it was. The Soviets had early gotten rid of those German rocket men they had secured. Until 1960, possibly because they thought the Americans knew something they didn't, the Soviets wasted considerable effort on developing Navaho-type cruise missiles. Since they were already developing large rocket engines for ballistic missiles, this was sheer waste, without the "fallout" that made the misguided Navaho project pay off for the Americans. Worse, they failed to scale down their first ICBM, the R-7, as the Americans did the Atlas, when small powerful warheads became available. The R-7 proved a fine space launcher, but a poor weapon, requiring lengthy preparations to fire, impossible to put in hardened sites, and so big it had to be based on railroad lines.[26]

The American decision to build an IRBM had only a modest impact on the military balance, but eventually led to a development of far greater importance—the Polaris submarine-launched missile. The initiative for the IRBM came from scientists and political leaders, not from the armed forces or industry. It was not universally popular. Gardner, and many in the Air Force, including Schriever, did not want it, lest it dilute concentration on intercontinental missiles, and it involved dependence on overseas bases the Air Force had long wanted to escape. Of course, that view did not supersede interservice rivalry. If an IRBM had to be built, Schriever and the Air Force wanted the job. The possibility of helping the British take on the project was studied, but they lacked the ability to do it, while the Army missile group was a strong rival contender for the job. Bitter rivalry led to the "solution" of having both services build IRBMs—the Air Force's Thor and the Army's Jupiter. The latter was really a joint Army–Navy project, for Jupiter was designed so it could be launched from submarines, although the Navy did not like taking a liquid-fuel rocket to sea. Both missiles were developed rapidly; they were really quite similar. Thor, a scaled-down Atlas, had the advantage of being air-transportable, while Jupiter, a scaled-up Redstone, could be made relatively mobile on the ground, although in the end no one made any use of that. It was assumed, until Sputnik, that only one missile would actually be deployed; it was increasingly likely that Thor would be chosen. The Navy dropped the Jupiter project. Its Special Projects Office, under the extremely able Vice Admiral William Raborn, had seized on developments in solid fuels. It had already been interested in "Jupiter-S" a solid-fuel successor to Jupiter, but it would be a big, clumsy weapon, using clusters of existing solid-fuel rockets; a very large submarine could carry just four Jupiter-S missiles, which were not expected to become operational before 1965. In 1955, a more powerful solid fuel was developed. During 1956, it became apparent that this and the availability of lighter warheads meant that a far more compact solid-fuel submarine missile could be built, much sooner than Jupiter-S. So the Navy canceled both the naval version of Jupiter and Jupiter-S. In January 1957, it initiated a completely independent program, "Polaris," which proved amazingly successful. Under Raborn's able leadership, and using new management techniques, Polaris became one of the rare defense programs to come in early and under budget. It was the first U.S. missile program to strongly affect the strategic balance.

The British had been interested in Thor at an early stage, and, in March 1957, the President and Prime Minister Macmillan reached an early outline agreement to base an IRBM, probably Thor, in Britain, to be operated by the Royal Air Force. By then, ironically, the Americans were losing faith in the value of the IRBM.

The development of Atlas, Thor, and Jupiter did not go smoothly, apart from interservice quarrels. Atlas suffered many failures during 1957, and flew full range only in November 1958, over a year after the first full range flight of the R-7. Only the fourth Thor test, on September 20, 1957, was a success. Jupiter, more successful, went full range on May 31—but the Air Force, which was slated to operate whatever IRBM was picked, did not like it any better.

The defense budget came under heavy public and Congressional pressure in 1957. The Administration had to fight to prevent more severe cuts. (After Sputnik, many of those attacking the Administration for its allegedly inadequate attention to defense would conveniently forget that they had taken a very different line earlier.) Because of that, and internal conflicts, the missile effort slackened slightly. Talbott's successor as Air Force Secretary, Donald Quarles, was a dogmatic believer that it was already impossible for either side to win a nuclear war and was indifferent to the precise strategic balance. He was willing to postpone an operational ICBM capability and favored stopping either Atlas or Titan development. In March 1957, the planned development budget for Fiscal Year 1958 was cut by 20 percent, and cut further in May. Secretary Wilson reduced overtime work, and the priority of Titan, and later limited the production of Titan and the IRBMs while testing went on. The cuts were not in effect for long, but they, and the handling of the earth satellite program, did the Eisenhower Administration immense political harm.[27]

Notes

1 Peter Calvocoressi, *Survey of International Affairs 1952* (London: Oxford University Press, 1955), p. 2. The following discussion emphasizes the Cold War struggle as one between *blocs*, in which the United States and the Soviet Union were the leading, but not the only, elements. Far too much commentary in the last forty years or so has portrayed the Cold War as a sort of Soviet–American duel, which is not only incorrect but was *not* how it was seen in the 1940s and 1950s.

2 Saki Dockerill, *Eisenhower's New Look: National Security Policy 1953–1961* (New York: St. Martin's Press, 1996), p. 27; *Foreign Relations of the United States 1952–1954, Volume VIII* (Washington DC: Government Printing Office, 1993), pp. 1196–1205; *Foreign Relations of the United States 1952–1954, Volume II* (Washington DC: Government Printing Office, 1984), pp. 329–349. Volumes of the Foreign Relations series will hereafter be abbreviated *FRUS* after first citation.

3 For a classic statement of this view of the Dulles–Eisenhower relationship, cf. Herman Finer, *Dulles Over Suez* (New York: Quadrangle, 1964), which, although intelligent in many of its observations, propounds the totally wrong-headed thesis that Dulles misled Eisenhower into opposing the Anglo-French-Israeli attack on Egypt in 1956.

4 Nikita Khrushchev, *Khrushchev Remembers: The Last Testament* (Boston: Little Brown, 1974), p. 363; Chow Ching-wen, *Ten Years of Storm* (New York: Holt, Rinehart & Winston, 1960), p. 294.

5 Selwyn Lloyd, *Suez 1956* (London: Jonathan Cape, 1978), p. 258; Charles Bohlen, *Witness to History* (New York: Norton, 1973), pp. 456–457.

6 John Lewis Gaddis, *Strategies of Containment* (New York: Oxford University Press, 1982), p. 179.

7 Emmett John Hughes, *The Ordeal of Power* (New York: Atheneum, 1963), p. 105; *Foreign Relations of the United States 1952–1954, Volume XV, Part I* (Washington DC: Government Printing Office, 1984), pp. 694, 805–806, 891.

8 Lloyd, *Suez 1956*, pp. 219, 250; Peter Rodman, *More Precious than Peace* (New York: Scribners, 1994), pp. 85–86; Adams, *First Hand Report*, p. 124; Robert R. Bowie and Richard H. Immerman, *Waging Peace* (New York: Oxford University Press, 1998), pp. 221, 228.

9 Richard M. Leighton, *Strategy, Money and the New Look 1953–1956* (Washington DC: Office of the Secretary of Defense, 2001), pp. 9–11, 16–20, 550; Robert J. Watson, *Into the Missile Age 1956–1960* (Washington DC: Office of the Secretary of Defense, 1997), pp. 3–10, 88–89.

10 Dockerill, *Eisenhower's New Look*, p. 21; *Leighton, Strategy, Money and the New Look*, pp. 9, 36–37; Robert Watson, *The Joint Chiefs and National Policy 1953–1954* (Washington DC: Historical Division, Joint Chiefs of Staff, 1986), pp. 15, 26, 32, 255. Arthur Radford *From Pearl Harbor to Vietnam* (Stanford, CA: Hoover Institution, 1980), gives insights into Radford, although, unfortunately, the Admiral could not write more than part of his memoirs before his death, and concentrated on Vietnam, the "hottest" topic when he was writing.

11 *FRUS 1952–1954, Vol. II*, pp. 265–267, 551–555, 576–586; *Foreign Relations of the United States 1955–1957, Volume XIX* (Washington DC: Government Printing Office, 1990), pp. 25–27. Bowie and Immerman, *Waging Peace*, pp. 47–49, 149; Leighton, *Strategy, Money and the New Look*, p. 338.

12 *Foreign Relations of the United States 1955–1957, Volume II*, pp. 79. 135–138; Adams, *First Hand Report*, p. 133.

13 *Foreign Relations of the United States 1955–1957, Volume XIII* (Washington DC: Government Printing Office, 1988), p. 687; *Foreign Relations of the United States 1958–1960, Volume VIII* (Washington DC: Government Printing Office, 1993), p. 209; Alistair Horne, *Harold Macmillan* (New York: Viking, 1989), Vol. II, pp. 41, 117.

14 *FRUS 1955–1957, Vol. XIX*, p. 407.

15 *FRUS 1952–1954, Vol. XIX*, pp. 145, 190, 227, 266–267, 379–385, 555, 560–561, 653, 724; *FRUS 1955–1957, Vol. XIX*, pp. 35, 141.

16 *FRUS 1952–1954, Vol. II*, pp. 409, 721; *Foreign Relations of the United States 1952–1954, Volume XIII* (Washington DC: Government Printing Office, 1982), pp. 1252, 1261, 1435; *FRUS 1955–1957, Vol. XIX*, pp. 35, 126–127; *Foreign Relations of the United States 1952–1954, Volume XVI* (Washington DC: Government Printing Office, 1981), pp. 621, 654.

17 *FRUS 1952–1954, Vol. II*, pp. 555, 586, 715–717, 776–778; *FRUS 1955–1957, Vol. XIX*, pp. 85–86; *Foreign Relations of the United States 1958–1960, Volume III* (Washington DC: Government Printing Office, 1996), pp. 85–89.

18 Bowie and Immermann, *Waging Peace*, p. 125; *FRUS 1952–1954, Vol. II*, p. 461; *FRUS 1952–1954, Vol. XIII*, p. 1441; *Foreign Relations of the United States 1952–1954, Volume XIV, Part 1* (Washington DC: Government Printing Office, 1986), p. 617.

19 Louis L. Gerson, *John Foster Dulles* (New York: Cooper Square, 1967), p. 331 n. 16; *FRUS 1952–1954, Vol. II*, pp. 421, 555, 836; *FRUS 1955–1957, Vol. XIX*, pp. 27, 136; *FRUS 1958–1960, Vol. III*, pp. 192–194, 202–203; *FRUS 1952–1954, Vol. XIV, Part 1*, pp. 175–179, 294–296, 401–407, 409–411, 533: *FRUS 1955–1957, Vol. II*, p. 343.

20 Dockerill, *Eisenhower's New Look*, pp. 3–5, 40–42, 197, 201; *FRUS 1955–1957, Vol. XIX*, pp. 60–61, 302, 306, 313, 432, 526–527; *FRUS 1958–1960, Vol. III*, pp. 233, 247; Douglas Kinnard, *President Eisenhower and Strategy Management* (Lexington, KY: University Press of Kentucky, 1977), pp. 8, 29, 50, 54, 64, 70; Dwight D. Eisenhower, *Eisenhower: Mandate For Change* (New York: Signet, 1965), p. 570; *FRUS 1952–1954, Vol. XIV, Part 1*, p. 831; *FRUS 1955–1957, Vol. II*, pp. 123–127, 273–276, 336–337, 350, 358, 370–380, 445–447, 459; Ingo Tauschweitzer, *The Cold War US Army* (Lawrence, KS: University of Kansas Press, 2008), pp. 3, 28–32, 48; Bowie and Immerman, *Waging Peace*, pp. 45, 179–180; Watson, *History of the Joint Chiefs of Staff, Vol. V*, pp. 8–9, 26, 29–33; Leighton, *Strategy, Money and the New Look*, pp. 39–41, 91, 216–220.

21 *FRUS 1955–1957, Vol. II*, pp. 358, 431, 446–447; *FRUS 1955–1957, Vol. XIX*, pp. 206, 526–527; *FRUS 1958–1960, Vol. III*, pp. 121–122, 128–131; Byron Fairchild and Walter S. Poole, *The Joint Chiefs and National Policy 1957–1960* (Washington DC: Historical Division, Joint Chiefs of Staff, 2000), pp. 11, 15, 19–20, 29; Watson, *Into the Missile Age*, pp. 110–111, 228.

22 Kenneth W. Condit, *The Joint Chiefs of Staff and National Policy 1955–1956* (Washington DC: Historical Division, Joint Staff, 1992), pp. 25–26, 30; Watson, *The Joint Chiefs and National Policy 1953–1954*, pp. 93–103, 324–325; Fairchild and Poole, *The Joint Chiefs and National Policy 1957–1960*, pp. 11, 143–143; *FRUS 1955–1957, Vol. XIX*, pp. 5, 415; *FRUS 1952–1954, Vol. II*, pp. 599–604, 635–636, 715; Tauschweitzer, *The Cold War US Army*, pp. 40–44.

23 *FRUS 1952–1954, Vol. II*, pp. 685–686, 694, 785–802, 832–834; *FRUS 1952–1954, Vol. XIV, Part 1*, pp. 516–517, 526–536; *FRUS 1955–1957, Vol. II*, pp. 26, 138, 403; Leighton, *Strategy, Money and the New Look*, pp. 335–356; Watson, *The Joint Chiefs and National Policy 1953–1954*, pp. 46–54; Bowie and Immerman, *Waging Peace*, pp. 167–169, 172–177; Gayle B. Montgomery and James W. Johnson, *One Step From the White House* (Berkeley, CA: University of California Press, 1998), pp. 130, 174–176, 185. Leighton and Bowie and Immermann trace the origins of the Joint Chiefs of Staff's proposals to somewhat different origins.

24 Alan Levine, *The Missile and Space Race* (Westport, CT: Praeger, 1994), pp. 12–21, 23, 27–29; Edmund Beard, *Developing the ICBM* (New York: Columbia University Press, 1976), pp. 6–8, 37–44, 49–56, 62–72, 75, 84, 89, 96, 102, 104, 130–144; Jacob Neufeld, *Ballistic Missiles in the United States Air Force* (Washington DC: Office of Air Force History, 1990), pp. 24–33, 36–38, 44–92.

25 Levine, *The Missile and Space Race*, pp. 29–33; Beard, *Developing the ICBM*, pp. 144–185; Neufeld, *Ballistic Missiles in the United States Air Force*, pp. 93–128, 255–269.

26 *FRUS 1955–1957, Vol. XIX*, pp. 25, 41–56, 115, 407; Eisenhower, *Mandate for Change*, pp. 546–547; Leighton, *Strategy, Money and the New Look*, pp. 423–438; Levine, *The Missile and Space Race*, pp. 19, 23, 34–36, 46, 74, 92, 162–163; James R. Killian, *Sputnik, Scientists and Eisenhower* (Cambridge, MA: MIT Press, 1977), pp. 67–68; Neufeld, *Ballistic Missiles in the United States Air Force*, pp. 120–122, 128–136; Beard, *Developing the ICBM*, pp. 186–194.

27 Levine, *The Missile and Space Race*, pp. 36–44; Leighton, *Strategy, Money and the New Look*, pp. 440–449; Watson, *Into the Missile Age*, pp. 89–101, 158–165, 175–178; Humphrey Wynn, *The RAF Strategic Nuclear Deterrent Forces: Ministry of Defence: Air Historical Branch* (London: Her Majesty's Stationery Office, 1997), pp. 280–283; John Boyes, *Project Emily* (Stroud: History Press, 2008), pp. 23–26, 29–30, 46.

3

THE ENEMY

Khrushchev's USSR

The Cold War enemy was changing, but not, unfortunately, in a way that made life simpler for the democracies. The Soviets instituted reforms that may have averted a looming catastrophe, and while not saving them in the long run, made them a more formidable enemy for a time. Much of this was due to Nikita Khrushchev, the most unusual and most colorful of Soviet rulers. For a time, perhaps, he was genuinely popular among Russians, although many always regarded him as an "uncultured" boor.

Stalin's death, or murder, was followed by a lengthy struggle for succession, which alone would have ensured a sort of breathing space and a slight "thaw" in the Cold War. (By making it hard for the Iranian Communists to get help or even advice from Moscow, this may have strongly influenced the struggle for Iran in 1953.) The other Soviet leaders briefly combined to dispose of the most dangerous contender for the succession, the Soviet Himmler (as Stalin had once jokingly referred to him, when speaking to the Western leaders in an unguarded moment), Lavrenti Beria. He was finally arrested and executed, in classic Stalinist fashion, it was "discovered" that he had been a British agent since 1920! The rest of the succession struggle, however, was conducted in a less violent, and by Soviet standards positively gentlemanly fashion. The victor, Khrushchev, was, rarely for a Communist leader, of working-class origin, a southern Russian from the Donetz basin. He had only joined the Communist party in 1918, having been a Menshevik, not a Bolshevik, sympathizer before the revolution, a dark and deadly secret during his lifetime. Before going into politics, he had wanted to become an engineer, and considered emigrating to the United States. (In that hypothetical better alternate universe where Hitler became a moderately successful if eccentric painter, Stalin a priest, and Mao Zedong head librarian of Beijing University, Khrushchev might have become a

Detroit car designer.) He had rapidly risen to become party boss in Ukraine. His record in the Great Purges was no worse than, and perhaps better than, other Soviet leaders; the Purges, at least, seem to have bothered him. Although brutal enough in the "assimilation" of East Galicia in 1939–1941, and in crushing Ukrainian nationalist resistance after World War II, he was perhaps relatively more "remote" than most leaders from the terror apparatus, as some of his early biographers, the Medvedev brothers, put it. Stalin had liked him as a jolly drinking companion, and the least threatening of his would-be successors—he may also have liked him because he was as short as the dictator. A political commissar with several Soviet "fronts" (the Red Army equivalent of Western army groups) during World War II, although blamed for the disastrous defeat at Kharkov in May 1942, he was particularly associated with Marshal Rodion Malinovsky, who would become Minister of Defense in 1957. From 1949 Khrushchev was the Moscow region Party Secretary and was also in charge of agriculture, at which he became considered a specialist. Although dreaming up one of the most characteristically Stalinist ideas for "reforming" agriculture, the "agrogorods"—consolidating farming into "agricultural cities"—he seems to have been aware, unusually for the Soviet elite, of the disastrous state of farming. Unfortunately, he was also heavily influenced, like Stalin, by the neo-Lamarckian quack biologist Trofim Lysenko.

His successes at averting agricultural catastrophe, along with his cleverness at political maneuver, were the key to his political triumphs. As First Secretary of the Communist Party from 1953, he promoted and profited from the shift of power from the government and police back to the Party. He attacked his chief rival, Georgi Malenkov, criticizing Malenkov's allegedly excessive solicitude for light industry and consumer goods at the expense of the traditional Soviet emphasis on the maximum possible growth of heavy industry. He, and others, bitterly attacked Malenkov's suggestion, in March 1954 (echoing a speech Eisenhower had made in December 1953) that nuclear war was out of the question because it would wreck civilization. Malenkov was forced to publicly renounce this.[1]

Khrushchev averted agricultural collapse with several drastic measures. First, he let up on restrictions on the private plots of collective farmers—plots that, on just 3 percent of the farmland, produced 30 percent of the USSR's food—by reducing taxes and in-kind payments for the peasants. He also promoted enormously greater use of corn—mostly for animal feed; like most Europeans, Russians did not care to eat corn—importing better strains from the United States.

But the biggest and for a time most successful venture of all, undertaken against skepticism and considerable opposition from other Soviet leaders, was the exploitation of the "Virgin Lands," areas of the southern Urals, south Siberia and northern Kazakhstan not previously farmed, with fertile soil but irregular and low rainfall. Using as a skilled nucleus the Volga Germans exiled to Kazakhstan during World War II, and specially mobilized workers to supplement a massive stream of permanent Russian and Ukrainian peasant settlers, hundreds of new state farms were built, planting only wheat. They were given most of the newest agricultural machinery, at the expense of allotments to the traditional centers of farming. The plan was a gamble, and a stopgap. It was originally expected that, after a few successful seasons dependent on good rainfall, the exclusive planting of wheat would be replaced by proper crop rotation and the dry-farming methods safe and dependable agriculture required in most of the new farmlands.

The first harvest, in 1954, was a success, that of 1955, a failure, but that of 1956 was a great success, cementing Khrushchev's political triumph. The new lands supplied, in 1956 and for several more years, half the grain raised in the Soviet Union. Characteristically, however, Khrushchev and other Soviet leaders forgot the original temporary nature of arrangements for the Virgin Lands, and continued exclusive wheat-raising with methods relying on continued good rainfall. The result, when drought began, was something like the American Dust Bowl of the 1930s, but far worse. (Apparently no one in the Kremlin read Steinbeck's *The Grapes of Wrath*.) From 1962 on, there was a titanic ecological disaster in which vast amounts of precious topsoil were blown away, and the Soviets were forced into the costly humiliation of buying American wheat. The corn campaign also proved oversold in the long run. It was planted everywhere, even in utterly unsuitable northern areas like Siberia and the Leningrad (St. Petersburg) region, with much waste. Just as the Virgin Lands, properly handled, might have produced a reliable source of food, the Soviets missed the chance of creating a proper "corn-belt" in the warm southern areas—south Ukraine, the Don and Lower Volga, and the North Caucasus—really suited to the plant.[2]

Thus Khrushchev, while generating some short-run successes, did his part in undermining the future of the Soviet system, and his actions were characteristic of his general approach. Although highly intelligent, he was temperamental and inclined to extremes. He was more of an improviser and gambler than other Soviet leaders, apt to rush full steam ahead instead of carefully analyzing a problem, and (even more so after 1957) prone to listen to what he wanted to hear. He lacked the patience for lengthy programs that might be sound but lacked a quick payoff. He was, however, far more intellectually flexible than his colleagues, and perhaps less of a control freak than other Soviet leaders, readier to see the value of carrots as well as sticks, and more willing to allow his subjects a long leash. Still, he was not a true decentralizer. (No one in the Kremlin read Drucker's *Concept of the Corporation*, either.)

He was a Communist ideologue, but a less rigid one, capable of commenting that "It's of no use having the correct ideology if you are walking around without any pants on" (some Western "democratic" politicians have not yet figured this out). He was easier to work with, and under, than other Soviet rulers: his subordinates referred to him as the "First" (*pervi*) rather than the "boss" (*vozhd*) or even "master" (*khozayin*) as they had Stalin. Unlike Stalin and others, he did not object to associating with the public, and mixed well with foreigners, especially foreign Communists, and welcomed traveling outside the Soviet sphere. He even had an almost sportsmanlike approach to some of the minor aspects of international relations, allowing, for example, the award of the Tchaikovsky prize to the American Van Cliburn in 1958, which would have been utterly inconceivable under Stalin. It does seem that he had retained relatively more decency and humanity than Stalin's other lieutenants. While having some anti-Semitic tendencies, he was embarrassed by them.

He was, however, in the last resort, a Communist true believer. And, once a particular problem or crisis had been solved, perhaps by an ideologically strained compromise or deviation, he could not let well enough alone, but felt compelled to resort to a more orthodox, comfortable line. For example, having avoided disaster by letting up on private plots, he would later crack down on them, and having allowed more freedom to writers, would periodically clamp down again.

Foreign policy remained dominated by ideology. As Khrushchev himself frankly said on New Year's Eve, 1957, "when it comes to fighting imperialism, we are all Stalinists." That should have been plain enough, but it was, and still is, hard for many Westerners to assimilate the point that within the Soviet orbit Khrushchev was a genuine reformer, relatively humane, and vastly easier for his subjects to live under, but remained a deadly enemy of the West. This was something, also, obscured by Khrushchev's memoirs, which make him more moderate than he was, and by highly selective readings of his foreign and defense policies. (In particular, Khrushchev portrayed himself as completely ruling out nuclear war as unwinnable, although in truth his views when he was in power were ambiguous.)[3] Until the end of his rule, and indeed after, many Westerners were sure that he was a moderate, peaceable fellow. Any Soviet actions that seemed to contradict that pleasing picture were attributed to the malignant pressure of, usually unnamed, "Stalinists." Arguments for concessions to the Soviets were often rationalized as an alleged way to keep this "Brand X" version of Soviet leader from toppling the reasonable Khrushchev. (Sometimes "Brand X" was specified as Frol Kozlov, Khrushchev's most probable heir up to 1963, who was in fact the "First's" loyal lieutenant.) Actually, all the most menacing Soviet actions of the late 1950s and early 1960s were pushed, and usually originated by Khrushchev himself, sometimes against the resistance of more prudent elements, some of whom were more "Stalinist" than he was in general tendency.[4] Later, as the crudest sort of mirror-imaging became popular, unpleasant Soviet actions would be ascribed to the Soviet "military–industrial complex."

Khrushchev would be a formidable enemy, posing difficult problems for Eisenhower and Dulles. For much of the early 1960s, he would run rings around Eisenhower's fantastically glamorized successor; only the much greater power at American command and growing Soviet–Chinese hostility would prevent disaster.

The general tenor of Soviet society had changed greatly after Stalin. The most extreme terror, and the ridiculous claims that Russians, or some other people on the territory of the modern Soviet Union, had invented just about everything, together with attacks on everything "Western" from jazz to science fiction, were stopped. Stalin's last exercise in paranoid conspiracy claims, the "Doctor's Plot," was declared a fraud, and concessions made to consumer interests and the development of light industry, although these would be attacked by Khrushchev and his allies in the campaign against Malenkov, they were continued when Khrushchev won. (Extending similar concessions to the satellites, and the irresolute response of the East German authorities, triggered the East German uprising of June 1953.) Beria's internal empire was reduced, the Soviet secret police, the MGB, being removed from the Ministry of Internal Affairs, and renamed the KGB. The "Ministry of Medium Machine Building," responsible for making nuclear weapons, was also removed from the Ministry of Internal Affairs, and amnesties began to slowly reduce the huge concentration camp population, picking up speed from 1955.

At the Twentieth Party Congress, in February 1956, the previously implicit "de-Stalinization" became overt. Khrushchev's supporter, Deputy Prime Minister Anastas Mikoyan, and then Khrushchev himself, directly attacked Stalin, admitting for the first time, a small fraction of his crimes and blunders, although only those committed after 1934, and against Communist Party members. The attack on Stalin—partly a way to undermine those more closely connected to the tyrant and his worst (from a Communist point of view) actions, and partly perhaps a result of pressure from below—millions returning from the Gulag were now able to talk—was an implicit promise to Party members, at least, that they would enjoy some personal security. There would be no massive purges, and the police would be restrained. At the Congress, the Soviets repudiated Stalin's doctrine that the class struggle became more intense as "socialism" was built, the rationale for the Great Purges and the worst terror, and suggested that there might be more than one road to "socialism" and, even, that a peaceful transition to "socialism" was possible. (However, Soviet interpreters later suggested that the absorption of the Baltic States, and the takeover of East-Central Europe, especially Czechoslovakia, were examples of the "peaceful road.") The Twentieth Party Congress also repudiated the doctrine that war was inevitable as long as capitalism existed, suggesting that Khrushchev might have taken over Malenkov's ideas about nuclear war as well as some of his internal policies.

The attack on Stalin, and implicit promise of further liberalization, had unanticipated consequences, some of which rebounded against Khrushchev. In East-Central Europe, it led to serious unrest in Poland, which was terminated without Soviet military intervention, and sparked an outright revolution in Hungary in October 1956, brutally crushed by the Red Army. Outside the Soviet sphere, the "Secret Speech," which was soon anything but secret, seriously injured Communists in Western Europe, where they and their sympathizers were stunned to find the Soviet leaders openly admitting the crimes they had earlier denied. In the English-speaking world, however, where Communism and blatant apologetics for the USSR had long been discredited, Khrushchev's moves provided an opening for a whole new road to denial of reality, promoting delusions about the Soviet system's ability to reform itself and pursue peaceful policies.

The crises in East-Central Europe, and further steps by Khrushchev, caused opposition to him in the Party Praesidium (as the Politburo was called between 1952 and 1966), which led to a nearly successful coup against him. In May 1957, Khrushchev proposed a major revision of the planning system and made unrealistic brags about an imminent cure for the housing shortage, and, even more, surpassing the United States in at least some major categories of agricultural production. While Khrushchev was visiting Finland in June 1957, the chief plotters against him—Malenkov, Molotov, Kaganovich, and Voroshilov—persuaded Premier Bulganin and two other Praesidium members to join them, giving the anti-Khrushchev faction a majority in the Praesidium. Later, Foreign Minister Shepilov, a non-voting candidate member of the Praesidium, who had been a Khrushchev supporter, went over to them. On June 18, they sprang an ambush on Khrushchev (though the latter may have gotten some slight advance warning) demanding he resign as First Secretary. But he turned the tables on them. He mustered support from the military, police, and the horde of lower-level Party officials who owed their positions to him, and secured an appeal to a plenary decision of the entire Party Central Committee. The military helped fly in members from the provinces to Moscow, and that gave him victory over the "Anti-Party Group" as it was later identified; its members were eliminated, but in the new style. Some, at least, were surprised to find themselves merely exiled to minor posts far from Moscow or retired rather than killed.

The victor enlarged the membership of the Praesidium, and packed it with his mediocre followers. Henceforth he relied on advice from them, when he took advice, and from two remaining Old Bolsheviks, Mikoyan and Otto Kuusinen, who were among the most moderate members of the Praesidium. Mikoyan had been the sole Soviet leader to oppose military action in Hungary; he would oppose, albeit ineffectively, Khrushchev's most aggressive foreign moves in the next few years, although he was the most enthusiastic supporter of the Cuban revolution among the Soviet leaders. Khrushchev now turned on his ally, Minister of Defense and war hero Marshal Zhukov, the most popular member of the Praesidium. He may have been genuinely convinced that Zhukov was a dangerous "Bonapartist," bent on overthrowing the civilian leadership. Probably, the Marshal had no such aim, but merely wanted more extensive rehabilitation of military victims of the Purges, and to reduce the power of political officers. He was accused of promoting his own "cult of personality"—one of the retrospective attacks on Stalin—and on October 25 was forced to retire. He was replaced by Malinovsky.

Along with the triumph of Sputnik earlier that month, this put Khrushchev at the peak of his power and popularity. Indeed, this was the peak of the Soviet system. The economy was functioning well, or at least as well as it ever had, or ever would, with a high rate of industrial growth, and the food situation as good as it had ever been since collectivization. Life was getting visibly better and freer, and was expected to continue to do so. The Communist regime had now been in power for two generations. It was the only government most Soviet citizens had ever known. Even the probably substantial part of the population that continued to hate it had long since become resigned to it. To the great majority, even of them, it was "their" government. It was at the peak of its prestige in the rest of the world, much of which increasingly believed, or at least feared, that the Soviets, not the Western democracies, were the "wave of the future."

In March 1958, Khrushchev forced out Bulganin, who had been the "Anti-Party Group" candidate to replace him, and took the job of Premier for himself. Later in 1958, he disposed of the powerful police general Ivan Serov, a strong ally earlier, but a dangerous character who had been deep in some of the bloodiest acts in Soviet history. While completing his power position, Khrushchev embarked on new reforms. He terminated the sixth Five-Year Plan in September 1957 and switched over to a new "Seven-Year Plan" to start in 1959. A new agricultural reform, dissolving the Machine Tractor Stations, proved less successful. They had owned and controlled the machinery used by collective farmers. While transferring the machines to the farms was a good idea it was executed badly, and far too fast. The collective farms were forced to buy the equipment outright, and much was damaged in the process, hurting farm production. Somewhat more successfully, in late 1958, Khrushchev instituted reforms in the Soviet judicial system, although perhaps in the end having little real effect.[5]

Khrushchev in Foreign Affairs

Even Molotov, the most "Stalinist" of the rival successors, having reclaimed his old job as Foreign Minister, had favored a reduction of tensions and some breathing space when Stalin died. Others of the short-lived collegial leadership were inclined to go farther. The Soviets quickly repudiated the "germ warfare" hoax launched in 1952; those immediately in charge of it were arrested. Women who had married foreigners were allowed to leave with their husbands, and diplomatic relations resumed with Israel. The Soviets withdrew the claims to Turkish territory made after World War II. The Soviets cut back on the extraction of reparations from East Germany and the economic exploitation of the other satellites. Over the next few years this trend continued, to the point that by the late 1950s they were subsidizing the satellites rather than the other way around. The Soviets finally withdrew from their Manchurian bases and terminated the joint-stock Soviet–Chinese enterprises the Chinese had disliked. But further attempts to improve relations, often generous by Soviet standards, would founder on Mao's growing hostility and arrogance.

Further changes in policy were generally pushed through by Khrushchev over Molotov's opposition, notably the Austrian State Treaty, which withdrew all Allied forces from Austria and neutralized that country. The Soviets hoped this move would be an implicit suggestion to West Germany to stay out of NATO. In response to the Paris Agreements and the end of the Western occupation of West Germany, the Soviets established relations with the German Federal Republic, released the last German prisoners of war, and formally terminated their own occupation of East Germany. Ending Stalin's policy of making only bilateral alliances, the Soviets created the Warsaw Pact to counter NATO; actually, its original purpose seems to have been to provide a paper bargaining counter to be traded for the dissolution of the actually existing NATO. The Soviets withdrew from their base at Hango/Porkalla in Finland, and, in early 1956, dissolved the Cominform organization of European Communist parties. From 1955, they sharply reduced the swollen ground forces built up in Stalin's last years—probably the greatest burden on their economy. Khrushchev and Bulganin began making state visits far from the Soviet bloc, hobnobbing with non-Communist leaders and even crowds. They attempted to come to terms with the heretic ruler of Yugoslavia, Tito.

All this fueled the idea in the West that the Cold War had fundamentally "thawed" and even that it might be nearing its end. But that was a highly optimistic conclusion. Khrushchev's fundamental attitudes, and those of most if not all of the Soviet leaders, had not changed a bit. His basic approach to foreign policy was unpromising. To be sure, he had had little to do with it when Stalin was alive, but he had thought, then, that Stalin was overcautious! In 1940, he had been disappointed when Stalin ended the war with Finland before it was conquered and reduced to a puppet state. In 1945, he thought that Stalin should have gone ahead with the planned invasion of the northern Japanese island of Hokkaido, instead of canceling the operation after Hiroshima. In 1950 he had thought Stalin unduly cautious after the Americans entered the Korean War. He had suggested putting Marshal Malinovsky in command of the Communist forces, and sending a Soviet tank corps to Korea. That would have won the Korean War right away, and probably have led straight to World War III. In 1953, he vigorously opposed abandoning East Germany in a deal with the West, tentatively suggested by Beria, and possibly considered by Malenkov.

Khrushchev's steady aim was to induce, later to force, the disintegration of NATO; and, when the time was ripe, use nuclear blackmail against the West. The Soviet bloc would execute a leap southward, bypassing containment and the alliances constructed since the war by alliances with pseudo-neutralist, non-Communist ex-colonial countries, hostile to the West, which needed Soviet help to realize their ambitions. That policy, a reversion to and expansion of Lenin's policies in the early 1920s, *not* aiding Communist revolutions in the underdeveloped countries, was the main element in Khrushchev's policies toward the underdeveloped world. He did not reject Communist seizures of power there, and welcomed them when they did occur, but he did not expect or bank on them in the near future. This policy started with the "Czech" arms deal with Egypt in 1955—Czechoslovakia being used as a front and precaution against a violent Western reaction—and evolved into an uneasy alliance. Similar relationships developed with Syria, Iraq after the 1958 revolution there, Indonesia, Ghana, and Guinea.

Soviet arms helped overturn the uneasy balance in the Middle East and to produce the Suez–Sinai War in 1956, although that war was not desired by the Soviets and, in part, took them by surprise. Khrushchev's response to the Anglo-French attack was a threat to attack Britain and France with missiles, which were not yet operational. Although that bluff was not the cause of the Allies' decision to back down, Khrushchev, and most of his intended audience in Asia and Africa, assumed it was, and it encouraged similar moves in the future. He had already observed, and exploited, the short-lived fuss over the "bomber gap" in the United States. That too encouraged the policies he would follow from late 1957 on, based on claims to possess ICBMs he did not have.[6]

The Soviet ICBM

When Stalin died, the Soviets had few nuclear weapons and no assured, effective way to deliver them to North America. Attempts to develop heavy bombers went badly. It was not surprising, therefore, that the Soviets stressed missile development, in which they might, indeed did for a time, get a lead. Their missile development program developed in a simpler way than the Americans', without the interservice clashes. It went into high gear in 1953. It was run like the U.S. Army's Ballistic Missile Agency (ABMA) rather than the Western Development Division. An artillery general, Mitrofan Nedelin, was in charge. But the Germans drawn from the V-2 program played a lesser role than the von Braun team at ABMA, and after 1950 were not important. Instead of the complex interplay of rival programs that split the small American effort, the Soviets simply built bigger and bigger missiles. After the R-5 missile, with a 700-mile range, flew in early 1954, a final decision was made to go ahead with the huge R-7 ICBM, carrying a five-ton warhead. Its design was frozen in February 1954, and never scaled down, as the Americans did the Atlas later that year. The enormous missile that resulted was a clumsy weapon, but could lift great payloads into space, making possible the great size of Soviet satellites and space probes and the many firsts the Soviets would score in space from 1957 to 1962. It was powered by RD-107 and RD-108 engines (slightly different variants of the same design), which were basically clusters of improved V-2 engines fed by a single turbopump, generating 228,000 pounds of thrust, far more than any engine the Americans were even contemplating. The Americans assumed that the Soviet engines were, as they considered conventional, huge single-chambered engines, which made the Soviets seem more advanced than they were. The R-7's structure was also heavy by Western standards.

The Soviets began test firings in May 1957, launching a successful full-range flight on August 21, 1957. But they continued to suffer serious problems with accuracy and reentry. Constructing an operational base, at Plesetsk, also proved very slow.

The Soviets also developed short-range ballistic missiles that could be fired from a surfaced submarine. They were actually slightly ahead of the Americans in gaining a submarine-launched missile capability, albeit a very limited, technically backward one, that was soon overtaken by the far superior Polaris ballistic missile submarine system.

The Soviets' successful ICBM test attracted remarkably little attention or concern, rather to the surprise of President Eisenhower. Just over six weeks later, however, the Soviets, taking part in the International Geophysical Year, used an R-7 to launch the first artificial earth satellite, Sputnik I. They had announced their intention to do this well before, in April 1955, and disclosed the wavelengths on which it would broadcast in June 1957, but the result was a terrific shock in the West.[7]

Notes

1 William Taubman, *Khrushchev: The Man and His Era* (New York: Norton, 2003), esp. pp. 240–241, 264–266; Roy and Zhores Medvedev, *Khrushchev: The Years in Power* (New York: Norton, 1978), pp. 4–17, 44; David Holloway, *Stalin and the Bomb* (New Haven, CT: Yale University Press, 1994), pp. 333–339; Robert Conquest, *Power and Policy in the USSR* (New York: St. Martin's Press, 1961), pp. 26–28, 231, 260; Leonard Schapiro, *The Communist Party of the Soviet Union* (New York: Vintage, 1971), pp. 555–566.

2 John Keep, *Last of the Empires* (New York: Oxford University Press, 1995), pp. 108–113, 116; Roy and Zhores Medvedev, *Khrushchev: The Years in Power*, pp. 29–37, 57–62, 117–128, 164; Taubman, *Khrushchev*, pp. 262, 265–268, 480.

3 Jonathan Haslam, *Russia's Cold War* (New Haven, CT: Yale University Press, 2011), p. 139; Keep, *Last of the Empires*, pp. 42–118; Archie Brown, *The Rise and Fall of Communism* (New York: Harper Collins, 2009), pp. 253–264; William Odom, *The Collapse of the Soviet Military* (New Haven, CT: Yale University Press, 1998), pp. 67, 113; Jan Sejna, *We Will Bury You* (London: Sidgwick & Jackson, 1981), pp. 22–24, 28; Taubman, *Khrushchev*, pp. xiv, xx, 326, 331.

4 Aleksandr Fursenko and Timothy Naftali, *Khrushchev's Cold War* (New York: Norton, 2006), have fully demonstrated this.

5 Taubman, *Khrushchev*, pp. 271–273, 278, 282, 294–306, 311–323, 361–376; *Russia Under Khrushchev*, ed. Abraham Brumberg (New York: Praeger, 1962), pp. 43, 61, 72–73, 111, 211; Schapiro, *The Communist Party of the Soviet Union*, pp. 564–567, 610–611; Brown, *The Rise and Fall of Communism*, pp. 278–292; Conquest, *Power and Policy in the*

USSR, pp. 222–233, 281, 292–293, 298–323, 348, 360; Holloway, *Stalin and the Bomb*, p. 343; Haslam, *Russia's Cold War*, pp. 165–173; Keep, *Last of the Empires*, pp. 49–58, 81, 106; Roy and Zhores Medvedev, *Khrushchev: The Years in Power*, pp. 66–82, 85–93; Fursenko and Naftali, *Khrushchev's Cold War*, pp. 146–149, 151–153.

6 Fursenko and Naftali, *Khrushchev's Cold War*, pp. 27, 33–34, 39, 41–42, 48–64, 124–127, 133; Taubman, *Khrushchev*, pp. 141, 290–297, 326–359, 379–380; Haslam, *Russia's Cold War*, pp. 155–157, 170; Arnold Horelick and Myron Rush, *Strategic Power and Soviet Foreign Policy* (Chicago, IL: University of Chicago Press, 1966), pp. 18, 29, 31; *A Cardboard Castle?* ed. Vojtech Mastny (Budapest: Central European University Press, 2005), pp. 3–5, 8, 13; Uriel Ra'anan, *The USSR Arms the Third World* (Cambridge, MA: MIT Press, 1969), pp. 7, 87–89, 113–115, 126 n. 99, 172.

7 Levine, *The Missile and Space Race*, pp. 21–23, 33, 45–46, 51–52, 56–57; Steve Zaloga, *The Kremlin's Nuclear Sword* (Washington DC: Smithsonian Institution Press, 2002), pp. 12–17, 23–29, 36–54.

4

THE SPUTNIK SHOCK

On October 4, 1957, a modified R-7 ICBM put Sputnik I, the first artificial earth satellite, into orbit. The small aluminum alloy sphere, weighing 184 pounds, and carrying just two radio transmitters (it carried no other instrumentation) set off a veritable explosion in the West. It was a shock at several levels. It was so large, far bigger than the satellites the Americans planned to launch as part of their Vanguard program, that it had to have been launched by an ICBM—one larger than the Americans were building. (That it was *too* big was not suspected at the time.) The fact that the Soviets led in the ICBM race, which, to Eisenhower's surprise, had eluded the news media and the public earlier, now sank in. As if Sputnik I was not a sufficient shock, on November 3, the Soviets launched a much larger, heavily instrumented Sputnik, weighing 1,120 pounds and carrying a dog. (Humorists in the West dubbed it "Muttnik.") It remained attached to the R-7's spent sustainer stage, so over 8,000 pounds had gone into orbit. Some in the West, at the time, thought that it had been launched by a new rocket, perhaps using some sort of "superfuel," or even by a nuclear rocket. A delighted Khrushchev secured a Lenin prize for Sergei Korolev, who directed the Soviet program.

All of this posed several definite, if not immediate dangers. First, *if* the Soviet ICBM was reliable and effective, and could be mass-produced, and the Americans failed to catch up or take successful countermeasures, the Soviets could, within some years, transform their lead in development into a massive ICBM force superior to the Americans. That would create a "missile gap," from 1959–1964, during which the Soviets would outnumber—and enormously outnumber—the Americans in ICBMs. (The "missile gap" was thus a prediction, *not* a statement of the current military balance.) It might lead to an actual "deterrent gap" and even a Soviet first-strike capability. The distinction between a "missile gap" and "deterrent gap" must be stressed. The Eisenhower Administration, like practically everyone in the West, expected, for a time, that a missile gap would develop, but was fairly sure that it could avert the Soviets' gaining an effective first strike capability.

The second great problem was a "space" or payload gap. The R-7 was so much more powerful than any American rocket, that at least for some years, it alone, much less anything else the Soviets came up with, would let the Soviets send far bigger loads into space. It could, and did, let them score any number of "firsts"—notably, sending the first probes to the Moon in 1959, and putting the first men into orbit in 1961—and exploit any military advantage that might be found in space. Unlike the missile gap, the space gap was very real. Only in 1963 did the Americans match the Soviet ability to send heavy loads into space. But American superiority in electronics, and the large number of satellites the Americans sent up, meant that, in practice, they outpaced the Soviets in terms of scientific results and the effective utilization of space.

What was known was bad enough, but many feared that the Sputniks might be just the first and least of a whole range of technological firsts; rumors and projections at the time suggested that they might be ahead in developing exotic chemical fuels, and nuclear-powered planes and rockets. They were widely believed to be far advanced in work on the "T4A," the long-rumored Soviet version of the Sanger manned intercontinental rocket bomber, on which the Germans had done some work during World War II, and in which Stalin had taken an interest. There were reports that the Soviets were testing a 50,000-pound thrust nuclear rocket engine (the Americans would not have such an engine until 1969) and working on one with 2.2 million pounds of thrust! (The F-1 engines used in the Saturn V moon rocket developed 1.5 million pounds of thrust.) Few would have believed at the time that the Soviets were either not working on such projects or were far behind the Americans.

But the issues of the missile gap and space exploration, important as they were, was just part of what appeared to people at the time as a colossal crisis. Even when it was understood, as it soon was in the United States (but *not* in Europe) that there was no immediate danger, and that the West would retain strategic superiority in the near future, there was a feeling of great disillusionment and worry. The Soviets, it seemed, had beaten the West, and the United States in particular, at its own game—technology. They, not the democracies, enjoyed the glory of launching what was immediately dubbed the Space Age. And it seemed that they threatened to overtake the West not only in a narrowly military field, but on a broad range of technological and economic endeavors. Many in the West, unlike some of Khrushchev's colleagues, took seriously the "First's" boasts, on the fortieth anniversary of the Bolshevik Revolution, that the Soviets would overtake the United States in the production of critical items within fifteen years.

None of this was a purely American notion. There was a common mood of near panic throughout the Western world. *The London Times* wrote of a world transformed, in political and social terms, by Sputnik. Prime Minister Harold Macmillan remarked in November 1957 that "Never has the threat of Soviet Communism been so great." Macmillan, a conventional Conservative, was one of those who swallowed the increasingly popular idea that the Soviets might overtake the West economically. At the other end of the British political spectrum, the leftist *New Statesman*, in its issue of January 4, 1958, sneered that the American Gaither Report proved that Soviet preponderance was already so great that, at least until 1961 American survival would depend on Soviet benevolence—a quality few others discerned.

Unlike the far left, or most Europeans, however, most of the British people reacted to the perceived greater threat by becoming more pro-American. A majority of Europeans, except in Italy, who reacted more strongly than Americans to Sputnik, actually came to think, for the next several years, that the Soviets had already overtaken the Americans in military strength. Some were openly angry at the Americans for letting the Soviets get ahead of them. But they did not give way to complete panic. Although the mainland NATO countries became extremely skittish about allowing American IRBM bases in their countries, and seemed to distance themselves from the Americans, NATO did not collapse, suggesting that Dulles' worries about America's allies might have been exaggerated.

The American reaction was explosive enough. Walter Reuther, head of the United Automobile Workers (then at the peak of its power and prestige), one of the greatest American labor leaders, and a leading liberal, described Sputnik as a "bloodless Pearl Harbor" and declared that American workers would make any sacrifice needed to catch up with the Soviets—a perfect example of the spirit of most Americans at the time. (Khrushchev once sourly remarked that "in Russia we hanged the likes of Reuther back in 1917.") Edward Teller, the famed physicist credited with being the "father of the H-bomb," and *The Reporter* magazine also invoked the Pearl Harbor analogy. There was no little fear that this might be too optimistic—that Sputnik, and the Soviet missile superiority it seemed to portend, might be just the prelude to a real Pearl Harbor, that, unlike the original, the United States would not survive. Senators Henry Jackson and Stuart Symington, genuine hard liners on defense, who, unlike many other post-Sputnik critics, had consistently complained that the Eisenhower Administration was not spending enough on missile development, were particularly vehement. Jackson described Sputnik as a devastating blow to American prestige, and warned that we were losing the race for the ICBM. Symington, an ex-Secretary of the Air Force widely credited with exaggerated knowledge, commented that Sputnik was "one more proof of growing Communist superiority in the all-important missile field. If this now-known superiority develops into supremacy, the position of the free world will be critical." Symington would be the greatest thorn in the side of the Eisenhower Administration for the next two years, pushing the most pessimistic projections of Soviet missile strength. (Later, after the missile gap was exploded, and political fashions changed, he blamed the CIA for misleading him, although he had belittled its estimates as overoptimistic at the time.) The journals *Aviation Week* and *Missiles and Rockets,* long critical of the Administration, fed the attacks on it, as did some ex-officials, notably Trevor Gardner, although his observation that it had restarted the ICBM effort was generally ignored. The normally reliably Republican Luce Time-Life empire turned against the Administration; *Life* even printed an article in its issue of November 18, 1957 titled "The Case for Being Panicky." "Sophisticated" journals of opinion chimed in. In December, the *New Republic* published a two-part article by the well-known political scientist Hans Morgenthau titled "The Decline of America."

The critics profited from the initial bungling of the Eisenhower Administration, which was further exaggerated by selective reporting of remarks from people who had little relevant to say. Ike's first television address in response to Sputnik seemed evasive and some poorly chosen wording misleadingly implied that he was ill-informed about missile development. Sherman Adams' declaration that the Administration was not interested in an "outer space basketball game," and the remark of Clarence Randall, an Eisenhower adviser on international trade, that Sputnik was a "silly bauble," did not make a good impression. Neither did the comment of Admiral Rawson Bennett, the head of naval research, that Sputnik was a "hunk of iron almost anybody could launch," a remark actually intended to encourage those working on the Vanguard project. Administration spokesmen tried to counter the critics by inflating expenditures on research and development by reclassifying expenses more properly classified as procurement, production, and even housekeeping at research facilities as "R and D," but this backfired when these tricks were soon exposed. Some of the Administration's more extreme defenders were less than no help, idiotically suggesting that Sputnik was a "fake," or that it was somehow the product of espionage. Many whined that the Soviet achievement was really due to their grabbing the Germans who had developed the V-2 missile; in fact, it was the Americans who had gotten, and used, most of the German missile experts. Even the normally careful Secretary of State seemed to briefly give credence to this. But such nonsense was quickly exposed.

The Administration soon took up a more prudent and intelligent response. On October 11, Eisenhower remarked that Americans should not be either complacent or hysterical, while Dulles suggested that Sputnik might be a good thing, a kick in the pants that might prevent complacency in the West; both emphasized that the United States was still distinctly superior militarily and would remain so in the near future. During November 1957, the President and Dulles conceded more reason for worry, the Secretary of State remarking on November 4 that the Soviets probably led the United States in certain fields, as did Eisenhower, who finally conceded that Sputnik had some military significance. The President, however, was sidelined on November 25 by a stroke, the last major illness of his presidency, although as usual he made an amazingly swift and complete recovery.

Still, the Administration never overcame the early reverses. The *New York Times*, in November, typically warned that the United States was in a "race for survival," and reported the estimate of Wernher von Braun, responsible for the development of the V-2 and now the chief civilian at the Army Ballistic Missile Agency, that we were five years behind the Soviets in missile and space matters. Most of the American scientific community, including many later bitterly critical of the whole missile gap episode, believed that the Soviets were ahead of the Americans in missiles, although there was no consensus on the extent or importance of the Soviet lead. Moreover, although von Braun, Gardner, and others offered clear testimony to the contrary, the political opposition firmly fixed in the public mind the idea that the lag was the fault of the current Administration. The Democrats artfully hid the fact it was the Eisenhower Administration that had gotten the ICBM and satellite programs going in the first place, and that any development lag was actually the fault of the Truman Administration. Attacks on the incumbent Administration became steadily more ferocious; it was criticized for recklessly relaxing the ICBM effort by its cutbacks in 1957, and mismanaging the satellite program by choosing the "civilian" (actually Navy-associated) Vanguard project over the Army's rival "Project Orbiter," and blundering in promoting duplicate IRBM programs. More generally, the failures of missile development were blamed on a failure to curb interservice rivalry and some, usually unexplained, because nonexistent, bad organization of missile development programs.

There were calls for a missile czar, far greater funds for missile development, and a "Manhattan Project" approach, although this faltered when Gardner and von Braun warned that the missile and space effort was too far advanced for that to be an appropriate move. (Eisenhower himself had pondered this on October 11, before rejecting it for just those reasons.) Many scientists accused the Administration of not sufficiently funding scientific work in general. Some people, notably ex-President Truman and the influential columnist Walter Lippmann, blamed Sputnik on "McCarthyism," claiming that official persecution had driven the best scientists from missile and satellite work, a claim for which there was no evidence. Some alarms, over the next few years, were truly extreme. Notable examples include Drew Pearson's book, *America—Second Class Power* (1958), which was breathtakingly dishonest, but is a useful indicator of the atmosphere of the era, and Alexander de Seversky's *America—Too Young to Die* (1961). By contrast, sober works like Hanson Baldwin's more balanced *The Great Arms Race* (1958) received relatively little attention. Not only the Eisenhower Administration came under attack.

Many blamed Sputnik on the failure of the American educational system, and there was a belated spate of publicity for people who had railed for years, with reason, about the state of education, ranging from Rudolf Flesch to Admiral

Hyman Rickover. It was characteristic of the time that Robert A. Heinlein's 1958 novel, *Have Spacesuit, Will Travel*, wittily parodied the dismal state of American schools. Many, in the following years, compared them unfavorably with Soviet schools, typified by Arthur Trace's 1961 book *What Ivan Knows that Johnny Doesn't*, whose title itself was a takeoff on Flesch's well-known 1955 book, *Why Johnny Can't Read*. The critics attacked the sight method of teaching reading, progressive education in general, insufficient attention to mathematics and science, and failure to concentrate on developing gifted children. Although all this had little to do with Sputnik and the missile race, the criticisms were well founded enough to impress many people, including the President, who endorsed them in a speech.

Further, there was a vast attack on the real and supposed social evils of the time—not so much poverty, ignorance, crime, or racial discrimination, as might be supposed, but "conformity," "status-seeking," "consumerism" (in the sense of obsessive grasping after material luxuries), "materialism," and the inability of the "mass man" or "organization man" to meet the Soviet and other challenges. Clichés for years among intellectuals, they now received a mass audience. There was a convergence of both liberal and conservative tendencies, for many conservatives shared these ideas, while some contemporary liberals combined them with what would later be seen as an old-fashioned moralism. There was also a convergence of liberal demands for reform and greater military strength that would seem very strange in later years. Sputnik and its aftermath revived, and helped drive leftward, American liberalism. It seemed to discredit, not just the Eisenhower Administration, but the post-New Deal, middle-of-the-road American society that it had epitomized.

Later, there was an increasing discussion of the persistence of poverty, discrimination, corruption in government, unions and show business, and other evils. Those things had not, contrary to later legend, gone unnoticed earlier, but they were increasingly seen, in 1958 and after, not just as problems to be cured by economic growth, education, and modest reforms, but as part and parcel of the existing order of things, which was failing in its own terms—a factor in the growth of political radicalism that was beginning in this era and that became far more visible in the 1960s. A subtle but critical transformation took place. The late 1940s and 1950s were increasingly pictured statically, as some sort of frozen status quo, instead of being seen as the era of amazing and rapid progress that it really was. Such misconceptions about the postwar era, despite what should have been their almost self-evident absurdity, would be uncritically swallowed and repeatedly regurgitated decades later.[1]

The Gaither Report

The Administration was hampered by one of its earlier precautionary moves, which had produced the "Gaither Report"—"Deterrence and Survival in the Nuclear Age," officially submitted on November 7, 1957, although Eisenhower had received summaries of its chilling conclusions on November 4. It had been prepared by the Security Review Panel, of the Office of Defense Mobilization's Scientific Advisory Committee, nominally chaired by H. Rowan Gaither, the head of the Ford Foundation. Due to Gaither falling ill, the Panel was effectively headed by a businessman, Robert Sprague, and the final report was largely written by Paul Nitze, who had led the National Security Council under Truman. The report had grown out of a review of civil defense initiated in April, which had been enlarged into a review of the whole of American defense. Although Eisenhower had not wanted such a wide-ranging review, he carefully considered it. The Gaither Report was alarming, even terrifying, forecasting a mortal threat starting in 1959–1960. It deemed the Soviets far stronger than earlier supposed, both militarily and economically. Although the Soviet Gross National Product was just one-third of the American, it was rising half again as fast, and the military threat was great. The Soviets were probably ahead in ICBMs, and the report pointed to serious vulnerabilities of the Strategic Air Command, and the lack of an early-warning system. The report recommended an immense military buildup, ordering far more IRBMs (240 instead of 60) and first-generation ICBMs (600 instead of 80) than the Administration had envisioned, and building a national fallout shelter system. The National Security Council intensively discussed the report on November 7. Eisenhower was clearly disturbed. Other reports he had seen confirmed the problems with SAC, but he and Dulles believed that the Gaither Report underestimated the effectiveness of bombers as against missiles in the next few years, and the advantages of our overseas bases. Moreover, some intelligence, largely based on the U-2 flights, which the Gaither panel had not seen, left him more confident than it had been. Dulles thought that some contingencies envisaged in the Report so remote they were not worth the cost of prevention.

The Secretary of State's opinion of the Report was probably not improved when he conferred with Sprague personally early in January 1958, and found the man so frightened that he recommended resorting to preventive war, or at least "hot negotiations," before Soviet strength became overwhelming.

It would be Khrushchev, not the Americans, who would be launching "hot negotiations" in 1958.

While not rejecting the Gaither Report in total, the Administration did not accept it as a general blueprint. But its existence soon became known. Whether or not to publicly release it, or part of it, became a lively political issue. Eisenhower did not make it public, but its substance leaked out during December 1957. Its conclusions were little questioned, which did not help the Administration which was already taking a pounding in the hearings of Lyndon Johnson's Preparedness Investigating Subcommittee of the Senate Armed Services Committee.[2]

The Administration's own estimates were not entirely consistent, and, although generally less alarmist than the Gaither Report, von Braun, or the partisan critics, were not complacent either. The President was considerably more worried than he let on in public. On October 15, he had met the Science Advisory Committee of the Office of Defense Mobilization, which had sponsored the Gaither Report. He asked the scientists present whether American science as a whole was being outdistanced. The physicist Isidore Rabi, who had become friendly with Eisenhower during the latter's unhappy tenure as head of Columbia University, rated the United States as still ahead, but the Soviets were more heavily emphasizing science, and would overtake us in ten years unless action was taken. Rabi and others suggested making James R. Killian a Presidential Science Advisor, creating a Presidential Science Advisory Committee, and providing more funds for basic research. Eisenhower readily accepted these proposals.

On October 23, a panel of experts convened by the CIA told the younger Dulles that the United States was lagging two or three years behind the Soviets, who might have an "initial operational capability" (IOC) of a dozen ICBMs at the end of 1958. They believed that the Soviets were running an orderly, not a "crash" program. The CIA's National Intelligence Estimate of November 1957 predicted an IOC of ten missiles in 1959, but the Soviets would have 100 in 1960, and 200 by 1962, versus an expected 24 American ICBMs in 1960 and 65 in 1961! Nevertheless, the NIE, like most of its predecessors, concluded that the Soviets were unlikely to start or incur grave risks of war over the next five years. James Killian, assuming his duties as the President's adviser, was somewhat reassured, on December 28, by a report on the missile program that indicated it was going satisfactorily, and that, while the United States was probably behind the Soviets, it was because it had started later, not because of inferior technology.

In his State of the Union Address on January 9, Eisenhower conceded, as he would do several times in 1958, that there was a "consensus of opinion" that we were "probably somewhat behind the Soviets in some areas of long-range ballistic missile development." Some days later, at an NSC meeting on January 16, it was reported that Soviet missile testing had dropped off, an indication, Eisenhower thought, correctly, that they had run into trouble. The physicist George Kistiakowsky, summarizing a report on February 4, judged that the Soviets were about a year ahead of us in propulsion, a year behind us in warhead development, and somewhat behind us in guidance.[3] Things were beginning to seem better. But, with the very big warheads the R-7 could carry, the Soviet warhead and guidance lag might not matter much, and the 20–30 tests the Soviets needed for operational deployment might be finished in just six months.

The ongoing Johnson Committee hearings, which lasted from November 25 to January 23, kept the Administration on the defensive. Johnson, hoping to become President, characteristically saw Sputnik and the missile issue as both a real national challenge and a political opportunity. Although some testimony refuted the more extreme charges against the Administration, Johnson and the Democrats avoided calling some inconvenient witnesses, and skillfully steered things so that the testimony of those who, like Gardner and von Braun, did draw attention to the point that it was the Truman Administration, not the current one, that was responsible for the late start in missiles and space, was overlooked. The hearings' impressive list of "recommendations" on missile and space matters was, in fact, largely cribbed by Johnson's staff from classified reports of what the Administration was already doing![4]

From "Flopnik" to Explorer

The poky American IGY satellite program seemed to be a disaster. Back in July 1955, the American government had decided to launch a satellite as part of the International Geophysical Year program. Several alternatives were offered to do the job. A Defense Department advisory group headed by Dr. Homer Stewart of the Jet Propulsion Laboratory rejected an Air Force proposal to put up a satellite with Atlas as violating its directive to avoid potential interference with military missile work. The main choice was between an early Army–von Braun proposal, Project Orbiter, and the Navy's Vanguard. Orbiter, an improved version of a von Braun proposal of 1954, could be ready by August 1957, or even in 1956, with a "crash" program. It would launch a small satellite with an uprated Redstone carrying three upper stages of clusters of small solid-fuel rockets. The Naval Research Laboratory offered a more advanced satellite, with a complete electronic tracking system, "Minitrack," to follow it, using a three-stage launch vehicle derived from the Viking research rocket, which had been very successful at very low cost.

The Vanguard vehicle seemed more efficient and more advanced, and promised more possibilities of development, than the Orbiter lash-up. (The upper stages of Vanguard were in fact developed into the "Able" and "Delta" space launchers.) The Minitrack system, the better instrumented satellite, and a grave underestimate of its cost were the prime reasons for choosing Vanguard, although political factors—a dislike of the Army's German team (present although unadmitted) and a belief that the NRL project at least looked more civilian than Orbiter, which used a war weapon, may have had some influence. Vanguard proved unlucky, slowed by unrealistically small initial appropriations that snowballed into huge cost overruns, and other trouble. The excellent team the Martin company had formed to build the Viking had largely been switched to work on the Titan ICBM, and Titan conflicted with Vanguard, which required redesign.

Vanguard's first stage flew successfully three weeks after Sputnik. The first flight of the whole vehicle, which, it was hoped, might have the bonus of orbiting a four-pound "minimal satellite" much smaller than the ultimate model, was given excessive publicity by the Administration. It inadvertently implied that a successful satellite was expected. On December 6, Vanguard TV-3 rose a few feet. Its engine stopped, and it crashed in a spectacular burst of flame. The press and public experienced "Flopnik" as a major national humiliation, and the rest of the world followed suit. The United States could not even orbit a mere "grapefruit." The year 1957 ended in the most demoralizing possible way.

A real defeatist neurosis might have gotten out of hand. (The next Vanguard, in February, also failed.) Wernher von Braun and the Army Ballistic Missile Agency rode to the rescue, and von Braun was allowed to pursue his true love, space exploration. Only now, more than a decade after arriving in the United States, were von Braun and his men given a really major task. For a time he even became an American hero, a development viewed ruefully in Britain, where the V-2 attacks were a vivid memory. The British joked, parodying the title of a biography of von Braun, "I aim at the stars—but sometimes I hit London!"

The Army agency had preserved the possibility of Orbiter. Stewart had advised von Braun to do this in October 1955, a month after Vanguard was chosen. The Army had continued to develop the Orbiter vehicle as the "Jupiter C," to test nose cones for the Jupiter IRBM. The Redstone was lengthened and given more powerful fuel, with two "live" upper stages of clustered solid-fuel rockets to provide the speed for testing the IRBM warhead. A live fourth stage of just one "Baby Sergeant" rocket would let the Jupiter C orbit a satellite. To prevent ABMA from pulling a fast one, the Army ordered that only a dummy stage be used! Three flights in September 1956 proved the Army's case for "ablative" nose cones, which were adopted for the Thor as well. A renewed proposal in June 1957 to have the Jupiter C loft a satellite was turned down, but in August General John Medaris, the clever, slippery, and ambitious head of ABMA, who shared von Braun's dreams of space, had the nine remaining Jupiter Cs put in protected storage against the day when the Army would be called to launch a satellite. He expected Vanguard to fail.

Wilson's successor as Secretary of Defense, Neil McElroy, was at ABMA when Sputnik went up. Von Braun and Medaris told him that they could get a satellite up in 90 days. On October 8, Eisenhower let the Army get ready, as a back up. Medaris, on his own, had already had a Jupiter C taken out of storage. On November 8, ABMA was finally ordered to launch a satellite. The Jet Propulsion Laboratory repackaged instruments from Vanguard for the Army's Explorer satellite. It carried a pair of radios to report its outer surface and interior temperatures, micrometeorite impacts, and detection of cosmic rays. A Jupiter C (officially called a Juno I when carrying a live fourth stage and a satellite, a name that was little used) put Explorer I into orbit on January 31, 1958. There was much public relief, although some chagrin at Explorer's small size—as Adlai Stevenson glumly joked, it was 'long, thin, and not much to it." But the little American satellite made the first great scientific discovery of the Space Age—the Van Allen belts of radiation trapped in the Earth's magnetic field.[5]

The Buildup

Contrary to what is sometimes said, Sputnik had a major impact on defense plans. Eisenhower approved most recommendations for a speedup of the missile programs. The restrictions on overtime work, the focus of much political criticism ended on November 22. The first-generation ICBMs, Atlas and Titan I, were too far along to be accelerated further, but in December it was decided to procure far more of them. Earlier, only 80 Atlases and Titan Is had been programmed; now nine squadrons of Atlases alone would be formed. Plans for the first-generation ICBM force, however, fluctuated wildly over the next year. There was much argument over how many of each to build and which to emphasize, especially over the technically superior, but lagging Titan (which some wished to cancel entirely). There were complex changes to plans for the configuration of missile sites and control centers and how to "harden" them against Soviet attack; some alterations were due to new data from nuclear tests. A second-generation of ICBMs, Titan II (virtually a completely new missile) and Minuteman, a small solid-fuel ICBM made possible by the breakthrough that produced Polaris, were in prospect. The Administration approved developing Minuteman in February 1958. The reconnaissance satellite program was greatly accelerated, as was Polaris.

In December 1957, the Administration made a radical change of plans for the submarine-based missile. Polaris would be rushed into operation in 1960, not 1963, by accepting a more limited capability and using modified attack submarines instead of boats designed as missile carriers from the start. A limited-range Polaris A-1 missile, using a less powerful fuel and a more primitive guidance system, capable of flying only 1,200 miles instead of the originally planned 1,500, would be ready in time. An attack submarine under construction, renamed *George Washington*, was cut in two and a 130-foot section spliced in to carry 16 Polaris A-1s. Three Polaris subs were ordered, but it was already expected that many more would follow. The acceleration of Polaris was the most important change triggered by Sputnik. Another decision, made on November 25, probably partially politically motivated, and that almost certainly would not have been made without the shock of Sputnik, was to produce and accelerate both Thor and Jupiter as IRBMs, although the Administration was fast losing faith in the IRBMs' military value. (They seemed just too vulnerable to a Soviet first strike.) The Strategic Air Command's dispersal and alert status were radically improved and the development of the Ballistic Missile Early Warning System speeded up.

In March 1958, it was decided to stretch out Minuteman's development until a better solid fuel became available, and to early phase out Atlas for Titan II, which used storable fuels, and like Minuteman, could stay indefinitely in an underground silo. A further increase was approved at the NSC meeting of April 24. Eisenhower reluctantly approved plans for a 180-missile IRBM force (never actually carried out) and increasing first-generation ICBMs again from 120 to 180 missiles. The Polaris force was raised to five subs. The later Atlas missiles would be put in "semi-hardened" sites—they would lie in above-ground bunkers from which they would be elevated to fire.[6]

Reorganization

In addition to speeding up missile and related programs, the Administration embarked on several major reorganizational efforts. Its first step, in February 1958, was to create a new Advanced Research Projects Agency (ARPA) within the Defense Department—a small agency to evaluate and coordinate, but not actually direct, the research efforts of the armed forces and ensure that promising research that was not of interest to a particular service was supported. It was expected, at the time, that ARPA would take over all military space matters. A major reorganization of the whole Defense Department followed, designed to reduce interservice rivalry and duplication. Eisenhower expended much time and energy on this from November 1957 to April 1958. Under the new organization, all operational forces were allotted to unified commands; and orders would flow directly to those commands from the President and Secretary of Defense. The latter's position and military staff would be strengthened, while the Service departments—Army, Navy, and Air Force—would be removed from the chain of command. The Secretary of Defense, not the service departments, would handle appropriations. The positions of the Joint Chiefs of Staff and their Chairman would be strengthened, and all research would come under a civilian Director of Defense Research and Engineering. Eisenhower viewed this as only a halfway house to total armed forces unification, which he expected to take another generation. But it encountered considerable opposition in Congress, which stood to lose powers to the Secretary of Defense. The reorganization finally passed Congress in August. On the whole, it worked well, but helped make possible the disastrous sway of Robert McNamara, the arrogant Secretary of Defense under Kennedy and Johnson.

A contentious issue in 1958 was how to run the space effort, which, it was generally thought, ought to come under one agency. There were several candidates for the job. The Federation of American Scientists and an important and knowledgable political leader, Senator Clinton Anderson of New Mexico, favored putting it under an enlarged Atomic Energy Commission. An alternative civilian candidate was the National Advisory Committee for Aeronautics (NACA), a small government agency handling aviation research. It was already developing the X-15 rocket research plane, which was expected to reach a height of 50 miles and was arguably the first true spaceship, but was not seen that way at the time. However, NACA was not highly regarded by scientists or its chief customers, the armed forces, who still blamed it for not doing more to develop jet engines before and during World War II.

And it had no expertise in developing hardware or managing big programs. Alternatively, the Air Force (backed by Edward Teller) and ABMA wanted the job. The Army, however, had little expectation of actually getting it and settled for backing an enlarged ARPA as a space agency. The question had major implications. Either the AEC or the Air Force would be much likelier to push nuclear propulsion or other "radical" ideas than NACA or ABMA. NACA campaigned skillfully for the job, and the overall inclination in the Administration, from Ike on down, was for a civilian, space-only agency, a view especially pushed by the President's Science Advisory Committee and the Bureau of the Budget. Eisenhower approved using NACA as the nucleus for a new agency on March 5, 1958. The National Aeronautics and Space Administration emerged in October. It absorbed several other organizations, or chunks of them, in a process taking another two years, beginning with the highly esteemed Jet Propulsion Laboratory in December 1958. It finally acquired most of ABMA, including the von Braun team, in mid-1960. Military space work, which in practice meant running reconnaissance satellites, went to the Air Force in 1959.[7]

1958 at Home

The Sputniks and the missile gap, and a year of crisis in foreign affairs, were accompanied by a glum year in domestic affairs. The recession that had begun in August 1957, the worst since World War II, was the only black mark on the generally successful economic record of the Eisenhower Administration. During 1957, a downturn in housing, a decline in car production, and the collapse of demand in the capital-goods industry all coincided. The situation was aggravated by a ratcheting up of interest rates and exceptionally tight credit, and mistakes in tax policy, delaying the normal countercyclical moves in dealing with a recession. The President and his associates had continued to focus on the danger of inflation rather than recession, although the Eisenhower Administration's mistakes in this direction proved far less harmful than its successor's carelessness. Unemployment peaked at 5.3 million or 7 percent of the work force, in July 1958. A peculiarity of the recession was that, while industrial production sank 15 percent at the nadir of the downturn, it recovered rather quickly, and the Gross National Product actually rose. Farmers were relatively unaffected. Nevertheless, the worst downturn in twenty years was not a good advertisement for the Eisenhower Administration, or for that matter, capitalism.[8]

In April 1958 Eisenhower's popularity fell to the lowest level of his presidency. Only 49 percent of those polled thought he was doing a good job, although his popularity recovered smartly later and remained high for the rest of his term. The absurd "golfing and goofing" image of Eisenhower reached its height at this time. Some liberals, including the editors of the *New Republic* and *The Progressive*, were so scared in the post-Sputnik atmosphere and worried about Ike's health, that, in early 1958, they actually called on him to resign! Their other fears had temporarily overcome their normal and all too justified fear of Richard Nixon. Luckily for the United States and its allies, Eisenhower paid no attention. Beginning in June, the Administration was embarrassed by a "conflict of interest" scandal that ruined the President's capable but much disliked Chief of Staff, Sherman Adams. Adams had accepted costly gifts from a sleazy businessman, Bernard Goldfine, who he had known since he was Governor of New Hampshire. He was accused of intervening on Goldfine's behalf with the Federal Trade and Securities and Exchange Commissions. Even Eisenhower conceded that Adams had been imprudent. Although continued investigation did not prove any improper actions by Adams, it entirely discredited Goldfine, who landed in prison. It became apparent that Adams' judgment was questionable, at best, and he was a political millstone for the Republicans. Their candidates all over the country were scared. He had to resign in September. All this did not improve Republican chances in the November mid-term elections.

The President fought unusually energetically for Republican candidates, giving many variations of a standard speech from October 20 to Election Day. Dealing with the missile and space race energetically, he eagerly and accurately pointed out that the "missile gap," which he used in the sense of a developmental lag as well as a future projection of numbers of missiles, was the fault of the Truman Administration, not his, and that lag in development was being made up. In dealing with domestic affairs, his speeches seem far more interesting—and prophetic—than most utterances by presidents in similar campaigns. He vigorously attacked the Democratic Party, which, he observed, was really a rogue's alliance of two different parties—one of reactionary Southerners, the other of recklessly spending liberals, even radicals. If the Democrats won the off-year elections, and then the presidency, there would be an unstoppable growth of the Federal government implementing foolish policies, and inflation.

It cannot be said that these predictions proved incorrect.

Despite his efforts, the elections were an utter disaster for the Republicans, the worst since 1936. Only a few liberal Republicans, like Nelson Rockefeller, defied the tide. The Democrats won 13 seats in the Senate and 47 in the House, and five governorships. The Senate became 62–34 Democratic and the House 282–153, giving the Democrats, if they were united, the ability to override the President's veto. The elections ended the careers of several prominent Republicans, notably William Knowland. The President was especially upset when Knowland's attempt to switch from the Senate to the governorship of California ended disastrously. Although he had not gotten along well with Knowland as the Senate Majority Leader, Eisenhower had badly wanted him to win. Knowland's defeat incidentally eliminated Richard Nixon's greatest enemy within the Republican party; not only Republicans would have cause to rue it.

The President saw the defeat as a personal one; and it left him full of fore-bodings for the future of his country. No single thing seemed to explain it. The general adverse atmosphere of Sputniks and recession, the unpopularity of the right-to-work laws many Republicans were pushing—five out of six of such proposals were defeated in referendums—and unpopular farm policies all played a role.[9]

From late 1957, Eisenhower had taken up one "liberal" cause: improved education. He completely agreed with a series of articles in *Life* in March and April 1958 critical of the American educational system. The sense of crisis after Sputnik made it possible to break down long-standing obstacles to federal aid to education, notably the issues of aid to parochial schools and Southern segregation. Eisenhower successfully backed the National Defense Education Act, passed in September, providing loans and fellowships for science and language studies.[10]

The general feeling of worry and disillusionment after Sputnik had coincided with and promoted a resurgence of social criticism and a leftward lurch in politics in the United States—indeed throughout the West—as not only Eisenhower but his counterparts in the other democracies, and the policies and ideas dominant since World War II came under increasing attack. In the United States, there was a huge growth of the amount of, and audience for, the social criticisms developed by liberal and leftwing critics in the years before Sputnik. Mostly, but not entirely on the left—for quite a few conservatives, including Eisenhower and John Foster Dulles, showed some unease at the way American society was going, and agreed with elements of the fashionable thinking.

Boredom, or disgust with, some popular fashions and consumer obsessions, such as the flashy styles of consumer goods that Thomas Hines has described as "Populuxe" was also a factor. Some have suggested that the collapse of the car market, and the failure of Ford's new Edsel, was at least partly due to revulsion at the overdecorated, "gorp" ridden "Detroit Baroque" style and a readiness to try something new, e.g. small cars and imports. (An attack on "Detroit Baroque." John Keats' funny book *The Insolent Chariots*, became a bestseller in 1958.) In the same year John Kenneth Galbraith's *The Affluent Society* also became a bestseller. Ideologically and politically it proved enormously influential. Galbraith argued that our already "affluent" society had been focused on private investment and producing consumer goods at the expense of public investment in schools, parks, slum clearance, and what was later called "infrastructure." Taking for granted the validity of Keynesian economics, American economic supremacy, the overwhelming power and permanence of the great American corporations, and the power of unions, Galbraith held that economic growth was no longer that important. He urged far greater government intervention in the economy, an annual income plan to be paid for by higher taxes, including a national sales tax, and wage and price controls.

In the rest of the Western world, there was an open resurgence of socialist ideas, with renewed faith in nationalization and planned economies, which seemed to have been vindicated by the Soviet advance. Even in the United States, there was a quiet resurgence of radicalism, and a mixture of ideological softening and defeatism toward the Soviets. There was a definite weakening of anti-Communist sentiment, noted by contemporary observers such as Sidney Hook and *Commentary* and *National Review* magazines. There was even a revival of outright apologias for the Soviets, which culminated in the development of the "revisionist" view of the Cold War. Notable examples of this were C. Wright Mills *The Causes of World War III*, and a little later, William Appleman Williams' writings. The myth that the Soviet Union was "a visible demonstration of how an agrarian economy can industrialize by itself in two generations" (H. Stuart Hughes) reached its peak at this time. Or, as the famed sociologist Mills put it, the USSR was "only forty years removed from peasant, feudal backwardness." It was widely believed that this, and the Soviets' greater economic growth, put them in a better position to deal with the underdeveloped world. At least economically, the Soviets were a more suitable model for most of the world than the West. (Mills, who manifested a credulity that would have delighted a witch doctor, also imagined that "Russia is free of color prejudice.") The underdeveloped world, it was held, needed a "socialist" or at least a more state-guided form of development than the United States could provide or had been willing to back. Moreover, the United States had to show more enthusiasm for "neutralism." It was argued, somewhat inconsistently, that the Cold War was irrelevant to most of the world's people. Some suggested that the West would just have to accept and aid development-oriented dictatorships over supposedly ineffectual democracies in the underdeveloped world. Such ideas were often coupled with suggestions for a "Marshall Plan" for Asia, or Latin America, or Africa.

Unfortunately, the Marshall Plan had been a cooperative effort of advanced democracies to repair war damage. It was, unfortunately, irrelevant to the problems of the underdeveloped world. The other beliefs had even less to recommend them. Not only would the Soviet path prove a dead end, it had little relevance to the solution of the problems of underdeveloped lands. Imperial Russia had never been a country of that sort at all, and had been the fourth or fifth industrial power in the world by 1914, long before Stalin's renewal of the industrialization drive.

Strangest of all, perhaps, from the point of view of later decades, there was a growing belief, in 1958, and the following few years, that America was in moral decline, an idea common not only among conservatives but ardent liberals like John Steinbeck. They and others were troubled by the growth of moral relativism or a tendency to identify moral judgments with the approval or disapproval of one's immediate social circle rather than measuring actions against traditional moral standards. Many were upset by the rather minor scandals in the Eisenhower Administration, the arrogant corruption of Representative Adam Clayton Powell on the other side of the political spectrum, cheating and sex orgies in colleges, and the "payola" and quiz show scandals, which began to surface in April 1958, and that discredited the once widely admired Charles Van Doren, the son of a prominent literary family. The rather more serious corruption and organized crime role in some major unions like the Teamsters also got wider exposure.

Rock 'n' roll, or at least its lyrics, was widely deplored as morally degenerate, and not only by fundamentalist preachers and music critics. Even some liberals were upset by some of the sexual material now being published, notably Nabokov's *Lolita*.[11]

Perhaps the best comment on all this is that, over fifty years later, social mores have changed so completely that we cannot tell whether such criticisms were a case of crying wolf, or bitterly prophetic.

Notes

1 Levine, *The Missile and Space Race*, pp. 57–61, 77–78, 219 n. 18; Levine, *Bad Old Days*, pp. 113–116; Killian, *Sputnik, Scientists and Eisenhower*, pp. xv, 2, 7–11; D.F. Fleming, *The Cold War and Its Origins, Volume II* (Garden City, KS: Doubleday, 1961), pp. 885–887; Richard Stebbins, *The United States in World Affairs 1958* (New York: Harper, 1959), pp. 2–3, 15–16; Rip Bulkley, *The Sputniks Crisis and Early United States Space Policy* (Bloomington, IN: Indiana University Press, 1991), pp. 4–15, 160–162; Robert Divine, *The Sputnik Challenge* (New York: Oxford University Press, 1993), pp. xvi–xviii, 4–75; Horne, *Harold Macmillan, Vol. II*, p. 53; Peter Roman, *Eisenhower and the Missile Gap* (Ithaca, NY: Cornell University Press, 1995); Edgar Bottome, *The Missile Gap* (Rutgers, NJ: Fairleigh Dickinson University Press, 1971).

2 *FRUS 1958–1960, Vol. III*, pp. 1–9; *FRUS 1957, Vol. XIX*, pp. 638–661, 665–672; Watson, *Into the Missile Age*, pp. 136–141; Divine, *The Sputnik Challenge*, pp. 35–41, 77; Eisenhower, *Waging Peace*, pp. 219–223; Killian, *Sputnik, Scientists and Eisenhower*, pp. 6, 96.

3 Divine, *The Sputnik Challenge*, pp. 12, 30–33, 79–82, 113–114; Killian, *Sputnik, Scientists and Eisenhower*, pp. 144–146; *FRUS 1957, Vol. XIX*, pp. 665–672; *FRUS 1958–1960, Vol. III*, pp. 31–32, 65, 79–82.

4 Divine, *The Sputnik Challenge*, pp. 62–68; Bulkley, *The Sputniks Crisis and Early United States Space Policy*, pp. 185–206; Levine, *The Missile and Space Race*, pp. 66–67.

5 Levine, *The Missile and Space Race*, pp. 20–21, 51–55, 68–69; Watson, *Into the Missile Age*, pp. 141, 172–174, 178; Divine, *The Sputnik Challenge*, pp. 71, 94–96, 102; Bulkley, *The Sputniks Crisis and Early United States Space Policy*, pp. 89, 132–139; Constance Green, *Vanguard* (Washington DC: NASA, 1970); Clayton Koppel, *JPL and the American Space Program* (New Haven, CT: Yale University Press, 1982), pp. 83, 85, 87–88.

6 Fairchild and Poole, *The Joint Chiefs and National Policy 1957–1960*, pp. 43, 46, 49; Watson, *Into the Missile Age*, pp. 142–154, 166, 178, 184, 186–187, 192–196, 374–379; Divine, *The Sputnik Challenge*, pp. 68–70, 121–126; Levine, *The Missile and Space Race*, pp. 69–70, 81, 84; Neufeld, *Ballistic Missiles in the United States Air Force*, pp. 172, 175–176, 193–196; *FRUS 1958–1960, Vol. III*, pp. 42, 70–77; Eisenhower, *Waging Peace*, p. 254.

7 Watson, *Into the Missile Age*, pp. 187–191, 361, 390–396; Kinnard, *Eisenhower and Strategy Management*, p. 89; Fairchild and Poole, *The Joint Chiefs and National Policy 1957–1960*, pp. 4–7; Barck, *History of the United States Since 1945*, pp. 233–234; Levine, *The Missile and Space Race*, pp. 70–71, 102–105; Eisenhower, *Waging Peace*, pp. 246–253, 257.

8 Saulnier, *Constructive Years*, pp. 97–111, 224–225; Barck, *History of the United States Since 1945*, pp. 230–232; Eisenhower, *Waging Peace*, pp. 304–311.

9 Divine, *The Sputnik Challenge*, pp. 196–197; Oakley, *God's Country*, pp. 372–375; Eisenhower, *Waging Peace*, pp. 311–318, 375–381. Cf. Ambrose, *Eisenhower: The President*, p. 487, who, unreliable as unusual, leads his readers to believe that Eisenhower never worried about a missile gap.

10 Eisenhower, *Waging Peace*, pp. 241–243; Divine, *The Sputnik Challenge*, pp. 52–58, 159–168; Barbara Clowse, *Brainpower for the Cold War* (Westport, CT: Greenwood, 1981).

11 Levine, *Bad Old Days*, pp. 85, 107–111, 114–121, 150; Richard Pells, *The Liberal Mind in a Conservative Age* (New York: Harper, 1984), pp. 162–174, 348–358; Oakley, *God's Country*, pp. 410–412; C. Wright Mills, *The Causes of World War III* (New York: Simon & Schuster 1958), pp. 68–69, 105. Mills' book, like his later pro-Castro work, *Listen Yankee*, often foreshadows New Left ideas of the 1960s, although is much more influenced by fear of nuclear war.

5

THE "MISSILE GAP" AND SPACE RACE

The "shattering blow" of the Sputniks to Western morale, as a contemporary observer described it, initiated one of the grimmest years of the Cold War.[1] Some crises of the period were caused by local forces, but others would be related directly to the missile and space race between the Soviets and the Americans, and all, probably, were influenced by perceptions—however far removed from reality—of that race. For public perceptions of what was going on in this period were probably farther removed from reality than in any other part of the Cold War, with the exception, perhaps, of the delusionary era of détente in the 1970s. The widely expected "missile gap" would open—in reverse. The small and already shrinking lag in development would be closed, and the Americans would race ahead and build a great ICBM force, while the Soviets, at least in intercontinental weapons, seemed to stand still. The military balance throughout remained sharply in favor of the West, while, behind the scenes, the Soviet–Chinese axis was disintegrating. (The Soviets, did, however, start a little-noted, but massive buildup of medium- and intermediate-range missiles, well able to destroy Western Europe, Japan, and American overseas bases.)

While the missile gap myth was at its height, and for some time after, the Soviets tried to bluff the West into retreating, over Berlin and other issues. When the missile gap bluff was exposed in 1961, Khrushchev would try to maintain his offensive, first by exploding the largest thermonuclear bomb ever built, and later, by moving some of the readily available medium- and intermediate-range missiles to Cuba, from which they could hit the United States.

By 1958, Marshal Nedelin, the head of missile development, and others, had recognized that the R-7 was not a good weapon. Khrushchev's son, a missile engineer, had alerted his father to its problems. It was so huge, clumsy, and took so long to get ready that it was useless for retaliation—it was so clearly only a first-strike weapon that it was not even suitable as that. To build a force of several hundred R-7s risked provoking a preemptive attack, if it seemed likely that they were about to be fired, and American bombers might well catch them all on the ground. It was decided to procure just a few R-7s as ICBMs, use the rest as space launchers, and go on to develop more useful second-generation ICBMs. Korolev's next design, the R-9, was not very successful. The rival missile design bureau of Mikhail Yangel developed the superior R-16, but it was not ready for deployment until 1961.

But, soon after Sputnik, at the latest, Khrushchev, reflecting on the apparent success of his bluffing during the Suez crisis, and the American reaction to the brief "bomber gap" episode, and now to Sputnik I, realized that he could profit from the perception of Soviet missile superiority, even without having any ready as weapons. Everything possible would be done to push the missile gap myth. He would create the impression that he had, or more exactly would soon get, an ICBM capability, and that the West should get out of his way while it could still do so. In the last resort, in any crisis, he would have to back down, but he hoped the other side would be scared enough to cave in first. That did not happen, although, we shall see, it nearly did. In the latter part of the missile gap era, at least from 1959 to 1961, an American traitor, Colonel William Whalen, provided the Soviets U.S. intelligence estimates of Soviet strength. Even before Whalen began working for the Soviets, such estimates were regularly leaked to American newspapers; so Soviet claims could be pitched to sound plausible.

Already, in November 1957, at the Moscow conference of the world's Communist parties, the last meeting of a more or less united world Communist movement, the Soviets claimed a general shift of the "correlation of forces," which included all of the elements of the struggle for the world, not just the military balance, had taken place in favor of the Communist bloc. They claimed that they had eliminated American military superiority, and neutralized U.S. overseas bases. As the Berlin crisis began in November 1958, the Soviets announced that ICBMs were now in mass production, and soon began intimating that they already had an operational force, and had approximate military equality with the United States. In tandem with the ICBM claims, Khrushchev made repeated "country-busting" threats that he could easily destroy this or that NATO country harboring U.S. bases, e.g., that six bombs could destroy Britain.

After a brief relaxation in tensions in 1959, Khrushchev would go on, in November 1959, to claim to have a substantial ICBM force, and, in July 1960, claim that he could destroy the United States and hint that he had a fantastic new weapon aside from the ICBM. After the U-2 was shot down in May 1960, however, he generally backed away from the most exaggerated boasts. (By then, the Eisenhower Administration was sure there would be no missile gap.) After his revival of claims to Soviet superiority in July, he retreated to just claiming strategic parity with the Americans.[2]

Estimating the Threat

The Americans struggled to learn what was really going on. Their chief instruments were the U-2s, the radar station at Samsun in Turkey, and monitoring Soviet transmissions. All had serious limitations. The Turkish radar could track Soviet missiles through part of their flights, and Soviet telemetry was overheard, but it was not always certain whether or not a test had succeeded. U-2s had to be used cautiously—they only flew over the Soviet Union about thirty times in all—and could not reach all of Soviet territory. After several crashes, the U-2 was grounded and none flew over the USSR at all between March 1958 and April 1959. Later flights faced the danger that the newest Soviet missiles could reach the U-2's height with some control, so areas known to be defended had to be avoided. U-2 evidence was of a negative sort. It might show that the Soviets had not yet deployed ICBMs, but not whether they were about to do so, and it might be foiled by camouflage or other devices.

The Turkish radar and monitoring effort were not without dangers. During 1958 the Soviets were ready to play particularly rough on their southern frontier, where slow prop-driven U.S. electronic reconnaissance planes, flying just outside Soviet airspace, sometimes strayed across the border. (For public consumption, they were allegedly "studying electromagnetic wave propagation," but the truth was well known within the armed forces.) A C-118 transport supporting the intelligence efforts wandered into Soviet Azerbaijan and was forced down by MIG-17s on June 27. The nine men aboard were returned. On September 4, a C-130 on a monitoring mission crossed the Soviet-Turkish border and was shot down. All 17 men aboard were killed. This caused considerable anger in the United States. Many people, including President Eisenhower, suspected, apparently wrongly, that the Soviets had deliberately lured the plane into their airspace with a fake radio beacon. Some even called for breaking relations and embargoing trade with the Soviets. The Soviets had in fact regularly sent out signals on frequencies reserved for Turkish use by international agreement, but this had been known for some time. Their actions were irresponsible, but probably not part of a deliberate decoy operation. However, the whole business, and their lying about other facts involved disgusted many.[3]

In late 1957 and early 1958 George Kistiakowsky and others had begun to quiet the more extreme fears of a basic American technical inferiority in the missile field. But a Special National Intelligence Estimate in January 1958 was the most frightening of all official estimates in the missile gap era. It warned that the Soviets might have a small operational ICBM force—"initial operational capability" (IOC) as early as mid-1958, and a force of 100 ICBMs in mid-1959.

That might enable the Soviets to launch a devastating first strike on the Strategic Air Command, before an early warning system able to detect ICBMs was ready. So much depended on whether the Soviets could quickly finish testing, and mass produce their ICBMs. It was urgent to finish the Ballistic

Missile Early Warning System, disperse SAC, get our own ICBMs, and quickly deploy an attack-proof retaliatory force—the Polaris submarines. The missile gap thus offered two possible sub-threats—one, an early Soviet creation of a modest force able to attain complete surprise, sometime in 1959–1961, second, and later, building a massive force that would vastly outnumber its American counterpart from 1960–1964. The latter might not give the Soviets a decisive military advantage, since by then the Americans would have early warning, a dispersed bomber force and Polaris, but it was not a pleasant prospect.[4]

The very worst fears did not last long. At a National Security Council meeting of April 14, Allen Dulles reported that Soviet testing had fallen off, and a failure had definitely occurred. In fact, ICBM testing ceased for almost a year. After Sputnik III was orbited in May, no R-7s flew at all for the rest of 1958. The National Intelligence Estimate of June 1958 nevertheless concluded that the Soviets might have 10 ICBMs by early 1959, 100 by the end of that year, 500 in 1960, and 1,000 in 1964, but, knowing of the Soviet failure, Eisenhower rather discounted this. Many, however, considered the June 1958 estimate overoptimistic! Despite the evidence of a Soviet failure, the Air Force, against the CIA, maintained that the Soviets had completed the necessary testing, and were going into mass production. Higher estimates also emanated from the aircraft industry, and were leaked by the columnist Joe Alsop in July 1958. He reported estimates of a force of 500 missiles by the end of 1960, 1,500 in 1962, and 2,000 in 1963. Senator Symington, accepting estimates made by the Air Force and Convair executive Thomas Lanphier, met Eisenhower personally in late August to sell high estimates of the threat. The President was unconvinced. The National Intelligence Estimate of August 27 expected a Soviet IOC in 1959, although not excluding one in late 1958, and predicted a Soviet force of 100 ICBMs within a year of the attainment of an IOC, and a force of 500 by 1961–1962. It did, however, warn that the Soviets were moving faster on submarine missiles than expected.

The failure of the Soviets to test as expected, and inability to detect missile base construction, led to greater optimism. A December 1958 estimate revised the threat downward. The Soviets were expected to have 10 ICBMs sometime in 1959, 100 in 1960, 300 by 1961, 500 by 1962, and 1,000–1,500 by 1963, hardly eliminating the threat, but shoving it further into the future. In the same period, von Braun concluded that the Soviet lead was small, and not militarily important.

But the more optimistic National Intelligence Estimate enraged Symington and led to further leaks of higher estimates, and one of the biggest public eruptions of the whole missile gap era in the early months of 1959, with Democratic politicians and articles in liberal magazines like *The Reporter* and *The New Republic* bitterly attacking the Administration for recklessly underestimating the Soviet ICBM danger. Secretary of Defense McElroy publicly remarked, on January 27, 1959, that there was no evidence that the Soviets would even have operational ICBMs before the United States. But this and similar assurances were widely viewed as attempts to soft soap the public. McElroy told the National Security

Council, two days later, that the so-called "missile gap" had been narrowed and we were now estimating a longer period before a Soviet operational capability. But there were real differences of opinion in the Administration, and even Eisenhower had flashes of worry in early 1959. The Science Advisory Committee thought, wrongly, that the Soviets already had an IOC, which the CIA, whose views the National Intelligence Estimate reflected, denied. The public furor was fueled by a series of failures of American missile tests. But in April 1959, the Soviets resumed ICBM tests and it became clear that the optimists had been right. Moreover, the Soviets had failures in the new series of tests. Even the Air Force admitted that the Soviets would not gain an operational capability in 1959. The National Intelligence Estimates became more optimistic during 1959, and, after a last flurry of concern, by late in that year the Administration was fairly sure that there would be no missile gap. That became ever clearer during 1960, but did not stop John F. Kennedy, although he had been told of correct estimates, from unscrupulously using the missile gap in the election of 1960. Worse, unable to admit that he had lied (although President Eisenhower and General Schriever informed the public of the real situation before the former left office) Kennedy let the gap, which had degenerated from a mistaken but real fear to a shabby political hoax, remain an albatross around the neck of Western diplomacy until September 1961.[5]

The IRBMs

As the Americans tried to close the supposed ICBM lead, they sought to deploy an interim strategic missile, the land-based IRBM, which should be ready soon—despite extreme interservice rivalries and increasing doubts about the military effectiveness of the Thors and Jupiters. They would be based above ground on "soft" fixed sites, and have little warning time in the event of Soviet attack. Except in Britain, which had already accepted the Thors, it was hard even to get the necessary bases, but Secretary Dulles pushed for them, perhaps mostly as a political symbol. At a December 1957 NATO conference, most members were clearly reluctant to accept the missiles. Although Dulles got acceptance of IRBM bases in principle, which was considered a major success, most of the participants did not want them based on their own territory. The only really enthusiastic country was Turkey, which was the least desirable base from the American point of view; the Turks were *too* close to the USSR, and it was feared they might be irresponsible. Eventually a squadron of 15 Jupiters was based in Turkey, and Italy accepted 30, despite great domestic opposition. Although General Norstad, the NATO commander, wanted an enormously greater IRBM force, the general tendency, from the spring of 1958, was for the military in Washington to lose enthusiasm for a large IRBM force. The missiles were inaccurate as well as vulnerable to a first strike; civilian strategists were even more critical than the military. The Air Force, which had favored a 16-squadron force, reduced its target to eight squadrons—the long-planned four Thor squadrons in Britain, three Jupiter squadrons in Turkey and a European country, and a Thor squadron based in Alaska or Okinawa. Eventually any Pacific deployment was dropped and in the end just seven IRBM squadrons were deployed. By January 1959, SAC even recommended canceling the whole IRBM effort. It went on as a demonstration of resolve as much as everything else.

In 1958, however, it seemed desirable to get IRBMs to Britain, at least, and soon. The Air Force pondered a crash program, establishing an experimental squadron of just five Thors, American-manned, at one of the American air bases in Britain, by July 1958. In the end, it was decided to stick with the existing program of equipping RAF units with warheads remaining in American custody. Launching was supposed to require both American and British agreement, but the British knew how to get around the "two-key" system and could have armed and fired the Thors without American consent. The Thor program slipped behind, as did building the four bases required and training the RAF units. So, despite the priority given the task, and "Project Emily," a massive American airlift that rushed the Thors and other equipment and supplies to Britain beginning in August 1958—it took over 300 flights by the Air Force's biggest transport, the C-124—the Thors took much longer to get into operation than expected. They gradually became operational between June 1959 and April 1960. But, once available, they turned out to be of greater military value than had been anticipated or was realized by later historians. RAF technicians found ways to fuel and prepare Thors much faster than the Americans had expected, and maintained the force at a higher level of readiness than had earlier been supposed possible. So they were not nearly as vulnerable to a Soviet first strike as was generally assumed, then and later. The Soviets took a deep interest in the Thor bases; their airliners flying to London developed an odd tendency to stray well off course and fly over them.

The Jupiters in Turkey lagged far behind. Delays in training local crews forced the Americans to man the missiles themselves for a time. After they finally became operational in 1961, the Jupiters were hampered by severe corrosion problems. Unlike the RAF Thors, they really were of little value; their sole worth was in complicating Soviet targeting and possibly indicating that the United States might strike first in the event of a conventional Soviet attack on NATO. The Kennedy Administration regarded such a "first strike echelon" (as all the IRBMs were considered) as provocative. Some elements in it favored canceling the Turkish deployment entirely but the Administration feared offending the Turks and did not do so. The growing Polaris submarine force was a more than superior substitute for the land-based IRBMs, and they did not last very long. The British pondered a modernized Thor force, with a longer-ranged version of the missile using hypergolic fuels, perhaps based in underground silos, but finally decided against this. During 1962 they decided to phase out the Thors in 1963. During the Cuban Missile crisis, the 15 Jupiters in

Turkey became an embarrassment to the U.S. government—or at least that was how it chose to regard them—and, as a super-secret part of the bargain ending the crisis they were withdrawn. That bargain, and the previous history of the Jupiters, and to some extent the other IRBMs, would be the subject of some spectacular lying by the Kennedy Administration and its apologists.[6]

In the end, the Jupiters and the Thors proved far more important for civilian space efforts than they ever were as weapons.

American ICBM Development

By the time of Sputnik, Atlas and Titan I were too far along for there to be much possibility of speeding up their development once the minor cuts and restrictions imposed earlier in 1957 were reversed. Plans for deploying them, however, fluctuated wildly for three years. It was hard to decide how many first-generation ICBMs should be built, and how they should be based. The "mix" of missile to be procured, the proper configuration of missile sites and control complexes, and how much to "harden" them against attack were difficult issues and data from the last nuclear tests in 1958, before the three-year test moratorium, caused major changes in plans.

Various models of the Atlas differed greatly in "hardness," and all were inferior to Titan I in that and other respects; but Titan lagged behind Atlas by about two years, only flying full range in February 1960. The record of ICBM testing was followed with great concern. The Air Force even laid plans, never executed, for an "emergency" ICBM, Thoric, using a combination of the Thor IRBM and the upper stages of the Vanguard satellite launcher, in case the main ICBM effort went really badly.

The promise of second-generation missiles—Titan II, and later on the solid-fuel Minuteman—complicated matters, as did Polaris, the Army, as well as the Navy, pushing the submarine missile as a substitute for some land-based ICBMs. Titan II, proposed by Martin engineers early in 1958, was basically a new missile using storable fuels and more powerful, it could be fired right out of an underground silo. (Titan I had to be moved up out of a silo to the surface on an elevator.) The Science Advisory Committee, in February 1958, wanted to procure just 80 Atlases, and then switch over to Titan. Eisenhower, cool to building many first-generation missiles of any sort, which he expected to rapidly become obsolete, liked giving priority to Titan and solid-fuel missiles. In April, he approved a 13-squadron force of Atlases and Titans, reluctantly upping this, in December, to 20 squadrons (11 of Titans) for June 1963. The Air Force wanted no less than 17 Atlas and 12 Titan squadrons. Titan was a subject of much argument; the competence of the Martin program was much criticized. Some in the Defense Department, taking the view opposite of Ike's, favored canceling Titan, or at least Titan II, as allegedly a wasteful duplication of Atlas, while the Ballistic Missile Division (as the Western Development Division had been renamed) strongly backed Titan. In 1960, Eisenhower, very reluctantly, approved a further increase to 13 Atlas and 14 Titan squadrons, close to the mix ultimately deployed. The overall impact of the missile gap was to cause the Administration to order somewhat more of the soon to be obsolescent Atlases than it would have liked.

The Atlas program was sluggish and suffered many reverses, which were frightening news given the fear of the missile gap. The main or sustainer engine of Atlas B, the first model to fly full range in November 1958, proved unreliable. Only three of six Atlas C tests, between December 1958 and August 1959, were successful. Atlas D, the first operational model, finished testing only in December 1959. Developing a system to fuel it quickly and safely proved difficult, and bases and training proved costlier than estimated. The declaration that Atlas D was "operational" in September 1959 was advanced for political purposes. Three missiles were maintained on the gantries used for experimental launches at Vandenberg Air Force Base; they could only have been fired with several hours warning. The other Atlas Ds, operational from August 1960, were stored above ground with no blast protection. Only later models were "semi-hardened." Atlas was never a very reliable weapon. Titan I, whose tests started only in February 1959, proved more dependable. Operational only in 1962, it was the first ICBM that was a real contribution to Western defense.[7]

Solid-Fuel Missiles

The Minuteman missile, which became the backbone of the ICBM force, resulted from the unexpectedly rapid development of the breakthrough in solid fuels that made Polaris possible. Air Force Colonel Edward Hall, an able scientist who had directed the testing of Thor, convinced General Schriever of the possibility of a three-stage solid-fuel ICBM. Schriever successfully fought for developing Minuteman in February 1958, despite widespread skepticism in the Air Force and the opposition of the Department of Defense's Director of Guided Missiles. The Air Force envisaged a flight test by the end of 1960, and an operational force by July 1963 that would eventually number 500 or more (twice that number would finally be deployed). In October 1958, Boeing became the assembly and test contractor for Minuteman, which got a DX priority in September 1959 and became a crash program during the Kennedy Administration.[8]

The Polaris submarine-based missile, which inspired Minuteman, was the sole missile project (with the minor and overlooked exception of the RAF Thors) to add substantially to Western power in the "missile gap" era. It had been radically speeded up in December 1957; despite its high cost and complexity, Eisenhower strongly backed it.

Polaris was run on a wartime basis by Admiral Raborn's Special Projects Office, using new management techniques. But it was sheer hard work and spirited leadership that made Polaris come in ahead of time and on budget. It was not just another project, but a crusade, Raborn making clear to everyone in the program that the stakes were enormous. He lectured employees and their families, telling his audiences to grasp the backs of their necks—"Those are the necks that will be saved when Polaris is developed!" While the Electric Boat Company worked on the submarines—three shifts and overtime—missile work went on at top speed. There were setbacks; a serious explosion in a plant that made the propellant, and a difficult test history. Test vehicles were successfully fired from underwater tubes as early as March 1958, but the Polaris itself failed spectacularly. The first full-scale Polaris launched in September 1958 failed—and so did its four successors. A sixth missile, in April 1959, did succeed, and after that things went more smoothly. The *George Washington*, launched in November 1959, made its first patrol a year later.[9] Had the missile gap been real, Polaris might have been the salvation of the United States.

That the gap was not real became fully apparent during 1960. During that year the United States lost the U-2 as a source of intelligence on the USSR, but rapidly recovered thanks to a byproduct of the missile program—the reconnaissance satellite. In August the "Discoverer" satellite series (actually the public cover name for the "Corona" program) launched by a combination of the Thor and the specially developed Agena upper stage, finally succeeded after more than a year and a half, and a dozen failures.[10]

The Space Race during 1958

Sputnik sparked a race to be "first" in space, first in unmanned, later in manned flight. The stakes in the race lay in prestige, and general technological and scientific advances. But that was not immediately clear, for aside from reconnaissance, it seemed possible, in the late 1950s, that there might be other, early direct military applications in space. In 1958, and for several more years, it seemed that the Americans were not doing too well. Apart from the Americans' many and well-publicized outright failures, the Soviets were sending up far bigger payloads, and scoring spectacular firsts, even though the Americans sent up more satellites and made the more significant discoveries. The Soviets maintained their psychological advantage, although they launched only one space mission in 1958, orbiting Sputnik III, a 2,925-pound, well-equipped geophysical laboratory that made the Explorers and Vanguards look pitiful.

The Explorers and Vanguards were only erratically successful. Both the next Vanguard flight and Explorer II failed. On March 17, the second American satellite, Vanguard I was put into higher orbit than Explorer I. Almost literally "just a grapefruit," it weighed only 3.5 pounds and carried just heat-measuring devices and a radio transmitter. But, powered by solar batteries, it reported for seven years and tracking it disclosed the Earth's true shape and other important geophysical data, notably that the Earth's mantle was less plastic, and the density of the fringe of the atmosphere greater than had been thought. Between failures of launch vehicle or satellite, the Vanguard program put up only one more successful satellite, this full-sized, in September 1959. The Explorers had a higher success rate. Explorer III, put up on March 26, 1958, duplicated the puzzling results of Explorer I, registering an increase of radiation as it climbed; then its radiation counter had seemed to "die." (Vanguard I did not carry a radiation counter.) Helped by clues from earlier high-altitude research rockets that had not reached orbit, James Van Allen, who had helped plan the radiation experiment, correctly theorized that the counters had been overloaded by extremely powerful belts of protons and electrons trapped in the Earth's magnetic field. Improved equipment was devised for Explorer IV, successfully orbited July 26, to test the theory.

The radiation belts, initially named after Van Allen, and the problem of their nature, suddenly seemed to become a vital Cold War issue. Earlier, Nicholas Christofilos, a physicist at the AEC's Livermore Laboratory, had suggested that artificially injecting radiation into the Earth's magnetic field with high-altitude nuclear explosions could wreck radio communications over a vast area for some time. The discovery of naturally trapped radiation focused attention on the possibility that an enemy, by detonating a few bombs at high altitude or in near-earth space, could prevent detection of an attack, or alternatively that high-altitude explosions could form a defensive screen that would wreck the electronics of attacking missiles. It was vital to explore the problem, and beat the deadline imposed by the forthcoming test ban, since the Soviets, thanks to Sputnik III, might know more than the Americans. On July 31 and August 10, in the last nuclear tests of the "Hardtack" series, already planned in 1957, Redstones launched from Johnston Island in the Pacific lofted H-bombs to 48 and 28 miles. They blanked out communications in the central Pacific for hours. In the hastily arranged "Argus" tests, three solid-fuel rockets launched from ships in the South Atlantic in August and September took one-kiloton bombs to 300 miles, increasing the strength of the radiation belts. But the concentration of electrons dissipated too fast to have the effects originally thought possible. After a later series of tests in 1962, after the Soviets broke the test moratorium, it became apparent that the "rainbow bomb" was not militarily important. Its effects were not entirely predictable, there were limits to how intense they could be made, and they could not be produced in the polar regions, which were the most critical points in nuclear warfare (but which the radiation belts did not cover).[11]

Developing New Launchers

The last Jupiter Cs were expended in failed satellite launches. These and the Vanguards were superseded by larger vehicles modified from military missiles, as Jupiter C had been modified from Redstone. Jupiter, Thor, and Atlas, combined with various upper stages—Able (the modified upper stages of the Vanguard launcher) and its later developments, Able-Star, Delta, and Agena. The latter, originally reserved for reconnaissance satellites, was released in 1959 for civilian purposes. Later, the Titan II ICBM would also be modified as a space launcher and Centaur and Burner upper stages would join the family of launchers. Following the example of Jupiter C, the missiles' fuel tanks would be enlarged, their engines improved, and strap-on solid-fuel rockets added, which, with the upper stages, provided space launchers that would be used for decades. The modified Jupiter—"Juno II"—first tested in December 1958, proved the least useful; its upper stages, although using better solid fuels than those of Jupiter C, proved underpowered. It was used to launch more Explorer satellites and Pioneer Moon probes, but was not very successful. The many modifications of Thor (eventually renamed Deltas) were far more effective. Used until the 1980s, and then revived after the *Challenger* disaster, the early Thor-Deltas and Thor-Agenas put up the first reconnaissance, communications, and weather satellites. The Atlas–Able combination proved a failure, but an Atlas became the first large American satellite. The whole sustainer stage of Atlas 10-B, carrying a small useful payload, went into orbit in December 1958. Atlas-Agenas would loft heavier satellites, Ranger and Orbiter Moon probes, and Mariner probes to Venus and Mars.

The First Race to the Moon

In 1958 the Americans hoped to beat the Soviets to the next objective in space but many engineers were skeptical of success. Nevertheless, the new Advanced Research Projects Agency authorized "Project Mona" in March, to send Pioneer probes to the Moon. The Air Force's Thor-Ables would send Pioneers into orbit around the Moon, while much smaller Army probes, launched by Juno IIs, were to near miss the Moon.

The program did not go well. The first Thor-Able blew up after lift off on August 17. Another sent up Pioneer I on October 11, but the upper stages provided less power than planned, and the probe, after reaching 71,700 miles from Earth, fell back. Pioneer II, in November, was another failure. A Juno II launched Pioneer III on December 6, but it failed to reach escape velocity and fell back. Further Pioneers misfired in 1959–1960, although Pioneer IV, going far off course, went into orbit around the sun in March 1959.

In that year, the Soviets, who had developed an upper stage for the R-7, launched Luna I, near missing the Moon in January. Later in that year, Luna II hit the Moon, and in October 1959, Luna III flew round the Moon, and photographed its far side, never seen before. The Soviets had won the first race to the Moon.

Although NASA eventually absorbed all American space efforts other than military reconnaissance, for a time it was not certain that its domination would be complete. And the chief military rivals devised their own long-range programs for space in late 1957 and 1958. They are of interest for showing the optimistic expectations of the period. The Army plan, developed by von Braun, envisaged soft-landing a probe on the Moon in 1960, establishing a four-man space station in 1962, a manned Moon landing in 1966, followed by a permanent space station and lunar outpost by 1973 and manned trips to the planets. Cost estimates were also highly optimistic; the Army estimated it could have a small Moon base by November 1966 for just $6 billion. The Air Force's April 1958 five-year plan also called for a permanent Moon base. Some in the military thought a lunar base could have a direct military role; space, and particularly the Moon, was the "high ground" that would control the Earth. Some argued for basing part of the nuclear deterrent on the Moon. It would require only small missiles to attack Earth targets under permanent observation. A Soviet surprise attack would be rendered impossible; to block American retaliation the Soviets would have to destroy American Moon bases days before striking on Earth. In practice, however, offensive or retaliatory missions could be done more easily on Earth; and space-based defenses against ICBMs, while they might be possible eventually, were far ahead of the available technology. General Schriever, the chief author of the Air Force program, did not develop arguments for a Moon base on such ideas but argued that such a base would advance technology and aide things that would have military applications. But, in fact, many officers were interested in space exploration for its own sake.

The Eisenhower Administration would not accept such long-range programs, but, during 1958, it authorized three items of long-range interest, which NASA would inherit from their original military owners—the Saturn super-booster, the giant F-1 rocket engine, and the Centaur upper stage, which proved crucial for the Apollo program and other space developments. ARPA, in August, authorized the Air Forces to develop a liquid hydrogen-powered upper stage, Centaur, for space probes. Its development proved long and hard, but inaugurated the use of liquid hydrogen as a fuel.

The Air Force and the Army Ballistic Missiles Agency had contemplated developing rockets far bigger than ICBMs for years. The Air Force did not envisage a specific vehicle, but pushed for far bigger engines, culminating in the 1.5 million pound thrust F-1, which would power the Saturn V Moon rocket. ABMA, which depended on the Air Force North American Aviation Rocketdyne division nexus for its engines, envisaged clustering existing or soon to be available engines in a space booster, at first called Super-Jupiter, and later Juno V. After various mutations, this was approved in August 1958. Later it became the first vehicle in a family of super-boosters called Saturn. The original Juno V/Saturn became the Saturn I and IB.

NACA and the Air Force had worked on winged maneuverable space vehicles well before Sputnik. But the power to get them into orbit was far off. Even before Sputnik, the Air Force had pondered simpler craft that would reenter the atmosphere like the nose cone of a missile; they could be developed soon and lofted by ICBMs. Plans for manned "capsule" flights were agreed on in August 1958, first for suborbital flights lifted by Redstones or Jupiters, later orbital ones carried by the Atlas. In November 1958, this was dubbed Project Mercury. In 1961, after a much longer, costlier development than expected, it put the first Americans into space. The Eisenhower Administration was reluctant to pursue a further course of manned space flight beyond Mercury, but was open to Jet Propulsion Laboratory/NASA plans for further probes to the Moon, Mars, and Venus.

The Soviets planned a series of major probes to Mars and Venus, using the R-7 with an improved second stage and a new third stage. But their many attempts at planetary probes, in the early 1960s, would fail due to a design flaw in the new stage, and grossly unreliable electronics. The new stage usually did not fire in free fall; when it did, the probes suffered communications failures. The Soviets' manned program, which received the go-ahead at about the same time as Mercury, proved far more successful. The Vostok (East) craft was a capsule, like Mercury, but a better and safer design; the Soviet engineers had much higher weight limits within which to work. It gave the Soviets the chance to put the first men into orbit.[12] In addition to other Soviet firsts—the first satellite, the first to reach escape velocity, the first to hit the Moon, the first to see its far side—this convinced most of the world that the Soviets were still ahead, probably far ahead, in space through the early 1960s. Even before the "payload gap" was closed, however, the Americans had detected the Van Allen belts and Solar X-rays, introduced solar cells to power satellites, made the first television pictures of Earth, launched the first weather, communications, and polar orbiting satellites, and made the first recovery of vehicles from orbit.

One aspect of space flight the Eisenhower Administration never took proper credit for was the development of manned, reusable winged spacecraft—the X-15. Usually described as a "rocket research plane" it was really the first crude spaceship; it left the limits of the atmosphere, usually set at a height of 50 miles, several times. This was obscured by the fact the first Vostok and Mercury flights reached space a year before the X-15, and the odd public relations policies of NASA and the Kennedy Administration. NACA had envisaged the need for a hypersonic research craft that could fly to 50 miles, and perhaps later reach orbital velocity, as far back as 1952. The X-15, finally a joint NACA–Air Force effort, was built by North American Aviation. After delays and difficulties occasioned by the failure of the preceding rocket research plane, the X-2, and a lack of the data it should have supplied, the difficulty of working with Inconel-X, the new nickel-chrome-steel alloy of which the X-15 was built, and problems with the X-15's engine, the first of the three that were built emerged from the factory in October 1958. But it began limited flights only in 1959.[13]

Even less publicity went to the nuclear propulsion programs initiated by the Eisenhower Administration and derailed by later ones before they bore fruit. The joint AEC–Air Forces Project Rover, the nuclear reactor rocket, had set in April 1956 an unrealistically early target date for demonstrating feasibility by 1959. Budget cuts, the realization that there was no real ICBM application for nuclear propulsion, and a recognition that the early target date was utterly unrealistic, led in 1957 to pushing back a demonstration of feasibility to 1960–1962, ground testing to 1963, and actual nuclear rocket flight only in 1968. Work was centralized in the AEC's Los Alamos laboratory, while a special test site was built in Nevada. After Sputnik, interest in the nuclear rocket increased. Its chief advocates in Congress, Senators Clinton Anderson and Henry Jackson, urged giving it a DX priority, but without success. Perhaps unfortunately, responsibility for the nonnuclear side of the project was shifted from the Air Force to NASA in October 1958; a long, often bitter quarrel over how to conduct development divided the AEC from NASA for years. But the project declined in importance. In 1959, the Administration cut its budget. Probably more important, in early 1959, NASA decided that nuclear engines would be started only in orbit or near orbit, to minimize the consequences of an accident. Moreover, the project terminated development of the laminar-flow "Dumbo" reactor that had promised the possibility of an earth-to-orbit nuclear rocket, leaving the nuclear rocket of value only for long-range space-to-space work. A long series of "Kiwi" ground test reactors were built, with much difficulty and many failures. Even as the project finally succeeded, in the mid-1960s, its budget was slashed again, and objectives cut back. Finally, in 1971, with the space program being cut back, the nuclear rocket effort was sacrificed entirely to save the Space Shuttle. The Soviets had a nuclear rocket program, but pursued it haphazardly, perhaps merely as a check in case Project Rover succeeded; it early stuck at problems the Americans solved.[14]

A more radical idea, dubbed "Orion," sometimes called, perhaps euphemistically, the "nuclear pulse rocket," received attention in the post-Sputnik atmosphere. Orion involved propelling a spaceship with nuclear *bombs*. While working on the Manhattan Project, Stanislaw Ulam and the physicist Frederick de Hoffman realized that a spaceship could be driven by successive small nuclear blasts. Debris and plasma from explosions at the right distance, hitting a specially designed "pusher plate" attached to the ship by shock absorbers would drive the ship. There was little interest in this until the mid-1950s; nuclear fuel was scarce and weapons had priority. But data from nuclear tests indicated it was not obviously impractical; investigations were pursued at a low level of funding. After Sputnik, radical ideas got a better hearing. ARPA allotted more funds in April 1958. Theodore Taylor, a brilliant nuclear weapons designer who had specialized in very small tactical weapons, became Project Engineer. He was joined by the physicist Freeman Dyson. Rapid progress was made in identifying and resolving the main problems of Orion—ablation of the pusher plate by explosion effects, designing the shock absorber system, and the ejection system for the bombs ("pulse units"). A model powered by high explosives, "Hot Rod" or "Put Put," reached heights of 200 feet. Then the program stalled. NASA was not very interested, while the Air Force, which got the project from ARPA in 1960, had no official "mission" for it, and some chief scientists in the Defense Department opposed it. Further progress required actual nuclear explosions and a full-scale ship would be huge and costly. Orion finally ran afoul of the 1963 treaty banning nuclear testing in the atmosphere and space, which was interpreted as forbidding it. So Orion, a strange but promising effort, ended in 1965.[15]

Notes

1 Stebbins, *The United States in World Affairs, 1958*, p. 3.
2 Levine, *The Missile and Space Race*, pp. 73–76; Zaloga, *The Kremlin's Nuclear Sword*, pp. 48–50, 61–62, 68–70; Horelick and Rush, *Strategic Power and Soviet Foreign Policy*, pp. 35–40, 42, 47, 82, 105–121; John Prados, *The Soviet Estimate* (New York: Dial Press, 1982), p. 77; Philip Nash, *The Other Missiles of October* (Chapel Hill, NC: University of North Carolina Press, 1997), pp. 36–40.
3 Stebbins, *The United States in World Affairs, 1958*, pp. 74–75; Larry Tart and Robert Keefe, *The Price of Vigilance* (New York: Ballantine, 2002).
4 Levine, *The Missile and Space Race*, p. 77; Prados, *The Soviet Estimate*, pp. 75–78; Divine, *The Sputnik Challenge*, p. 171; Watson, *Into the Missile Age*, p. 306.
5 Watson, *Into the Missile Age*, pp. 306–308, 314–315, 349–358; George Kistiakowsky, *A Scientist in the White House* (Cambridge, MA: Harvard University Press, 1976), p. xi; Divine, *The Sputnik Challenge*, pp. 171–183; Roman, *Eisenhower and the Missile Gap*, pp. 35–49; Prados, *The Soviet Estimate*, pp. 78–90; *FRUS 1958–1960, Vol. III*, pp. 69, 130–139, 179–180, 325–330; Levine, *The Missile and Space Race*, pp. 78, 86–92.
6 Divine, *The Sputnik Challenge*, pp. 73, 115, 126; Boyes, *Project Emily*; Levine, *The Missile and Space Race*, pp. 79–81; Watson, *Into the Missile Age*, pp. 512–523; Humphrey Wynn, *The RAF Strategic Nuclear Deterrent Forces*, pp. 280–297, 340–362; Neufeld, *Ballistic Missiles in the United States Air Force*, pp. 172, 186, 223, 227, 232; Stebbins, *The United States in World Affairs, 1958*, p. 25; Nash, *The Other Missiles of October*, pp. 12–13, 15–19, 22, 45, 50, 53–56, 68–71, 175; Michael Armacost, *The Politics of Weapons Innovation* (New York: Columbia University Press, 1969), pp. 181, 184–204. Boyes' book shows that the Thors were of more military value than generally supposed.
7 Levine, *The Missile and Space Race*, pp. 81–82; Divine, *The Sputnik Challenge*, p. 126; *FRUS 1958–1960, Vol. III*, pp. 41–43; 70–77, 153–162; Neufeld, *Ballistic Missiles in the United States Air Force*, pp. 187–223; Watson, *Into the Missile Age*, pp. 361–366.
8 Watson, *Into the Missile Age*, pp. 191–192; Levine, *The Missile and Space Race*, pp. 83–84; Neufeld, *Ballistic Missiles in the United States Air Force*, pp. 182, 186, 227–230, 237; Roy Neal, *Ace in the Hole* (New York: Doubleday, 1962).
9 Levine, *The Missile and Space Race*, pp. 84–85; Watson, *Into the Missile Age*, pp. 374–375; Harvey Sapolsky, *Polaris System Development* (Cambridge, MA: Harvard University Press, 1972); Divine, *The Sputnik Challenge*, p. 120.
10 Levine, *The Missile and Space Race*, pp. 89, 100, 114–115.
11 Levine, *The Missile and Space Race*, pp. 97–99; Constance Green, *Vanguard*, pp. 217–255; Jack D. Manno, *Arming the Heavens* (New York: Dodd, Mead, 1984), pp. 55, 72–85; Donald R. Baucom, *The Origins of SDI* (Lawrence, KS: University Press of Kansas, 1992), p. 15.
12 Levine, *The Missile and Space Race*, pp. 99–102, 105–112, 115–117; Divine, *The Sputnik Challenge*, pp. 97–99, 108.
13 Levine, *The Missile and Space Race*, pp. 147–153; Milton Thompson, *At the Edge of Space* (Washington DC: Smithsonian Institution Press, 1992).
14 James Dewar, *To the Ends of the Solar System*, 2nd ed. (Burlington, ON: Apogee Books, 2007); Levine, *The Missile and Space Race*, pp. 159–171.
15 George Dyson, *Project Orion* (New York: Owl Books, 2003); Levine, *The Missile and Space Race*, pp. 172–174.

6

THE MUDDLED EAST

The Middle East Crisis of 1958 and the Lebanon Landing

The first major crisis of the "missile gap" era arose, and this was typical of the period, not out of a direct Soviet–Western clash but out of local politics, the local politics, in the case of the Middle East, and the folly of the advanced industrial countries of Western Europe and Japan (not yet the United States) in letting themselves become dependent on that labyrinth of hatreds for the lifeblood of oil. It was also one of several cases in which, contrary to a general impression, America's allies, in this instance the British, most notably, but not only in the Suez–Sinai War of 1956, were readier to use force than the United States.

Contrary to what was and is widely supposed, the fact that the problems of the Middle East, and other areas, were mostly not created by the Soviets or Chinese or the local Communists, however they exploited them, was fully understood by the American leaders. As Secretary Dulles remarked at a National Security Council meeting on March 20, 1958:

> [I]n the three situations which mostly greatly concern the United States today—namely, Indonesia, North Africa and the Middle East—the directing forces were not Communist, but primarily forces favorable personally to a Sukarno, a Nasser or the like. Developments in those areas had not been initiated by Soviet plots.

He even suggested that the Soviets would be reluctant to initiate Communist takeovers of the sort seen in Czechoslovakia, even if they were possible—although his brother sharply disagreed with that.

Long before 1958, it should have been obvious that the Middle East was a seething mass of overlapping hatreds—above all, a hatred of any Western influence (not just "imperialism"), of Israel, of radical Arabs for conservative regimes (which often loathed each other) and of the Muslim Arab majority in the region for religious and ethnic minorities (Christians, Kurds, and others) and Iranians, and indeed for Muslims of different sects. The importance of the Arab–Israeli conflict, while serious enough, has often been exaggerated. Indeed, through much of the 1950s, although there was little sign that it would be resolved, that struggle was often effectively stalemated. Israel's victory in the First Arab–Israeli war, and the regime of arms control established by the Western powers in 1950, discouraged a renewal of fighting. The Arab–Israeli conflict was not the central issue of the era in the Middle East. It was often distinctly subordinate to the struggle between the Arabs and the "imperialist" powers, or seen, by many Arabs, just as part of the same fight—Israel being just a Western imperialist beachhead in the Arab world. As Nasser put it in his *Philosophy of the Revolution*, "Even Israel itself is but a result of imperialism." It was less important than the struggle between radical nationalists and conservatives among Arabs. Curiously it was that quarrel, not, as is often erroneously supposed, the Arab–Israeli clash, that opened the way for Soviet entry into the Arab world. The radical–conservative struggle, expressed in a whole series of revolutions—in Egypt in 1952, Iraq in 1958, Yemen in 1962, and Libya in 1969, played out on "national" or state lines as well—Egypt, after the revolution of 1952, leading the radical side; Iraq, up to 1958, leading the conservative side. (Later on, in the 1960s, the Egyptians would wage war against the Yemeni royalists, who were backed by the later leaders of the conservative side, the Saudis, a war far bloodier than all the Arab–Israeli wars.) The conservative Arabs themselves were split by old dynastic grudges. The Saudis hated the Hashemite kings of Jordan and Iraq, and the Hashemites' British allies, who backed Oman and other small states with which the Saudis had territorial disputes, to the point that the Saudis, in the 1950s, sometimes backed the Egyptians against their fellow monarchs.

The postwar era had seen the transformation of nationalism in the Middle East and North Africa into a far more radical form. Arab, and Iranian, nationalism was an old story by World War II, but it now became far more extreme. Although the Wafd in Egypt and similar groups in other countries, and the Iraqi dictator Nuri es-Said, were nationalistic enough by the standards of the rest of the world, they had not been fanatically anti-Western, and had, usually, been willing to bargain and compromise with the Western powers, and, in some cases, ally with them against the Axis or Soviets. But the Egyptian Officers Movement, the Baath parties in Syria and Iraq, and similar groups elsewhere, like some nationalists in Southeast Asia and a distinct minority of Indian nationalists, were far more violently anti-Western. During World War II, men like Nasser, Sadat, and Sukarno were ready to welcome the Nazis and the Japanese military as liberators from Western domination.

Morality aside, people who believed such things were not exactly oversupplied with brains or a grasp of reality, but they increasingly dominated Arab, and some other, nationalist movements. They eclipsed the older Arab nationalists to such an extent that they and their Western apologists often appropriated the title of "Arab nationalist" for them, as though there had never been any Arab nationalist movement before. If anything, they would become more and more hostile and fanatical even as the French were expelled from Syria and Lebanon and the British departed Palestine and sought more equitable relations with the Arab states. They often entertained very strange ideas about the West, its aims, and its attitudes. (Many Iranian nationalists were even more paranoid, believing that all Iranian political factions other than their own were British agents, and attributed every conceivable misfortune to a British plot, even believing that the British caused droughts in Iran.) It was, of course, true that the Arabs and Iranians had real grievances and reasonable ambitions. Any Egyptian government would have sought to get its hands on the Suez Canal revenues, and no self-respecting Iranian could have liked the Anglo-Iranian Oil Company. But the importance of such issues to the life of the Middle Eastern peoples was vastly overrated.

The radical nationalists went beyond seeking national independence, and envisioned the unification of the Arabic-speaking people, and "Arab socialism," which, while accepting the Stalinist pattern of industrialization, rejected Marxism. In practice, "Arab socialism" meant the nationalization of business and amounted to ineffective control of the economy by army officers, the only people with experience in running large organizations. It is an interesting indicator of the basic problems of the Middle East that the rest of the region rejected the successful Turkish pattern of modernization although it would seem to have been a more natural model than any other.

Rejecting connections with the West, as far as possible, they professed "neutralism" in the Cold War, but that was soon transformed into what was often called "positive neutralism"—in effect, unadmitted alliance with the Communist bloc against the West. (Technically, "positive neutralism" was an Indian coinage, but was given a different twist by others.) To be sure, most Arabs did not like the Soviets, or Communism. Social relations with Russians were notably bad, and Arabs often disliked them as people more than Western Europeans or Americans. The Soviets, for their part, were often disgusted by Arab behavior. Even Soviet diplomats found it hard to swallow their rage when high-ranking Egyptians, with amazing tactlessness and stupidity, praised Adolf Hitler to their faces! At lower levels, Russians often referred to Arabs as "*chernozhopi*" — literally "black asses," the Russian equivalent of "nigger," and regarded Arabs as, at best, incompetent bunglers. Local Communist parties were generally unpopular and persecuted in the 1950s and 1960s, although there were exceptions. Communism gained a certain amount of support in Syria and Iraq, and for a time Communist seizures of power were not out of the question. Such possibilities, maintaining the general alliance with the radical nationalists, and handling the latter's persecution of the local Communists, posed difficult dilemmas for the Soviets.

For their part, many Westerners in the 1950s, and even much later, were blind to the reality of Arab, and Iranian, hostility. Often they simply failed to perceive the mobilization of the masses, and assumed that the traditional, narrowly based political elites would stay in control, or vastly underestimated the pace of political change. Many could just not grasp that Muslims—even in the 1950s political leaders and factions that were basically secularist found it prudent to at least pretend to be good Muslims—could ally with the "atheistic Communists." (Others discounted the religious element in hostility to the West.) Many were incredulous that accurate descriptions of Soviet imperialism, not just in Europe and East Asia, but against fellow Muslims in Central Asia and the Caucasus, had no effect. They just bounced off the consciousness of most Arabs and Iranians (and, for that matter, many other Asians and Africans). Others ascribed all Arab anger at the West to the latter's support of Israel, or swallowed, sometimes with varying amounts of indigestion, the most exaggerated charges against Western imperialism. Some who found it hard to accept the depth of hostility to Israel believed that some deal, combined with Western aid, could placate the Arabs and win them over—an idea common in the Eisenhower Administration, in its first years.

In the West, between the World Wars, there had grown up an influential current of opinion that accepted any claims made in terms of nationalism, self-determination, or anti-imperialism. A whole guilt complex had grown up about imperialism, race, and related matters. For many liberals and leftists, Asians and Africans, and/or "non-whites" in general, were not real people at all, but symbols of the evil of their own societies, automatically placed beyond criticism by their status as "victims." They no more saw them as people, good and bad, intelligent and stupid, than the most bigoted racialists—perhaps less so. Later, with the use and expansion of the term "Third World" (not yet used by English-speakers in the 1950s) Latin Americans would be subtracted from the West and added to the mix of victims, while the concept of imperialism, itself increasingly inflated, was already being partly supplanted by the even vaguer, more amorphous usage "colonialism." That would eventually provide a way to bracket rule over foreign peoples with other sorts of Western expansion, notably the settlement colonies that had produced the United States, Canada, Australia, Brazil, and other nations, and subtly or not so subtly delegitimized them. That result was still far off in 1958, but already vast amounts of misinformation were injected into Western debates.

The Cold War in the Middle East to 1957

The Middle East, and especially bases in Egypt, had played a major part in Western military planning in the late 1940s, although, before the Korean War, the Americans rejected a major defense role in the area, relegating that to the British and local forces. But extending anti-Soviet alliances to the region, and creating a Middle East Command, failed because of bitter Egyptian hostility to the British Suez Canal base, their main installation in the region, and general Arab hostility to the West and disinterest in the Cold War. (Some Arabs opposed the UN side in the Korean War because they blamed the UN for the creation of Israel!)

Surprisingly, at first sight, the deadlock over the Suez base was broken by the first radical nationalist breakthrough, the Egyptian revolution of 1952. Even the British welcomed the overthrow of the old regime, for which no one had had much respect. The new regime, dominated at first behind the scenes, then openly, by Colonel Gamal Nasser, instituted some badly needed reforms and actually seemed, for a time, more flexible than its predecessor in international negotiations. It got particularly enthusiastic support from the United States, although maintaining a savage propaganda campaign against Britain. Radio Cairo, in June 1954, broadcast that "Every Arab now realizes the glaring fact that the West now wishes to settle in our land forever. The West wants to remain the master of the world, so that it may colonize, enslave and exploit it." Israel, in this line, was just the "step-daughter" of imperialism. The Egyptians did their best to stir violence against Britain, not only in the Arab world but in sub-Saharan Africa, and aided the Cypriot terrorists.

Able, charismatic, a skillful demagogue, and movie-star handsome (he looked like the American actor Cesar Romero) Nasser became the dominant figure in Arab, not just Egyptian, politics until his death in 1970. He early got some overt American aid, and a handsome bribe from the CIA, which he used to build a mosque; it affected his behavior not at all. (This does not seem to have shaken that agency's remarkable faith in bribes.) But he became more willing to talk about the Suez issue, while the British finally recognized that the political situation had changed, and that the current military situation rendered a large-scale presence in the Suez Canal base an unnecessary expense. It was unlikely to be of use in a general war, and some of its functions could be shifted to Cyprus. Nasser even led the British to think that if agreement was reached, he might be open to some kind of defense tie with the West. In July 1954, despite the doubts of Prime Minister Churchill, and the hostility of the "Suez Group" faction of the Conservative Party, it was agreed that British troops would leave. Some civilian technicians would maintain the base, which the British could use in the event of an attack on the Arab countries or Turkey.

In 1953, Secretary Dulles had realized that defense arrangements with the Middle East must be based on the non-Arab "Northern Tier"—Turkey, Iran, and Pakistan. There might be a few exceptions, but, at best, the Arab states could only be kept neutral in the Cold War. The British, however, rejected that conclusion, insisting on bringing Iraq and Jordan into a Northern Tier alliance—the "Baghdad Pact." The United States did not join the Pact.

Nasser, unfortunately, was not the genial Arab Nehru many imagined. His true views had been revealed in his book, *Philosophy of the Revolution*, first published in early 1954, which envisaged Egypt as the center of a united Arab world, which, if possible, would extend its influence over the whole Islamic world and Africa, and use the oil resources of the Middle East and control of the Suez route, which already carried half of Europe's oil, against the West. After the Suez base agreement, propaganda against Britain actually became more violent. The Americans too found that hopes for an entente with Nasser, or solving the Arab–Israeli conflict, had been in vain. If Nasser ever considered such policies, as is sometimes claimed, he had quickly dropped the idea. He tried to secure American arms aid early in 1955, but the Americans made clear that such aid would be concentrated on defensive weapons, and must be supervised by an American mission, as stipulated by Congress, which Nasser refused to accept. There are strong indications that his seeming interest in American aid was a deliberate deceptive move to confuse the Western powers while raising his price with the Soviets; his real aim was a deal with them. Nasser became even more hostile to the British and their allies. He violently opposed the Baghdad Pact. All Arabs must be "neutral" in the Cold War; any allied with the West were "strikebreakers," if not traitors. A little Cold War started between Egypt and Iraq. Common hostility to the Baghdad Pact helped bring Egypt and the USSR together.

The latest Western attempt to resolve the Arab–Israeli conflict collapsed. To placate the Arabs, the Americans cold-shouldered Israel—Eisenhower's Administration was the least friendly to Israel of any after 1948—but discovered that this gained nothing. Their "Alpha Plan" involved resettling Arab refugees, and compensating them for their lost property (all at American and British expense, of course) while Israel would cede small chunks of land to the Arab countries to provide an Arab corridor through Israel. The deal also included an agreement for the division of Jordan River water and joint development there. Nasser, however, insisted that the Israelis cede the whole Negev region and allow the return of all refugees to their old homes. The Israelis would not accept any refugees, or cede any territory, and insisted on direct talks with the Arab states, which Nasser refused. The Egyptians allowed Palestinian attacks on Israel; a particularly violent Israeli retaliatory raid on Gaza further envenomed the situation, and provided an additional justification for the long-prepared arms deal with the Soviets, announced in September 1955.[1]

It bartered Egyptian cotton for fairly late model Soviet arms (nominally supplied by Czechoslovakia) at half price. The Soviets had expected an arrangement with Egypt since 1953, although not without some misgivings. Molotov and others disliked alliances with Nasser and similar types elsewhere, considering them a poor investment that might involve the Soviets in untimely confrontations with the West; and, with good reason, they distrusted the strength, reliability, and intelligence of the Egyptian and similar regimes. A good case can be made, and was by some Western observers even during the Cold War, that, in the end, Molotov was proved right, although perhaps only by a narrow margin, for Soviet aid to and alliance with Nasser's and similar regimes did cause the West terrific headaches and perhaps came close to inflicting catastrophic damage. But in the end they did not do so, and perhaps cost the USSR more than it gained.

Nasser, for his part, had had good reason to handle things slowly up to 1955. He was getting some aid from the West, and did not wish to take major risks before the British left Suez. And he was well aware of what the CIA had done in Iran and Guatemala.

The "Czech arms deal," soon followed by a similar deal with Syria, revolutionized the situation in the Middle East, among other things overturning the Tripartite arms regulation regime instituted in 1950 and enormously inflaming the local arms race. It revived the chances of an early Arab–Israeli war. The Western powers regarded it as a grave threat, but finally took no counteraction lest Nasser be driven even farther into the Soviets' arms.[2]

Assistant Secretary of State George Allen, visiting Cairo for the Alpha Plan, mildly protested to Nasser about the arms deal and explained American worries about an arms race. Nasser exploded,

> We are accustomed to imperialism. We have had five hundred years from the Turks and eighty years from the British. But under them, at least, we had our own Arab schools and local administration. And now that we can call our nation free from that imperialism, you Americans are the worst of all imperialists. Why? You want to know why? I'll tell you. Because it was you, America, who established the state of Israel. That, my dear Mr. Allen, means that in Arab lands you introduced not merely a foreign administration but a completely foreign people! You also saddled us with Arab refugees. This American imperialism is the worst kind we Arabs have ever experienced.[3]

After this, optimism about Nasser was really inexcusable, but it took some time, and more provocations to really enrage the British and Americans into regarding Nasser as simply an enemy. They blamed him for the final failure of the Alpha Plan, attempts to overthrow the Libyan government, and preventing Jordan from joining the Baghdad pact. The British also believed, wrongly, that Nasser was responsible for the dismissal of General Glubb, the British officer who had commanded the Jordanian Army. Over the next few years, they and the Americans may have overestimated the extent to which Nasser deliberately worked with the Soviets, but their basic perception of his hostility was hardly mistaken. Both countries settled on a policy of "neutralizing" or curbing him. The British leaders would have liked to overthrow or assassinate Nasser, but the Americans would not go so far. They saw no viable replacement for him, and vaguely hoped to bring him around at some point. But the prospect of the Western powers financing the construction of the Aswan High Dam did not mollify him. The Americans and British were determined to overthrow Nasser's ally, the Syrian government, which seemed a weaker target—one for which a replacement seemed to exist.

Secretary Dulles finally made clear that the United States would not aid the Aswan Dam project, which, like Nasser, was extremely unpopular in the United States. That triggered, or provided an excuse for, Nasser's nationalization of the Suez Canal on July 26, 1956.[4] This enraged the Western powers, and even some neutrals, but in and of itself, would not have provoked war. Egypt was due to get the Canal in 1968, and most lawyers thought that the Egyptian action was not illegal. But it disregarded the interests of the rest of the world in the Canal as an "international public utility." The British and French—the latter blamed Nasser's support for the rebels for their troubles in Algeria—feared, as Prime Minister Eden put it, Nasser's "thumb on our windpipe"—feared becoming the prisoners of Nasser, or other similar leaders, or even ultimately the Soviets, who would control the oil route to Western Europe if not the oil itself. Eden, who likened Nasser to Mussolini, personally warned Khrushchev in July 1956 that Britain would go to war over its oil supply. The British and French were determined to make Nasser "disgorge," if not to use the current crisis to get rid of him, period. They prepared for military action. The Israelis, fearing what would happen after the Egyptians and Syrians assimilated their new Soviet weapons, were ready to join in. They had a ready set of justifications for war—"fedayeen" raids, long-standing blocking of Israeli-bound ships from the Suez Canal, and the Egyptian blockade of the port of Eilat.

But the Americans did not think Nasser's action illegal, and Eisenhower—if not Dulles—ruled out using force, if negotiations failed, as they did, after several wearisome months during which the British became thoroughly disgusted, and alienated from the Americans. Neither the Americans nor the Western Europeans handled themselves well. The latter misunderstood the American position, and assumed that in the end the Americans would come around and at least let them go ahead with an attack on Egypt. (Dulles personally, like many other Americans might have been inclined to do just that.) They arranged a *sub rosa* alliance with Israel. The Israelis would attack, and the British and French would intervene on the pretext of separating the combatants to keep the Canal open.

The Soviets, of course, backed Egypt during the dispute over the Canal seizure. Like Nasser they underrated the danger of war, apparently assuming the Anglo-French military buildup was a bluff, and were coping with dangerous crises in Poland and Hungary. Neither the Soviets nor Nasser expected the Israeli attack that began on October 29, but both wrongly supposed that Egypt could handle such an attack.

Neither expected the Anglo-French attack that followed on October 31, and neither had any illusions that the Egyptians could cope with that. The Americans had not expected it either, supposing that if the Allies did act, they would wait until after the American elections on November 6. To the shock of the British and French, the Americans as well as the Soviets opposed them. British opinion, originally united against Nasser, was now badly split. Although most people probably backed Prime Minister Eden, some Conservatives opposed him, as did the leaders (not all the rank and file) of the Labour and Liberal parties. The Commonwealth was also split, only Australia and New Zealand supporting Britain, while, except for West Germany and some of the small Northern European democracies, world opinion seemed to back Egypt.

American opinion, although less emotional, was also split. The armed forces, and some liberals, as well as conservatives, favored the Allies. But Eisenhower, easily gaining reelection, strongly opposed the Israeli and Anglo-French attacks. He, not Dulles, who was friendlier to the Allies, but was sidelined by illness on November 3, determined policy. The American government brought fierce financial pressures to bear on the Allies. On November 5, the Soviets proposed a joint Soviet–American intervention against the Allies and threatened to attack London and Paris with missiles. That was sheer bluff—they had no rockets capable of reaching those cities. The Americans made clear that they would not consider a joint intervention or ignore a Soviet attack. Under pressure—more from the Americans than the Soviets—the British and French caved in. They and the Israelis, who could almost certainly have smashed the Egyptians without their help, were forced to withdraw without any concessions from Nasser. A small UN force was established to maintain peace between Egypt and Israel; it would prove entirely ineffective.[5]

The Suez–Sinai War proved a disaster for the West, which was steadily brainwashed by effective propaganda into seeing Suez as the "last gasp of imperialism"—sheer nonsense as far as the British were concerned, and especially Eden, who had never been an "Empire" man. The most serious result, at first, seemed to be a catastrophic breach in the Western alliance, but a return of commonsense on both sides of the Atlantic, which had not been much in evidence recently, healed it with remarkable rapidity, at least between the Americans and British; the French were less reconciled.

Suez was a major blow to the Western position in the Middle East, even the whole world. The Western Europeans were perceived as both evil aggressors and basically weak, it was hard even for conservative Arab governments to work with them. Nasser became a mythic hero, a giant-killer. The planned coup against the Syrian government collapsed; the plot backfired, discrediting everyone to the right of the pan-Arabs in Syria. The Americans gained little credit with Arab opinion for their stand. Many Arabs just whined that they should have done more, and most preferred to credit the Soviet threats with forcing the Allies to back down. The Egyptian leaders knew better, but did nothing to correct public perceptions. Khrushchev's wishful thinking led him to suppose that his bluff had worked, with unhappy results for the next few years. Soviet influence and popularity did increase enormously. In the Middle

East, and much of the rest of the world, Suez vastly outweighed Soviet actions in Hungary, rather to Eisenhower's astonishment. The President bitterly told the British Ambassador, on November 9, that to Asians "colonialism was not colonialism unless it is a matter of white domination over colored peoples."

The mentality of many Arabs was neatly demonstrated by the Syrian ruler, Shukri Quwatly. On November 8, when the American Ambassador complained that the Syrian government had not supported rebuking the Soviets over Hungary, Quwatly did not complain, as he might well have, about the Anglo-American plot against him, but just ranted about Zionism, and that the "situation in Hungary is not our affair, and I do not care if fifty Budapests are destroyed."

Although Britain's influence in the Middle East was not entirely destroyed, as is sometimes said, it was vastly reduced. The ability, and in the long run the will, of Western Europe to act in the region, was severely damaged. The Europeans would forfeit control of their oil supplies, and the United States would be left largely alone as the only outside power to counter the Soviets and later threats. The bizarre situation in which the United States and the UN acted against the democratic allies, while being utterly ineffective against the Soviets in Hungary, had a demoralizing effect. The American insistence on "one law for all" did not encourage respect for international law, but the reverse.

Dulles almost immediately realized that American policy had been wrong, virtually apologizing to the British and French Foreign Ministers when they visited him in his hospital. Shortly before his death, Eisenhower reluctantly came to agree.

Any temporary moderation by Nasser soon passed, and the Americans realized, by late November at the latest, that he was still an enemy, acting once again against the West and local governments in Lebanon, Libya, and Kuwait.[6]

The "Eisenhower Doctrine"

The Eisenhower Administration estimated that there was now a "power vacuum" in the Middle East. With Britain and France "out," the region was wide open to Soviet power and Nasserite extremism. This perhaps overestimated the immediate Soviet threat, for the Soviets did not consider the situation really ripe, and were still worried about the situation in East-Central Europe.

Secretary Wilson, the Joint Chiefs, and others in the Administration favored the United States joining the Baghdad Pact, as did the British. Dulles rejected this, and the President agreed. The Pact was already discredited with Arabs, and was opposed by the Saudis. The new American policy was to back Saudi Arabia, with its supposed appeal to Muslims, not to mention oil, as a counter-pole to Nasser, who would be contained, not overthrown, and warn the Soviets from open intervention in the Middle East. Nasser would be discouraged to avoid reckless actions and too close association with the Soviets. Economic and military aid, and if necessary force, would be used. The new policy was rapidly formulated, and announced by Eisenhower on January 5, 1957. He asked Congress for a joint resolution as well as funds. Even before the press knew what he would say, it dubbed it the "Eisenhower Doctrine," a name the President disliked. Many people disliked the vagueness of the "Middle East Resolution's" direction against "forces allied to international Communism" but it easily got through Congress. It was less successful in the Middle East. The NATO countries favored it, as did Pakistan and Iran, but most Arabs opposed the "Eisenhower Doctrine." They resented being seen as a "power vacuum," and saw no Soviet danger. The "real problem" of course, was imperialism, colonialism, Zionism, and so forth. It was a call for the Arab governments to stand up, but most preferred to sit down. Only Iraq and Lebanon backed the "Eisenhower Doctrine." Even the Saudis stayed aloof. The Soviets, although not inclined at the moment to an active policy in the Middle East, made clear that they would back Egypt and Syria.

The new policy was not an immediate and total failure. It encouraged Jordan to move back toward the West, King Hussein dismissing his pro-Nasser cabinet in April 1957, but had little success thereafter. Pushing King Saud as Nasser's rival misfired completely. One of Eisenhower's silliest foreign policy moves, it was based on a total misreading of the mentality of most Arabs, who viewed the Saudis, quite correctly, as reactionary, sectarian tyrants. Saud himself was erratic and not very brave and from mid-1957 began seeking another rapprochement with Nasser. By the end of 1957 Eisenhower ruefully saw he had been wrong, dryly noting that Saud's proposed "solution" to Middle East problems was to wipe out Israel. "It would be difficult to write a considered reply."[7]

Syrian Crisis and United Arab Republic

From the summer of 1957, American policy began to collapse. A key secret element of it was a renewed attempt to overthrow the Syrian government—another misfire.

In August 1957, the coup was uncovered; the plotters were arrested and several American diplomats expelled from Syria. Syrian politics moved ever further to the left. The dominant elements were the radical nationalist Baath (to the left of Nasser) and the Communists, who were the best-organized group in the country, had a serious paramilitary force, and some strength even in the regular army. Al-Bizri, the chief of staff, was definitely pro-Soviet, and widely believed, by Nasser as well as Western observers, to be a Communist. The Americans, and several of Syria's neighbors (Israel, Turkey, and Iraq) thought there was a good chance that a real Soviet satellite regime would be established and too strongly to be overturned from within.

The Eisenhower Administration now took up a very tough line, perhaps the riskiest and most provocative of Eisenhower's presidency, and that led to possibly the only Soviet–American confrontation of the whole Cold War that the United States could plausibly be blamed for starting. All of Syria's neighbors were encouraged to mobilize strong forces on its borders. Hopefully, the Syrians would be goaded into outright military action, which would provide an excuse for Iraq, perhaps supported by Jordan, to invade Syria. Turkey would take part in the initial maneuvers, but not, if possible, the attack, lest Arab nationalist sentiments be inflamed. The Turks indicated that they might well act on their own to stop a Communist or pro-Soviet regime, but the American government did not want that. They also wanted to keep the Israelis out. But the Iraqi and Jordanian governments were reluctant to act, fearing their own public opinion, while the Saudis would not even denounce the Syrian government. The Turks mobilized, but the Soviets strongly warned them against any aggressive act, and sent a naval force to Syria in September. The pressure against Syria merely roused Arab opinion against Turkey and the West, and internal support for the rather divided Syrian government. Syria, in Arab eyes, was "martyred" by the "encirclement." The Saudis wound up expressing sympathy with Syria, as did Jordan. On October 7, Khrushchev issued a yet stronger warning against any Turkish action, and on October 13 the Egyptians landed troops in Syria. The Turks professed to be still ready to move, but the Americans did not want them to act unilaterally. Dulles, on October 16, did warn against a Soviet attack on Turkey, but also acted to restrain the Turks. The Soviets also decided to defuse the crisis in late October; they do not seem to have envisaged or encouraged an early Communist takeover, as the West and others feared.[8]

The Syrians were left splintered between Baath and Nasserites on the one side, and the Communists on the other. The latter's ally, al-Bizri, now Defense Minister, might become President in 1958. Baath took the initiative in calling in the Egyptians to shut out their Communist rivals. Nasser had not envisaged, or wanted, *early* moves toward Arab unity. He thought such a union needed years of preparation. With some reluctance, he accepted an early Egyptian–Syrian union, on his terms (not welcome to Baath) to shut out the Communists. The result was the formation of the United Arab Republic in February 1958, with which Yemen became nominally associated. Although the UAR had been formed reluctantly, for short-range, narrow purposes, Nasser and Egypt seemed to have scored another great triumph, and the dream of Arab unity seemed to many in the Arab world and elsewhere to be on the verge of achievement. Nasser, in 1958, was expected to be the Bismarck or Cavour—or Hitler—of the Arab-speaking peoples. Instead, the creation of the UAR was the zenith of the pan-Arab dream. It lasted just three years.

Although it was understood at the time by Western observers that the UAR had been formed only reluctantly by Nasser, and that it was a reverse for the local Communists and the Soviets (despite the latter's public acclaim for it), Western appraisals of the probable results were pessimistic. It might not be just what Khrushchev wanted, but it nevertheless strengthened his local non-Communist allies. The Hashemite attempt to form a rival "Arab Union" of Iraq and Jordan won few supporters; virtually all Arabs were now afraid to oppose Nasser, even the Saudis caving in. In March 1958, King Saud was deposed after a belated plot against the UAR in Syria backfired.[9]

Lebanon

The radical nationalist wave now threatened to submerge the most modern, pro-Western and only democratic—sort of—Arab country, Lebanon. The immediate trigger for the crisis in Lebanon, however, was its peculiar political situation. It was split down the middle between Christians, mostly Maronites, and Muslims. The Christians were dominant. Originally the country had had a Christian majority. But no census had been taken since 1936, and it was generally estimated that the Muslims by 1958 had a slight majority, albeit split between Sunnites and Shiites. (Muslims certainly would have had a majority had Palestinian refugees been counted, but they had no political rights.) The political system involved a number of complex and delicate compromises; by tradition, the president was a Maronite, the prime minister a Muslim, and there were other arrangements of a similar nature. While Beirut and the coastal towns were modern and cosmopolitan, much of the countryside was run by regional/religious bosses, whose traditional dominance was often hidden behind high-sounding "modern" party designations.

Muslims, poorer than the Christians, were strongly attracted by Nasser and the pan-Arab message, and Lebanon played a part in the Middle East out of proportion to its size and population. Beirut was a center of foreign intrigue and massive interference by Western, Soviet, and Arab agents. The Lebanese government, unmistakably pro-Western in the Cold War, had never been friendly to Nasser. Lebanon had been the only Arab country other than Iraq to welcome the Eisenhower Doctrine. The President, Camille Chamoun, was widely regarded as an American client. He was not, as is often said, a reactionary or Christian sectarian, but a liberal lawyer, a reformer, and modernizer, whose efforts to reform the political system crossed traditional bosses of all sorts, alienating some fellow Maronites (including the Patriarch of his own church) as well as many Muslims. Unfortunately, he was also a selfish egomaniac, bent on hanging on to power at almost any cost. The Lebanese constitution limited him to a six-year term, ending in 1958, and he could not run again until another six years had passed. In the elections of 1958, which saw a peak of foreign interference in which outsiders of all sorts brought in unprecedented amounts of cash, the CIA had succeeded almost too well. Even moderate Arab nationalists were swept aside by Chamoun's supporters, and his opponents further alienated. Chamoun now wanted to amend the constitution so that he could run for a second term in 1958.

This put the Americans, at least in their opinion, in a dilemma. If Chamoun ran again, he was likely to win, even in an "unfixed" election. He was too able, and his opponents too badly divided. The only possible alternative candidate with a chance of winning was the Army Chief of Staff, Fuad Chehab, another Maronite, but a man trusted by all sects. He was thought, however, to be unlikely to run. If Chamoun won, the Americans thought, it would be at the cost of dangerously straining the fragile Lebanese political system and widening religious divisions. Yet, they would have to back him, because if he failed at reelection, this would be a perceived reverse for pro-Western elements and a victory for Nasser. So they tried to discourage Chamoun from his course. This did not work. His domestic opponents resorted to force.

Civil war, long feared, broke out on May 8. Nasser's government probably did not instigate the revolt, but quickly supported it, infiltrating arms and men across the Syrian border, while the UAR Embassy distributed arms and money in the capital. The Americans thought that the small Lebanese army (only 9,000 strong, about three-quarters Christians) could do much more than it did to suppress the rebellion, but Chehab seemed to have little will to push things to a conclusion, apparently fearing that his army might split along religious lines. By May 13, Chamoun was inquiring about how the Americans might respond to a request for intervention.

The Eisenhower Administration was extremely reluctant to intervene, Dulles, if anything, even more so than the President, believing that there would be a violent reaction in the rest of the Arab world. Nevertheless, it might become necessary, and planning for it proceeded. The Americans warned Chamoun, on the same day of his inquiry, that they might intervene to support the Lebanese government, but not to secure an additional term for him. Lebanon would first have to complain to the UN Security Council, and get at least one other Arab state to support it. In preliminary discussions the Americans agreed with the British, who were expected to participate in any intervention, that they would keep the French, violently hated by Arabs over Algeria, out of any operation. They warned off Nasser. In the meantime, the Sixth Fleet moved toward Lebanon, and two American destroyers patrolled off Beirut; Army airborne battle groups in West Germany got ready, and police equipment airlifted to Beirut.

On May 15, Nasser, visiting the USSR, issued a joint statement with Khrushchev that associated the UAR with many Soviet positions in the Cold War, notably in attacking Western overseas bases, and on disarmament and nuclear testing. Things seemed to get worse and worse. Chamoun was unwilling to back down. On May 22, he complained to the UN about the infiltration from Syria. The Americans estimated that the rebels were preparing to cut Lebanon in two, as a preliminary to a final drive for victory. They hardened even more against Nasser.

Nasser, however, now seemed to become somewhat more cautious. On May 20, the American Ambassador had met him to convey the warning prepared by Dulles on May 15, that the United States intended to live up to its commitment to maintain Lebanon's independence and integrity. It allowed that the aid coming from UAR territory might not be authorized by its government, giving the Egyptian a face-saving way out. Nasser criticized Chamoun and his supporters while denying any support for the rebels by the UAR, although admitting that there might have been some crossing of the Syrian border and smuggling of weapons. He then suddenly became more reasonable, suggesting a settlement, in which Chehab would become Prime Minister, the rebels would be amnestied, and Chamoun would serve out his presidential term but not run again. This was close to what actually developed. When the Lebanon issue was finally discussed by the UN Security Council on June 10, it was agreed to establish a Military Observation Group for Lebanon. The Soviets abstained, and Nasser did not object. He may now have regretted his pro-Soviet line of May 15, and worried that Lebanon threatened to become a trap for him. If he was too pushy, the Americans might use it as an excuse to destroy his regime.

The UN observation group proved ineffective, if not downright incompetent. It claimed to be unable to find evidence of infiltration from Syria, although it had hardly tried to. Even UN Secretary-General Hammarskjold did not rely on its reports. Nasser now suggested that, after an amnesty, Chehab succeed Chamoun as President. Dulles continued to warn Chamoun that American support was not a "blank check," and that in the long run Western intervention would backfire against him. But Chamoun remained stubborn, while the military situation got worse. As late as June 20, the Dulles brothers agreed that "the situation was going down the drain" and there seemed no way to stop it. The Secretary of State was horrified by what he saw as the probable results of intervention, remarking to the British Ambassador on June 18 that if the Lebanese government called for armed intervention, and we responded, there would be a wave of anti-Western sentiment, which would sweep away our friends in Jordan, Iraq and Saudi Arabia, and turn the Lebanese against us. If we did not respond, we would get the same results in the Arab world, just less abruptly. However, if we failed to respond, the effect on our friends in countries peripheral to the Arab world would be very bad, while these friends would be encouraged if we went into Lebanon. He was frantic to resolve the issue with an internal Lebanese solution. In a discussion in the State Department, four days later, he gloomily remarked that "the only thing worse than intervening, if requested to do so by the Lebanese government, would be not to go in." As he elaborated, the Jordanian and Iraqi governments would be swept away and the Lebanese government would probably not survive our withdrawal. But if we did not respond to call for intervention, they would be overthrown anyway.

> In this respect, there was little difference either way. The real difference lay with the peripheral countries and in that case the consequences of our failure to act would not be limited to the Arab countries alone, but would undermine the Northern Tier, Sudan and Libya.

Further, failure to respond would destroy "confidence in us of all the countries on the Soviet periphery through the Middle and Far East." But, during early July, the situation seemed to improve. The Americans thought that Nasser was now stopping or reducing the flow of men and material into Lebanon, although he was not ready to stop the fighting, while Chamoun finally backed down on July 10, indicating that he would not try to succeed himself. It was expected that Chehab would run for president in elections scheduled for July 24. It now appeared that the Lebanese crisis would pass without dramatic action.[10]

Then the situation changed drastically because of events outside Lebanon—events that led to the grim joke in the West that the news media phrase, "leading Middle East statesman," really meant "elderly Arab politician about to be assassinated."

The Iraqi Revolution

Iraq had been the most important Arab ally of the Western powers. Unfortunately, its government rested on a very narrow, shaky base of support. The small political and social elite was identified with the British; both were thoroughly hated. The royal family, a branch of the same Hashemites who ruled Jordan, was regarded as alien. Wealth was fantastically concentrated; some 2,000 families owned 70 percent of the land. Most of what little industry existed was owned by 23 families. Rich people paid no taxes, and corruption was bad even by Middle East standards. The dictator, Nuri es Said, was an able man in some ways, but while some respected him, he was generally hated. The rest of the Iraqi politicians were regarded as a bunch of crooks. Nuri directed the considerable oil revenues toward rational plans for economic development, but opposed agrarian and other reforms. With a doubtful understanding of the origins of revolutions, he and British officials assumed that the population would remain passive until and after Nuri's economic plans paid off. They did not reckon with the political mobilization going on under the surface, not only in the masses, but, more immediately important, in elements of the army. The American government generally followed the British lead in Iraqi matters, although some American officials were uneasy.

On July 14, a military coup led by General Abdul Kassim overthrew the government. Nuri and almost all of his relatives, the King and most of the royal family, and supporters of the old regime were simply massacred, all with overwhelming popular support in Iraq, and general enthusiasm in the rest of the Arab world, evident even in monarchies like Jordan and Saudi Arabia.

Some in the West suspected Communist involvement, but this idea was not much shared by officials. The coup was thought by the British leaders to be just a Nasser plot; the Americans were not so sure of Egyptian involvement, but broadly classified the new regime as "Nasserite." The Iraqis should have been so lucky.

Kassim turned out to be no "Nasserite"—just the first of a series of blundering, mass-murdering tyrants considerably worse than Nasser, who made the old regime look like a paradise of freedom. Nasser had no hand in or advance notice of the Iraqi revolution. Khrushchev had expected it, but not so soon. He had more reason than Nasser, at least at first, to be pleased. Kassim did have a connection with the illegal Iraqi Communist party, which seems to have had a considerable amount of underground support. Although not a party member, the Soviets understood that he regarded himself as a Communist. Kassim may have seemed, at this point, to perhaps be playing a role somewhat like that Fidel Castro actually played in the Cuban revolution. But the evolution of his regime proved entirely different. The Soviets had had no direct hand in the revolution, but they, and Nasser, were anxious to protect the new regime against Western intervention.[11] (As we shall see, that was not a serious danger.) This, not events in Lebanon and Jordan, was the key to their policies in the summer of 1958.

The Lebanon Landing

On hearing of the Iraqi revolution, Chamoun promptly requested American military intervention in Lebanon (on the morning of July 14). Eisenhower virtually decided to intervene immediately, before consulting his advisers, but characteristically carefully conferred with them before giving the go-ahead. A meeting of Secretary Dulles and State and Defense officials agreed that if we did nothing Nasser would take over the whole area and the U.S. position in the Middle East and elsewhere would be undermined. General Twining referred to the possibility of a massive operation in which we would go into Lebanon while the British went into Iraq and Kuwait, and possibly Israel would move into Western Jordan and the Turks into Syria, but this was not pursued later.

At a morning White House conference, Allen Dulles summarized what was known about Iraq and the ongoing crisis in Jordan, where King Hussein had already been in trouble. The Israelis, he warned, were likely to take over Jordan if there was disorder there. Eisenhower commented that "this is probably our last chance to do something in this area. While this rebellion continues, we still have a basis for going in, but once it succeeds the situation will be different . . . we must move." Foster Dulles discussed the fundamental problem of Soviet reaction. They would make very threatening gestures, particularly affecting Turkey and Iran. What they

would do depended on their judgment of the balance of power for a general war. We are better off now, according to General Twining, than three or four years from now. At the present time, the Soviets do not have long-range missiles, at least in any quantity. Nor do they have a substantial long-range air capability. If we do not accept the risk now, they will probably decide that we will never accept risk and will push harder than ever, and border countries will submit to them. If we do not respond to the call from Chamoun, we will suffer the elimination of our influence from Indonesia to Morocco.

He had not become happier about the probable results if we did move. Outlining the dangers, he remarked that if we did respond, "we must expect a very bad reaction through most of the Arab countries"—although there was "an appreciable chance that Nasser may have overplayed his hand and that if we are firm, he may withdraw from what he is doing if the Soviets do not come in." He concluded that the losses from doing nothing would be worse than the losses from taking action. He noted that the Lebanon problem had seemed on the way to solution, "but with the events in Iraq that is no longer available to us."

Thus considerations of the general trend of the Middle East and demonstrating American power and determination, in a timely way, before the "missile gap" arrived, not the immediate situation in Lebanon, were controlling factors in the decision to intervene.

Eisenhower and Dulles, meeting the leaders of Congress that afternoon, spoke to them much as they had in the White House conference, although Dulles emphasized the Soviet role more than he had in private. As Dulles explained, if we moved quickly and decisively, the Soviets might pull back Nasser, and we could insure Lebanon's independence. If we did not go in, Lebanon would not remain independent, and the non-Nasser governments in the Middle East and adjoining areas would be quickly overthrown. He admitted that there would be a bad reaction to our intervention, and mentioned that before the Iraqi revolution things in Lebanon had seemed to be on the way to solution. When asked about Iraq, Dulles said, "we had no present plans because we do not know enough." House Speaker Rayburn and Senator Mansfield suggested we might be getting involved in a civil war while Senator Fulbright was querulous about a Soviet or Communist role. But there was little serious opposition.

The British Prime Minister readily agreed to the American action and Eisenhower's idea of keeping the British force in Cyprus in reserve, rather than committing it right away to Lebanon. The American government did not, in fact, want the British to join in Lebanon at all. In any case the British had other ideas in mind. Prime Minister Macmillan blamed Nasser for Lebanon and Iraq. In a phone conversation with Eisenhower on July 14, he suggested a much larger Allied operation, a "second Suez," aimed at acting in Iraq and Syria to not only restore the pro-Western regime in Iraq, but the whole Near East. Eisenhower was not at all receptive. He had given the Marines the order to land the next day. The operation had been long planned and the allotted forces already assembled; the Marines would be backed up by part of an Army division and part of the 82nd Airborne Division. The Joint Chiefs wanted a limited alert for the Strategic Air Command. Eisenhower agreed to send a few tanker aircraft to forward positions.

There was no blazing enthusiasm for the coming intervention. Eisenhower glumly told his Vice President, early on July 15, that in the Middle East, "the people are on Nasser's side." Although Secretary Dulles' considered opinion was that the Soviets would not react dangerously, he had, at least, a fit of nerves, telling General Twining, on the evening of July 14, that he was now very worried. Eisenhower addressed the American people on July 15, leading them to think that Soviet involvement was more direct and immediate than the U.S. government really thought. Contrary to what is often supposed, he did not then or later invoke the "Eisenhower Doctrine."[12]

The Marines came ashore on the beaches south of Beirut, to secure the city's airport. It was, fortunately, not exactly a repetition of Tarawa or Iwo Jima. They were welcomed by bikini-clad bathers; some young Lebanese helped the Marines get their jeeps ashore. Eisenhower had made clear that the intervention would be strictly limited in scope; only the airport and Beirut would be occupied. He reasoned that if the Lebanese government and army, with their rear secured, could not win out, we were backing a government with so little support that we should not be there. Although it was often supposed that the intervention force had some sort of nuclear capability, its Honest John missiles had stayed behind in Germany.

All seemed peaceful, but there was a potentially dangerous "glitch." Chamoun, apparently fearing an army coup, had delayed telling General Chehab of the American intervention until after the last minute! Ambassador McClintock, who had seen no local increased threat and saw the intervention as unneeded in terms of Lebanon alone, met Chehab only as the landing was underway. Chehab wanted the Americans to stay offshore on their ships, and McClintock agreed. Chehab objected to the Marines entering Beirut itself, but had to give in. Yet Lebanese tanks and artillery moved into positions on the airport road to block the Marines. Chehab insisted that he had not ordered this move. Fortunately, both sides behaved cautiously; Chehab hastily conferred with the American commanders and countermanded the orders to the Lebanese forces.

The American force was built up to a peak of 14,357 men on August 5. It stayed away from serious fighting. It did not try to crush the rebellion. Not all agreed with this policy. An experienced observer, the tactical expert General S.L.A. Marshall, who was not a plunger or a reckless man, thought that the rebel stronghold could and should have been easily dealt with; as he put it, two armored personnel carriers could have cleaned it up "without ever buttoning up." He thought that might have averted later trouble in Lebanon. The Sixth Fleet commander suggested removing most American forces from Beirut, and securing Tripoli, and the Lebanese border. The special emissary sent to supervise the intervention, Robert Murphy (the Administration had come to distrust McClintock), McClintock, and the task force commander, Admiral Holloway, all disagreed. Without the help of the Americans, which Chehab did not want, fearing his army would break up, he compressed, rather than eliminated, the rebel stronghold in the Basta district of Beirut, while work toward a political settlement went on. This was slow—Murphy gained a bad impression of both Chamoun and Chehab—but a special election was finally arranged, which made Chehab President. Soon after, the Americans began withdrawing. All were gone by October 23. One had been killed by a sniper.[13]

American aims had been strictly limited. The real issue, as Dulles remarked to Eisenhower on July 23, was not the Soviets, or domination of the area, but fanatical Arab nationalism. "We cannot successfully oppose it but we can put up sandbags around positions we must protect—Israel, Lebanon, and oil positions, around the Persian Gulf." He now doubted, however, that the Arabs would attain unity.

Although the British may have seriously considered intervening in Iraq, there was little interest in the idea in the U.S. government even in the brief period in which such a move seemed possible. That would have required, at a minimum, an invitation from some surviving elements of the old regime and some Arab support. It had become clear, all too quickly, that the new regime was securely in power and quite popular. Securing an invitation to intervene would have required communication with the dead. The Turkish government was ready to intervene in Iraq anyway, but the British and Americans thought this foolish and did their best to discourage the idea. Dulles suggested, at a National Security Council meeting on July 24, that Kassim's regime might not be stable in the long run. He was right, but that was not much help at the time.[14]

The Americans, albeit without much enthusiasm, went along with the British move into Jordan. Macmillan had rapidly acceded to a request from King Hussein that he send troops to Jordan; 2,200 paratroopers were flown in from Cyprus. This seemed to stabilize the regime there. The Americans rejected British suggestions that American forces join them in Jordan, but wound up having to help the British, operating on a shoestring, with logistics. Their lack of enthusiasm was based on the Dulles brothers' belief (widely shared at the time, although it proved incorrect) that Jordan, unlike Lebanon, was not a viable state and that after the British left King Hussein's government would collapse. Thus there was little point in intervention there, although the brothers agreed that the consequences of the fall of Jordan's government would be extremely dangerous. They and others believed that in that event Israel and/or Iraq would move in, the Israelis occupying the West Bank, and this would very likely trigger a full-scale Arab–Israeli war. The Soviets and Americans would back opposite sides, with grave danger of the war widening. The brothers took some comfort in the belief that the Soviets were afraid of a Middle East war at that time.[15]

Political reactions to the Lebanon intervention turned out to be not as bad as Secretary Dulles had feared. At home, many Democrats expressed some misgivings, but nevertheless went along; there was too much trust in Eisenhower's judgment to be much dissent. But there was some. The well-known international lawyer Quincy Wright claimed that the intervention was a breach of international law. Some who were not lawyers might have found that reassuring. Much other opposition consisted of mechanical repetition of long-standing charges that the Administration held beliefs it did not hold and blaming it for not doing things it had actually done or not accomplishing feats that no one knew how to bring off. On July 18, Walter Lippman, the influential if incredibly overrated commentator, claimed that American policy was based on the fundamental error of believing that all would be well in the Middle East, if only the countries there could be persuaded to join in a military alliance against the Communists. On July 29, Lippman solemnly explained that the real issue in the Middle East was not oil, which the Arabs had to sell to the West, or Israel, or even "the revolutionary force of Nasserism" but the Soviets' determination not to have U.S. military power on their southern flank. More rationally, Senator Humphrey remarked, not without reason, that the Lebanon landing was an "act of desperation." His solution for the Middle East was settling the Arab–Israeli conflict and economic development . . . Platitudes that would not change much in the next half century and more.

Some liberal and leftist opposition was more vehement, even hysterical. *The Nation*, on August 2, 1958, called the Lebanon landing as provocative as a Soviet landing in Guatemala. It was pointless because Arab unity was inevitable, and the United States, was, as usual, supporting evil reactionary forces instead of good progressive ones.

In Britain, the Labour opposition criticized the Anglo-American actions, Secretary Dulles was not pleased by the lukewarm reactions of other NATO countries. There was some unease in West Germany and Japan. Some normally friendly neutrals, like Sweden, were critical, as was, more predictably, India.

In the Middle East, the Northern Tier countries favored the interventions; Arabs were overwhelmingly hostile. But the cataclysm the Eisenhower Administration had feared, with pro-Western governments toppling and oil installations sabotaged, did not occur.[16]

Nasser was surprised by the Lebanon landing. He and the Soviets were upset, fearing that it was a prelude to a Western move into Iraq. The Americans, on announcing their action, proposed that a UN emergency force replace their forces in Lebanon. The Soviets vetoed this and demanded that the Americans and British depart.

On July 17, Nasser hastily flew to Moscow to seek help. Khrushchev sought to restrain him from ill-considered action, and urged advising Kassim to keep quiet and give the Western powers no pretext to move against his regime. (Kassim quickly assured the West that he would keep the oil flowing.) Although the two leaders were not really far apart, both primarily concerned with protecting the new Iraqi regime, Nasser seems to have been disappointed that Khrushchev did not offer still more support to Egypt and Iraq.

The "First" did order military maneuvers in the Caucasus, and maneuvers by the Bulgarian army, he made it clear to Nasser that this was a bluff—he would take no military action. According to Nasser's follower and biographer Mohammed Heikal, he told Nasser "Frankly, we are not ready for confrontation. We are not ready for World War III"—a choice of words, which, if accurately reported, casts an interesting light on Khrushchev's oft-alleged total rejection of nuclear war. He did rush aid to Egypt and Iraq.

He tried to capitalize on the missile gap belief, boasting on Soviet military strength in public and in a note to Eisenhower on July 19 calling for a summit conference connected to the UN to discuss the current Middle East crisis and curb the delivery of arms to the region. The conference would consist of the United States, USSR, Britain, France, and India, and would report to the UN Secretary General and Security Council. It would be reviewed by a panel of Arab nations, not including Israel. The Western powers rejected this, as they did a variant proposal advanced on July 23, Eisenhower arguing that the existing powers of the UN had not been used, that the big powers could not dictate to the Middle Eastern countries, objected to the absence of Israel, and bringing in India arbitrarily altered the composition of the UN Security Council. As usual in this era, the "diplomatic" exchanges trailed off into sterility.

Both sides in the Middle East crisis had attained their minimum aims, which had not in fact crossed. The West had secured Lebanon and Jordan, and prevented a "Nasserite" or more radical revolutionary wave submerging the whole Arab world, while the Egyptians and Soviets had "saved" the Iraqi revolution. Nasser would have liked to get a revolutionary regime in Lebanon—he did not want to absorb it into the UAR—but it was hardly essential for him. Khrushchev, unfortunately, was sure that his bluffing had deterred Western intervention in Iraq, which led him to follow similar policies in the future.[17]

Nasser, however, seems to have been less pleased with Soviet support. The Western moves, and Khrushchev's caution in actual action, seem to have encouraged him to move away from the Soviets. That factor was combined with the tenuousness of the pan-Arab dream. There was no bridge between the immediate local and sectarian concerns of most Arabs and their desires for unity. Most Arabs wanted it, but could not overcome the greed for power and the cutthroat scramble for it that was the "political tradition" of the Arab world. Nasser almost immediately clashed with Kassim. The latter relied greatly on the Iraqi Communists, and curbed Nasser's local supporters, who tried to overthrow him. Another little Cold War began between the UAR and Iraq. Nasser, getting American wheat shipments from December 1958, suppressed his own Communists and openly criticized the Soviets in 1959, although later in the year relations with the Soviets began to recover. The Eisenhower Administration, trailed by the British, had, already in August 1958, concluded that, while local conservative resistance to radical Arab nationalism had collapsed, and Nasser was basically hostile, some sort of limited détente might be possible with him.

He could be contained and kept away from the Soviets. He was preferable to Kassim—although Ike wryly joked that the choice between Nasser and Kassim was like a choice between Dillinger and Capone! Some elements in the Administration were less enthusiastic about the rapprochement with Nasser.

The real worry, for a time, was an actual Communist seizure of power in Iraq, although Kassim's supposed Communist beliefs did not prevent him from curbing the Party a bit from June 1959. The Iraqi regime remained hostile to Nasser, who wound up on the same side as the Western powers in a confrontation with Iraq over Kuwait in 1961. In that year, Syria broke away from the UAR. Dulles' belief that the Iraqi regime would not prove stable over the long run proved right. In February 1963 Kassim achieved an unenviable first: the first political leader to be assassinated on live TV (albeit only in black and white). But his Baathist successors did not get along with Nasser either, or, for that matter the Baathists running Syria.

Nasser, however, gradually moved back toward the Soviets. He might not like them much, but he was a prisoner of his own ambitions. He could not attain his goals without them—or, as it turned out, even with them. Egypt's intervention in the Yemen from 1962, a "proxy war" with the Saudis, failed despite the use of mustard gas against "fellow Arabs." He then blundered into a third Arab–Israeli war, which closed the Suez Canal for seven years. The Soviets gained a position in Egypt not very far from that of the British before 1954, until they were thrown out by Nasser's successor.

Nevertheless, the oil resources on which the West and Japan increasingly depended came under continuing threat for decades. Next to his patron, Winston Churchill, Anthony Eden arguably proved the most expensively vindicated statesman of the century.

For the United States and Lebanon, the Lebanon intervention proved successful, if only in the short run. It was well executed, much in contrast to the costly blundering of the later intervention in Lebanon in 1982–1983. Ambassador McClintock, who had not originally favored it, concluded in November 1958 that the presence of the American force had calmed things down, encouraging the rebels to become more moderate and helped enable a compromise. He thought it a successful case of "limited war" that had served to check Soviet and Nasserite aspirations. He observed, however, that the basic issues that had produced the crisis were unresolved. That, unfortunately, remained true. The landing had won time for the Lebanese to settle their own problems.

They failed to use it.[18]

Iran

The most important Middle Eastern state, non-Arab, seemed quiescent in 1958, but this was deceptive—like much that was later said about American relations with Iran. For the Eisenhower Administration, later blamed, not entirely accurately, for creating the Shah's despotism, was not pleased with its supposed handiwork. In contrast to later American administrations, it had no illusions about the Shah or the state of things in Iran.

It had overthrown Mossadegh's National Front government, but it had not, in fact, put the Shah in power. The Shah's behavior during the 1953 coup was hardly courageous, and up to April 1955, the real power in the government was not the Shah, but General Fazollah Zahedi. Zahedi, although anything but an attractive character, was not unreasonable. There was no bloodbath against Mossadegh's former supporters. Only Communists and some religious fanatics were harshly treated, a huge network of Communists in the army being uncovered in 1954. Some of Mossadegh's former supporters (he had lost much of his popularity toward the end) were willing to come to terms with the new government, but its foolish insistence on trying Mossadegh revived some of his popular support. He spent the rest of his life under house arrest.

It was *after* the Shah maneuvered Zahedi out of power that the Iranian government became more and more tyrannical, evolving from an ordinary authoritarian regime into what Homa Katouzian has dubbed a "petrolic despotism" in which oil revenues made the Shah independent of all social groups and rational considerations. The Shah, who imagined that Iranians loved him, was obsessed with developing military power, for which he then had neither the money nor technical support. (As Secretary Dulles sarcastically noted, he thought he was a military genius.) In the late 1950s, the regime's economic record was poor. Despite oil revenues, it ran continual budget deficits. It was unable or unwilling to tax wealthy landowners or embark on reforms, and up to 1961 there was little economic development. It was only in the 1960s, when his regime was becoming visibly unstable even to him, that he would launch the reforms of the fabled "White Revolution." The Shah did support the West in the Cold War and resisted Soviet attempts to win him over, but otherwise had little to recommend him.

The United States grew steadily more tired of financing the budget deficits of an oil-rich state and the Shah's demands for fantastic amounts of military aid. It welcomed, if it did not back, a plan for a coup by General Valiollah Qarani, the Vice Chief of Staff of the army and head of army intelligence, an able and popular man. He intended not to destroy the Shah, but force him to "reign rather than rule." But the Shah was tipped off about the plot—possibly by the Soviets, who preferred his despotism to a reformist regime under a popular leader. Qarani and 39 others were arrested in February 1958; the Shah's belief that the Americans were behind the plot may have saved the General from execution. The Americans rejected another coup plan by General Bakhtiar, the head of "Savak," the secret police. (The Shah disposed of him, too, a few years later.)

After this the Eisenhower Administration had little faith in Iran's future. Its forecasts in 1958 proved far more accurate in the long run than those entertained in the 1960s and 1970s. The Embassy, Undersecretary of State Herter,

George Allen, and the CIA all agreed that the Shah's regime was unstable. While a coup was not now likely in the near future, it was unlikely to survive without undertaking major reforms soon, and possibly not even then. The general view was that the Shah was likely to go, sooner or later, but there was little the United States could do about it, other than keep a ceiling on his military ambitions and influence him toward reforms.[19]

Notes

1 *FRUS 1958–1960, Vol. III,* p. 54. Peter Hahn, *The United States, Great Britain and Egypt* (Chapel Hill, NC: University of North Carolina Press, 1991), pp. 3–181; Salim Yaqub, *Containing Arab Nationalism* (Chapel Hill, NC: University of North Carolina Press, 2004), pp. 7–32; Nigel Ashton, *Eisenhower, Macmillan and the Problem of Nasser* (New York: St. Martin's Press, 1996), pp. 19–23, 41–51, 58; Patrick Searle, *The Struggle for Syria* (London: Oxford University Press, 1965), pp. 25, 100–102, 186–188, 196, 199–200; Keith Kyle, *Suez* (London: I.B. Tauris, 2003), pp. 36–39, 42, 50, 66–77; William Roger Louis, *The Ends of British Imperialism* (London: I.B. Tauris, 2006), p. 693; Watson, *Into the Missile Age*, pp. 48–51; Howard Sachar, *Europe Leaves the Middle East* (New York: Alfred Knopf, 1972). The works by Hahn, Yaqub, and Ashton are of special value.

 Much of the literature on the Middle East, but not only that region, especially that published from 1990 on, grossly misrepresents both American and British policies, but especially the former, belittling American "anti-colonialism." Sometimes this is done by playing games with definitions; e.g. Scott Bills, *Empire and Cold War* (New York: St. Martin's Press, 1990), p. xi, which "explains" that American policy in the postwar era was not anti-colonial because any "policy which did not seek to directly empower native nationalists cannot be considered anti-colonial" (i.e. any policy accepting gradual evolution or a period of tutelage). It should be noted that in fact the Americans did not show much interest in such gradualist policies in any case. For examples of the distortion of American policy, public attitudes, and John Foster Dulles' views in particular, cf. Stephen Kinzer's *The Brothers* (New York: Henry Holt, 2013), especially pp. 80, 87, 128, 203, 211–212, 217, 242. A less extreme example is Steven Z. Freiberger's *Dawn Over Suez* (Chicago, IL: Ivan Dee, 1992), p. 53, which indicts Dulles' alleged tunnel vision and alleged inability to see any other problem than Soviet involvement. On page 213 Freiberger states that "The United States could not see Nasser as an Arab nationalist; Washington believed he was either a Soviet tool or an anti-Western demagogue," as though Nasser could not be two or all three of these things! "Washington," including Dulles, certainly recognized Nasser as an Arab nationalist, whatever else they thought he was.

2 Searle, *The Struggle for Syria*, p. 196; Finer, *Dulles Over Suez*, p. 32; *FRUS 1955–1957, Vol. XIII*, p. 596; Christopher Andrew and Vassili Mitrokhin, *The World Was Going Our Way* (New York: Perseus Books, 2005), pp. 140–142, 146; Fursenko and Naftali, *Khrushchev's Cold War*, pp. 57–75; Ra'anan, *The USSR Arms the Third World*, pp. 14–15, 37–172; Gamal Nasser, *Egypt's Liberation: The Philosophy of the Revolution* (Washington DC: Public Affairs Press, 1955), pp. 98–99, 109–112.

3 Finer, *Dulles Over Suez*, p. 32; Hahn, *The United States, Great Britain and Egypt*, pp. 191–192; Kyle, *Suez*, pp. 72–77.

4 Adams, *First Hand Report*, pp. 251–252, 277; Robert Rhodes-James, *Anthony Eden* (New York: McGraw Hill, 1980), pp. 429–432, 443–450; Hahn, *The United States, Great Britain and Egypt*, pp. 191–206; Searle, *The Struggle for Syria*, pp. 269–280; Kyle, *Suez*, pp. 82–84, 91, 93–99, 100–102; Ashton, *Eisenhower, Macmillan and the Problem of Nasser*, pp. 61–79.

5 Hahn, *The United States, Great Britain and Egypt*, pp. 211–239; Trevor Dupuy, *Elusive Victory* (New York: Harper & Row, 1978), pp. 133–218; Hugh Thomas, *Suez* (New York: Harper & Row, 1967); Selwyn Lloyd, *Suez 1956* (London: Jonathan Cape, 1978); Jonathan Pearson, *Sir Anthony Eden and the Suez Crisis* (London: Macmillan, 2003). Dupuy and Thomas are probably the best accounts of the Suez–Sinai war. Kyle's *Suez* is useful and has much new information but is extremely biased against the Allies—as is most of the literature. There is a fixation on treating Suez as an episode of "colonialism" or decolonization (e.g. Louis, *The Ends of British Imperialism*, p. 10).

6 Hahn, *The United States, Great Britain and Egypt*, pp. 236–241; *FRUS 1955–1957, Vol. XIII*, p. 56; *Foreign Relations of the United States 1955–1957, Volume XVI* (Washington DC: Government Printing Office, 1990), p. 1098; Rhodes-James, *Anthony Eden*, pp. 612–613; Lloyd, *Suez 1956*, esp. pp. 242–252; Finer, *Dulles Over Suez*, pp. 463–475; Fursenko and Naftali, *Khrushchev's Cold War*, pp. 124–137; Yaqub, *Containing Arab Nationalism*, pp. 10, 64, 70–72. Cf. David Nicols, *Eisenhower 1956* (New York: Simon & Schuster, 2011) for a defense of Eisenhower's policies. A regrettable example of complete cluelessness about Nasser, and the forces that he represented, by a usually able historian, is John Lewis Gaddis, *We Now Know* (New York: Oxford University Press, 1997), pp. 173–178.

7 Fursenko and Naftali, *Khrushchev's Cold War*, pp. 139–145; Eisenhower, *Waging Peace*, pp. 177–183; Ashton, *Eisenhower, Macmillan and the Problem of Nasser*, pp. 103–112; Yaqub, *Containing Arab Nationalism*, pp. 81–120; Nadav Safran, *From War To War* (New York: Pegasus, 1969), pp. 70–71; Watson, *Into the Missile Age*, pp. 70–72, 203–204; *The Papers of Dwight D. Eisenhower, Volume XVIII*, ed. Louis Galambos (Baltimore, MD: Johns Hopkins University Press, 2000), pp. 572, 603.

8 *FRUS 1955–1957, Vol. XIII*, pp. 618, 635, 638–639, 648–649, 669, 674, 678, 680, 694–696, 700, 735–737; Yaqub, *Containing Arab Nationalism*, pp. 147–187; Ashton, *Eisenhower, Macmillan and the Problem of Nasser*, pp. 122–140; Searle, *The Struggle for Syria*, pp. 286–322; Malcolm Kerr, *The Arab Cold War*, 3rd ed. (London: Oxford University Press, 1970), pp. 5–9; Eisenhower, *Waging Peace*, pp. 196–203; Safran, *From War to War*, pp. 71–72, 114–115.

9 Kerr, *The Arab Cold War*, pp. 5–15; Yaqub, *Containing Arab Nationalism*, pp. 177–202; Ashton, *Eisenhower, Macmillan and the Problem of Nasser*, pp. 141–148; *Foreign Relations of the United States 1958–1960, Volume XII* (Washington DC: Government Printing Office, 1993), pp. 49–54; Eisenhower, *Waging Peace*, pp. 262–263; Stebbins, *The United States in World Affairs 1958*, p. 189.

10 *Foreign Relations of the United States 1958–1960, Volume XI* (Washington DC: Government Printing Office, 1992), pp. 8–16, 18, 28–30, 44, 45, 49–50, 54–55, 60, 67–69, 79, 86, 93–98, 101, 106, 120–122, 153–155, 166–168, 171–180, 200–201, 206; Erika G. Allin, *The United States and the 1958 Lebanon Crisis* (Lanham, MD: University Press of America, 1994), pp. 33–76; Yaqub, *Containing Arab Nationalism*, pp. 205–219; Eisenhower, *Waging Peace*, pp. 264–269; Stebbins, *The United States in World Affairs 1958*, pp. 194–195, 199–201; Watson, *Into the Missile Age*, pp. 207–209; Leila Meo, *Lebanon: Improbable Nation* (Bloomington, IN: Indiana University Press, 1965).

11 Fursenko and Naftali, *Khrushchev's Cold War*, pp. 157–159; Yaqub, *Containing Arab Nationalism*, pp. 219–222; Ashton, *Eisenhower, Macmillan and the Problem of Nasser*, pp. 165–167; *The Iraqi Revolution of 1958*, ed. Robert Ferrea and William Roger Louis (New York: I.B. Tauris, 1991); *Foreign Relations of the United States 1958–1960, Vol. XII* (Washington DC: Government Printing Office, 1993), pp. 87–89, 327.

12 *FRUS 1958–1960, Vol. XI*, pp. 206–209, 210, 211–215, 218–226, 231–236, 244–246; Eisenhower, *Waging Peace*, pp. 269–275; Watson, *Into the Missile Age*, pp. 210–213; Richard Lamb, *The Macmillan Years* (London: John Murray, 1995), pp. 34–39; Yaqub, *Containing Arab Nationalism*, p. 223; Ashton, *Eisenhower, Macmillan and the Problem of Nasser*, pp. 168–170; Fairchild and Poole, *The Joint Chiefs and National Policy 1957–1960*, pp. 151–155.

13 *The Ends of British Imperialism*, p. 832; Watson, *Into the Missile Age*, pp. 210–218; *FRUS 1958–1960, Vol. XI*, pp. 215–216, 245, 247–255, 333–334, 337–338, 358, 396–397, 418, 539–540; S.L.A. Marshall, *Bringing Up the Rear* (San Rafael, CA: Presidio Press, 1979), pp. 251–256.

14 *FRUS 1958–1960, Vol. XII*, pp. 73–75, 98, 102, 327; *FRUS 1958–1960, Vol. XI*, pp. 213, 240–242, 306–308, 310, 335; *The Ends of British Imperialism*, pp. 832, 841; Yaqub, *Containing Arab Nationalism*, pp. 227, 231–232, 241; Ashton, *Eisenhower, Macmillan and the Problem of Nasser*, p. 173.

15 *FRUS 1958–1960, Vol. XI*, pp. 211–121, 310, 319, 375, 377, 418, 461–462; Ashton, *Eisenhower, Macmillan and the Problem of Nasser*, pp. 170, 178; Yaqub, *Containing Arab Nationalism*, p. 231.

16 Fleming, *The Cold War and Its Origins, Vol. II*, pp. 920, 922, 926–929, 933–935; Stebbins, *The United States in World Affairs 1958*, pp. 194–195, 199–201.

17 Mohammad Heikal, *The Sphinx and the Commissar* (New York: Harper & Row, 1978), p. 98; *FRUS 1958–1960, Vol. XI*, pp. 257, 339–340, 354, 371, 379–380, 393–394, 406–407; Eisenhower, *Waging Peace*, pp. 282–283; Fursenko and Naftali, *Khrushchev's Cold War*, pp. 166–177, 182–184.

18 Kerr, *The Arab Cold War*, pp. 15–19; *FRUS 1958–1960, Vol. XII*, pp. 145–154, 157–159, 187–199; Fairchild and Poole, *The Joint Chiefs and National Policy 1957–1960*, p. 63; Yaqub, *Containing Arab Nationalism*, pp. 248–261; Ashton, *Eisenhower, Macmillan and the Problem of Nasser*, pp. 191–209.

19 *FRUS 1958–1960, Vol. XI*, pp. 626–627; Agnes Korbani, *The US Interventions in Lebanon 1958 and 1982* (Westport, CT: Greenwood, 1991).

7

BATTLE IN THE TAIWAN STRAIT

The Second "Quemoy-Matsu Crisis"

The Middle East crisis had hardly subsided when a second, more serious crisis erupted in East Asia—the second crisis over the small islands in the Taiwan Strait off the coast of China. It was one result of the fact that the Chinese Civil War had never quite ended, and the awkward situation in which the United States had been left by measures taken in the Korean War. In both crises the United States was in a fantastically difficult position, facing a China still allied to the USSR, and led by a tyrant as evil as Stalin and perhaps more irrational than Stalin had usually been. It was caught between the machinations of the Chinese Communists, the Chinese Nationalists' desire to drag the United States into war, its own estimate of the dreadful consequences if the loss of the offshore islands caused the Nationalists to collapse, the difficulty of defending them without using tactical nuclear weapons, and the reluctance of other allies to support it.

Origins of the Dilemma

The United States had never recognized the Chinese Communist government, although it had expected to do so after the Nationalists on Taiwan (still usually called Formosa by Westerners in the 1950s) were finished off. When the Korean War began, the United States put Taiwan under its protection, forcing the Communists to postpone, then cancel the invasion of the island originally scheduled for 1951. The Americans built up the Nationalist forces, which raided the mainland, harassed shipping, and effectively closed some mainland ports during the Korean War, something well publicized after Eisenhower openly "unleashed" Chiang Kai-shek (Jiang Jieshi) in the last part of the war, although raids had been undertaken earlier. The Korean War, continued

Chinese Communist hostility, and American domestic political pressures made abandoning Taiwan or recognizing the Chinese Communists unthinkable in the foreseeable future. The United States was in the awkward position of defending the remnants of the losing side in a civil war, and that side's preposterous claim to be one of the five great powers represented in the UN Security Council. There were certain favorable ambiguities in its legal position. Taiwan had not been formally recognized as part of China. It, and the small nearby Penghu (Pescadores) islands, had been annexed by Japan in 1895. In the Cairo Declaration of 1943, the Americans had promised to return Taiwan and the Penghus to China. But, while the Nationalists had occupied Taiwan in 1945, it was not formally ceded to them. The Japanese peace treaty deprived Japan of its legal title, but did not transfer Taiwan to any Chinese government. That left the possibility open for a future turn to either a "two-China" policy of recognizing both Chinese governments (the Nationalists of course ruling only Taiwan) or backing an independent Taiwan, for which there was much support on the island. The Taiwanese, who had revolted against Nationalist rule in 1947, did not love their mainland rulers. Secretary Dulles carefully left the way open for such policies throughout his stewardship. Whatever the Americans did, there was at first sight little that the Chinese Communists could do directly across a 100-mile wide strait dominated by American naval and airpower.

Unfortunately, the Taiwan Strait was not a neat dividing line between the two Chinese sides. Since 1949, the Nationalists had held several groups of small islands just off the coast, in territory unquestionably under Chinese sovereignty, some of which the Nationalists might conceivably use as bases to invade the mainland. As the Korean War ended and the Americans "released" Chiang, the Communists began clearing the Nationalists off the offshore islands. Most were of no importance, but it was recognized that some islands that the Communists might attack later were more significant. American policy, as of November 1953 was to aid the Nationalists to defend them, but not engage their own forces.

Contrary to a common belief, the Eisenhower Administration, unlike many right-wing Republicans like Senator Knowland, was not fond of the Chinese Nationalists. Neither the President nor the Secretary of State had a high opinion of Chiang Kai-shek or his government; some lower officials were even more unfriendly. As Dulles remarked, in secret testimony before the Senate in April 1953, in comments revealing the attitude of the Administration towards authoritarian allies in general, Syngman Rhee and Chiang specifically were

> not the people under normal circumstances that we would want to support. We would be trying to get someone else, but in times like these, in the unrest of the world today, and the divided spirit, we know that we cannot make a transition without losing control of the situation.

This was a classic statement of what has been described as the "bolstering" position toward anti-Communist authoritarians as opposed to trying to reform or liberalize their regimes. The Administration would increasingly tend toward the latter as the years passed, but given Chiang's iron rule, that change would not affect policy toward the Nationalists much.

But, as Eisenhower told Karl Rankin, the Ambassador to the Nationalists, in May 1953, Chiang was no longer important. Dulles described him as bitter, arrogant, and difficult, and suspected that he would try to drag the United States into a Third World War as the only way for him to regain China. At most, the Nationalist armed forces were regarded as a minor asset, and Taiwan a place where a relatively free Chinese culture might evolve to influence developments on the mainland. In the event of a world war, or a serious uprising on the mainland, it was just possible that the Nationalists might usefully intervene, but neither contingency was regarded as likely.

The main thrust of American policy was to contain China, and, by pressuring it, eventually detach it from the Soviets.[1]

The First Taiwan Straits Crisis

From May 1954, the Communists began a new series of assaults on the offshore islands, and gave prominence to "liberating Taiwan" in their propaganda. Mao's immediate aim was to use the offensive against the more important offshore islands to prevent, then break, the alliance between the Nationalists and the Americans. If he succeeded in that, however, Nationalist morale might collapse, some might defect, and Taiwan might indeed be "liberated." The Soviets backed the Chinese in the crisis, although they made clear that they did not want a major war to develop, and Mao's tactics seem to have puzzled them.[2]

It was the Nationalists, not the Americans, who sought a formal alliance. Ironically, Eisenhower only accepted it during the ensuing crisis, in October 1954, as part of a bargain by which the Nationalists graciously allowed an attempt to get the UN to "neutralize" the Taiwan Strait. Dulles once bluntly called it a "bribe."[3]

A long series of mutual provocations developed. The Nationalists harassed Communist-bloc shipping, and actually seized a Soviet tanker in June (the Americans insisted that they release it) while the Communists shot down a British airliner. American planes searching for survivors shot down two Communist planes two days later.

Eisenhower had concluded in May that some of the outlying islands were really integral with Taiwan's defense, if only because Chiang had made them so. He had stationed 43,000 regular troops and 1,100 guerrillas on Jinmen island, then usually called Quemoy, or Kinmen, by Westerners, and put 5,000 regulars on Mazu (Matsu) and 10,000 more on the Dachens (Tachens). But no clear decision had been made about what to do when the central crisis began. On

September 3, the Communists began shelling Jinmen, killing two American military advisers (others were evacuated).

A majority of the Joint Chiefs of Staff, who had been calling for a tougher policy in general, favored intervening with U.S. forces to hold at least some of the offshore islands. They admitted there was no tactical military reason for this, but, if the Nationalists lost Jinmen, especially, their morale, and the Nationalist government might collapse. Dulles and Eisenhower shared that diagnosis, fearing the effects of such a collapse in the rest of East Asia. The "domino" type of thinking might be questioned, but a strong argument can be made even today that, if the United States could not, somehow or other, have held Taiwan—an island well outside the sphere of Communist control—or, more cynically, keep it in line—that would indeed have been likely to demoralize and disrupt our allies. Others in the Administration, notably the Secretary of Defense, and Undersecretary of State Walter Bedell Smith, did not like any involvement in the offshores.

Dulles outlined the problem at the National Security Council meeting of September 22. We had to defend the offshores, particularly Jinmen, but this might involve us in a war in which most of the war would condemn us. He termed it a "horrible dilemma." Eisenhower glumly noted that even American opinion was not favorable to a strong stand; and going beyond the terms of the 1950 declaration on the defense of Taiwan required Congressional authorization. It was decided to go to the UN to obtain an injunction to maintain the status quo to "neutralize" the Taiwan Strait. The President rejected the advice of Admirals Radford and Carney and General Twining to let the Nationalists bomb the mainland.

Dulles' approach to the UN was rejected by *both* Chinese factions! Defending Jinmen remained controversial even within the Administration. Secretary Wilson pointed out, on October 18 that the proposed mutual defense pact with the Nationalists would be very dangerous unless the offshore islands issue was settled first; but Eisenhower decided to accede to the Nationalists' wishes while not making clear any commitment to defend any of the offshores. It seemed increasingly likely that holding Jinmen would require not just American intervention but also using tactical nuclear weapons, while, on October 2, Khrushchev had seemed to squarely back his ally. At an NSC meeting on November 24, Dulles expounded the dilemma: "the basic fact was that these islands could not be held against an all-out Chinese Communist assault short of involving the United States in a general war with Communist China." Eisenhower noted that that meant general war with the Soviets also; for, if the Soviets did not stand by the Chinese, "the Soviet empire would quickly fall to pieces." Dulles noted that the Nationalists hoped for a general war. He and Dulles seemed ready to let the offshore islands go to the Communist government if they could arrange some face-saving agreement, or even an agreement involving, as Eisenhower put it, "some loss of face" rather than go to a general war. Dulles was surprisingly frank about this point with the Nationalist ambassador. On November 23, the Communists had screwed up the pressure. Thirteen Americans captured during the Korean War, and held after the armistice, were now sentenced to prison as spies. American opinion was enraged, and Eisenhower had to reject Senator Knowland's call for a full-scale naval blockade of China. The Communists built new jet-capable airfields opposite Taiwan.

On December 20, the Americans concluded a pact with the Nationalists, and in January 1955, the Communists captured I-chang (Yikang) island, north of the Dachens. It was clear that American policy had to be settled and clarified. It was decided that the Dachens, the probable next Communist target, would be evacuated, but Jinmen and the Mazus would be held, with American intervention if necessary, but only so long as the Communists proclaimed that they aimed to liberate Taiwan. Dulles favored a clear public declaration to this effect, but Eisenhower preferred a fuzzier, more ambiguous line—perhaps, although he never really explained his reasoning—to reduce the chance of the Nationalists dragging the United States into war. That might, however, encourage a miscalculation by Mao. Both men agreed that defending the off-shore islands required Congressional authorization. A Sabrejet fighter wing was ordered to Taiwan (up to then American combat units had not been stationed there). Dulles tried to get the Soviets to restrain their ally, but there was no indication, over the next few weeks, of any difference between the Communist great powers.

On January 28, the Senate passed the "Formosa Resolution," which essentially gave Eisenhower a blank check. Dulles, had however, assured Congress that he did not think that the United States should be permanently committed to hold the offshore islands. Some prominent Democrats—Senators Humphrey, Fulbright, Mansfield, Kefauver, and Morse—strongly opposed the Resolution.

Eisenhower and Dulles, late in January, began to fear that the Soviets might be egging on the Chinese, precisely in order to get their ally entangled in a war that would divide the United States from its allies (both men were fully conscious of the unpopularity of American policy). Ambassador Bohlen, in Moscow, and Admiral Radford pooh-poohed the idea; Radford thought the enemy axis as a whole was too weak to consider war. If China alone fought the United States, it would be beaten easily, and that would do the Soviets no good. Intelligence estimates, in February and March, concluded that the Chinese Communists would probably refrain from actions that would definitely lead to full-scale war. But they might miscalculate. While the Soviets would try to avoid war, they would, in the last resort, stand by their allies should the survival of the Chinese regime seem in danger, although they would try to confine hostilities to the Far East.

Chiang agreed to evacuate the Dachens, in return for a promise to defend Kinmen and the Mazus (with the usual reservation). He was angry, however, that Eisenhower would give no public promise.

The Administration had considerable difficulty with the British. The Churchill government backed defending Taiwan—the Labour opposition largely opposed even that—but wanted the offshore islands written off.

Eisenhower, at a National Security Council meeting on February 17, reflected on the "terrible dilemma" we were in. If we announced that we would help the defense of the offshores, world opinion would not support us, but if we did not act, the Communists would take them, and Chiang's government would collapse. To summarize the whole dilemma facing the Administration—that if the offshore islands were lost, the Nationalists might collapse, with disastrous repercussions in the rest of East and Southeast Asia; that the offshore islands could not be defended without recourse to tactical nuclear weapons, which might lead to all-out war, that fighting over the issue, even without nuclear weapons, would be incredibly unpopular and alienate us from our allies; that the Nationalists were likely manipulating the situation precisely in order to get us into war; and that the Soviets might want just that!

Dulles returned from a visit to East Asia more worried than ever, concluding that the Communists were determined to take Taiwan, whose loss would undermine the whole Western position in the Pacific. On March 6 he told Eisenhower that Kinmen and the Mazus must be defended, which would require using "atomic missiles" but not "weapons of mass destruction" against Communist airfields and gun emplacements. On March 8, Dulles made a veiled reference to this in public. By the time of a gloomy National Security Council meeting on March 10, Dulles thought there was at least an even chance that the United States would have to fight. He thought Nationalist morale shaky. If even a small Communist force reached Taiwan itself, things might unravel. (He bluntly noted that one or more generals might be bought.) We should temporize about any action, however, until after the Paris Agreements, arranging West German entry into NATO and rearmament, were ratified by the Europeans.

At a meeting at the White House the next day, Dulles seemed a bit more optimistic. General Twining did not think a major attack on Taiwan possible—the Communists just did not have enough airfields nearby—but there was a dangerous buildup of artillery around Jinmen. Plans envisaged, in the event of a full-scale assault, the use of 10–15 kiloton weapons against coastal air bases, POL (petroleum, oil, and lubricants) sites, and gun emplacements. Dulles again emphasized that, if possible, atomic weapons should not be used for the next 40–60 days; we should do our best to avoid intervention of any kind. Eisenhower indicated that, if we had to act, we would try to use conventional weapons first, using atomic weapons "only at the end." From this time on, Eisenhower seems to have become steadily less enthusiastic, if possible, about defending the offshores. Dulles publicly hinted, on March 21, that the Soviets were more reasonable than the Chinese. Over the next few days he noted that references to the "liberation of Taiwan" in Communist propaganda had sharply dropped off. In public, however, the crisis seemed to grow sharper. A leak described the Chief of Naval Operations' opinion that we would be at war by mid-April. This was not a "calculated leak"—Eisenhower was infuriated—but at press conferences on March 26 and 30, the President seemed to be getting the public ready for the use of tactical nuclear weapons. The Chinese Nationalists contributed their share to ratcheting up tension. On April 2, their agents blew up an airliner carrying part of the Chinese Communist delegation to the Bandung Afro-Asian Conference. Eisenhower, on April 5, pressed Chiang to abandon the offshore islands, or at least evacuate the civilians and reduce Jinmen and the Mazus to outposts, while a U.S. Marine division and additional air units would be stationed on Taiwan for a time. Dulles and Eisenhower toyed with another idea, a "clean break"—the offshore islands would be entirely evacuated but as "retaliation" a naval blockade of part of the mainland coast would be established. Chiang rejected all such ideas.

On April 5, Eisenhower summarized the issues and policy in a memorandum for Dulles. He noted that "the world" generally regarded the offshore islands as part of the Chinese mainland. Our intervention would seriously divide our own people and be unpopular elsewhere. But there was a great danger to morale on Taiwan and elsewhere if we refused to participate, in their defense, while there would be an adverse reaction if we counterattacked the mainland. "We have had ample forewarning of the adverse character of world reaction that would follow any such action on our part—especially if we felt compelled to use atomic weapons—which we probably would in order to insure success." The conflict might spread, and we might be isolated in world opinion. "The principal military reason for holding these two groups of islands is the estimated effect of their loss upon Formosa." That day, Dulles, at a press conference, made clear that the United States was absolutely committed only to defend Taiwan and the Penghus.

That same day, however, there was good news. The Indonesian Ambassador in Washington confided to the Americans that his Soviet counterpart had let slip—he thought it an unintentional slip, though he could not be sure—that the Chinese Communists would not attack Jinmen and the Mazus. On April 23, Zhou Enlai, at Bandung, indicated that the Chinese were backing off, and on May 17, announced that China sought to liberate Taiwan only by peaceful means. The Chinese seem to have been impressed by the American threat to use nuclear weapons, and possibly by Soviet pressure, or at least obvious reluctance. Just how close the danger of war was in 1955 is not clear even today. Eisenhower and Dulles had erred in not making the pact with the Nationalists contingent on an iron-clad agreement to reduce forces on or evacuate Jinmen and the Mazus. Once the crisis began, Dulles and others may have been right to prefer a clear-cut commitment as safer than Eisenhower's policy of public ambiguity.[4]

Between Two Crises 1955–1958

After the tacit cease-fire in 1955, the Chinese, as part of the general, if temporary shift toward a "peaceful" policy, publicized from the Bandung

Conference, released the thirteen Americans convicted in 1954. Talks began between the American and Chinese Ambassadors in Geneva. (Steady diplomatic contact, although not of course formal relations, between the United States and Chinese Communists thus began in 1955, and not, as many later pretended, only with the Nixon Administration.) However, the Americans completely failed, over the next two years, to obtain the "mutual renunciation of force" agreement for the Taiwan Strait that they sought. The Eisenhower Administration took an increasing interest in the policies both Communists and Nationalists feared—the "two Chinas" and independent Taiwan alternatives. In the short run, however, it did not pull away from Chiang, stationing Matador nuclear cruise missiles on Taiwan in 1957.

Chiang Kai-shek, however, once again showed that he was the most reliable ally of the United States, in reverse—he could always be relied on to do the opposite of what was wanted. Instead of reducing the offshore islands to lightly held outposts, as the Americans desired and expected, he steadily reinforced them, especially Jinmen, so that 100,000 men, a third of his best forces, were tied down in vulnerable positions. Already, in October 1957, Secretary Dulles concluded that the defense of the offshore islands was now integral to Taiwan itself. In May 1958 the Joint Chiefs of Staff concluded that the United States could defend the islands only with air and naval forces, and if it did, it must use nuclear weapons from the start.

Relations on Taiwan, between Americans and Chinese—apparently both the dominant mainlanders and the native Taiwanese—were not good in this period. The shooting of a Chinese by an American in March 1957, and what Chinese regarded as the too lenient treatment of the case, led to a big anti-American riot in Taipei, in which, the Americans thought, the Nationalist authorities seemed to deliberately refrain from protecting American facilities. This may have encouraged the Communists.

Mao Zedong was increasingly at odds with the Soviets. He was angry, and got steadily angrier, at Khrushchev for the latter's "secret speech" criticizing Stalin. While agreeing with its substance, at least in part, he considered it a mistake to publicize Stalin's faults, and possibly suspected, wrongly, that it was subtly aimed at him. He was increasingly disgruntled with the Soviets in general, although they had been far more generous to him since 1953 than Stalin had been. He decided to break with the Stalinist model of development, and introduce his own, allegedly superior, and more radical program, the Great Leap Forward. It was supposed to let China overtake Britain economically in fifteen years; later that goal was to be attained in just three years. It would turn out to be one of the greatest catastrophes in Chinese history.

After Sputnik, taken in by Khrushchev's bluffs and boasts as much as the West, Mao thought the balance of power had swung in favor of the Soviet–Chinese axis—in November 1957 he spoke of the "East wind prevailing over the West wind" and regarded subsequent Soviet policies as too weak. In January

1958 he decided to launch a new crisis over the offshore islands, probably for a combination of reasons. His main reasons may have been domestic and anti-Soviet—to rouse Chinese patriotism to mobilize mass sentiment as a preparation for the Great Leap Forward, and as a gesture to embarrass Khrushchev. At one point during the subsequent crisis (according to his doctor, Li Zhisu, whose dates and accounts are rather vague) he said that he did not intend to take Jinmen, but simply keep the Americans and Soviets "dancing" and sabotage any Soviet plans for an arrangement with the West. But he may well have hoped to so demoralize the Nationalists that they might collapse, or, at least, stop an American move toward a two-Chinas policy—one objective he shared with his mortal enemy across the Taiwan Strait! But he did not decide on exactly what to do or when, until the 1958 Middle East crisis.

Then a bizarre incident led to a sudden summit meeting with Khrushchev. The Soviets had wished to build a low-frequency radio station in China to communicate with their submarines in the Pacific. The Chinese objected. When Khrushchev sweetened the deal by proposing the development of a joint Soviet–Chinese nuclear submarine force, Mao exploded with paranoid accusations that this was a plot to reduce China to some sort of colonial status. Khrushchev, shocked, flew to China, meeting Mao from July 31 to August 3. Although Mao seemed calmer in person, Khrushchev was alarmed by Mao's seeming insouciance about the possibility of nuclear war, and Mao behaved with incredible, childish rudeness. A chain-smoker, he deliberately blew smoke in the face of the "First," who was sensitive to smoke. More important, incredibly, he did not tell Khrushchev (despite what the Russian wrote in his memoirs) of the coming Taiwan Strait crisis! The decision, made in mid-July, to start it right away had been precipitated by the Middle East crisis, Mao desiring a gesture to support the Arabs. Mao did not intend the crisis to lead to war, or even a direct clash with the Americans. He viewed it as a probe that might, but not necessarily, lead to a landing on Jinmen.[5]

That was not true of Chiang. He had stuck his best forces, 90,000 on Jinmen alone, in an incredibly dangerous position precisely to ensure that the next crisis over the offshore islands would bring about at least a Chinese–American war, if not World War III.

Difficulties with Communist military preparations, apparently in moving up enough artillery ammunition, delayed the onset of the crisis. They had built more airfields in the Taiwan Strait area, and began patrolling more aggressively, with MIG-17s superior to the Nationalists' F-84s and F-86s. On July 29, MIGs downed two F-84s over the Strait. More critical, they had nearly ringed Jinmen with guns. By September 12, over a thousand artillery pieces, ranging from 76 to 155 mm in caliber, were in heavily built emplacements. Only half the guns could be fired at any one time, but there were more emplacements than guns, flanking Jinmen on the north and south, so the island could be shelled from an arc of nearly 180 degrees.[6] The Americans had noted the buildup and air fighting, but at first were inclined to regard Nationalist warnings as just more of the complaints and demands they were all too used to. Their plans to resume the Geneva meetings with the Chinese Communists, which had been suspended for a time, and move them to Warsaw, were overtaken by the crisis. Eisenhower did not receive convincing intelligence pointing toward a new crisis until August 6. The day before that, the Joint Chiefs had ordered an additional carrier group to the Taiwan area and shipping twenty F-86Fs armed with the new Sidewinder air-to-air missile to the Nationalists.

At the National Security Council meeting of August 7, the danger was still somewhat underestimated. Allen Dulles reported that while the Communists had built up their fighter strength, there had been no sign of bomber deployment. And there was no sign of a ground force or naval buildup; he deemed an attack on the offshore islands unlikely without such elements, although the Communists might hope to starve out Jinmen with a blockade. The Nationalists had overdramatized the situation for their own purposes, and were provoking the Communists by attacking mainland junks. Eisenhower remarked that, even with the Formosa Resolution, there would be no excuse for U.S. intervention unless we concluded that the Communist air activity was a preliminary to an attack on Taiwan. We had no warrant to defend the offshore islands unless an attack on them was a prelude to one on Taiwan. The next day, however, Secretary Dulles suggested that, unlike 1954, the offshore islands contained such a large proportion of Nationalist troop strength that an attack on them now constituted an attack on Taiwan itself. When he presented this view, the President at first sounded skeptical, but Dulles convinced him that the loss of Jinmen and Mazu would crush Nationalist morale. Dulles speculated that perhaps both Communist big powers were probing to see whether the Soviet possession of ballistic missiles had weakened our resolve. On August 11, Eisenhower told General Twining that there were sound military reasons for the Nationalists to abandon the offshore islands, but it would signal to all Asia that there was no hope of resisting the Communists. It was becoming clear that a serious crisis impended. In meetings on August 14 and 15, the Joint Chiefs advocated supporting the Nationalists against a blockade of the offshore islands, with American intervention if necessary to defend the islands against a major assault. But they did not favor stating this policy openly "partially because the Chinese Nationalists, if they know we are committed to the defense of the offshore islands, may start something on their own." Ike reflected "when, as in this case, we are being shoved into something that we do not think is correct because of someone else's intransigence, this is when the American public and press say that the United States has a vacillating policy." The offshore islands had no strategic value. Any U.S. response to a Communist attack should be within "fixed definite limits." Secretary of Defense McElroy described the Nationalist attitude toward the offshore islands as "psychopathic." The Joint Chiefs of Staff warned that effective American intervention would require nuclear bombing of mainland bases, at first of six to eight airfields near Amoy, but possibly deeper attacks into China, later. They reported that they could keep open the supply lines to the offshore islands, but not defend them against direct assault, with conventional weapons.

Suspicion and anger directed against the Nationalists was palpable in American deliberations from this point on. Even hardline military leaders had quickly concluded that Chiang was taking the Americans for a ride, seeking to sucker them into an all-out war. Only the most pro-Chiang elements in the State Department—Assistant Secretary of State for Far Eastern Affairs Walter Roberson, and the Ambassador on Taiwan, Everett Drumright—were inclined to defend Chiang. Some in the State Department, notably the Assistant Secretary for Policy Planning, Gerard Smith, deplored the whole idea of defending the offshore islands if it meant a resort to nuclear weapons, but they did not sway policy. On August 20, the Warsaw Embassy was told to renew talks with the Chinese Communists without delay.

The Americans diverted six F-100s intended for NATO to the Nationalists, lent them three tank landing ships, and sent a third aircraft carrier to Taiwan as well as Air Force units. The Joint Chiefs of Staff had concluded that a sea blockade could be countered by providing air and naval escort for Nationalist convoys.

Eisenhower and others prudently, if wrongly, assumed that the Chinese Communists would act at least with the Soviets' acquiescence, even if not in complete coordination with them. That Mao was not even warning the Soviets of his plans understandably did not occur to them! They were still sure that the loss of Taiwan, if the Nationalists collapsed, would lead to a "chain of disaster" that would undermine the whole position of the anti-Communists in Asia. They estimated that if the Communists were convinced the United States would stand aside, they would land on Jinmen and perhaps the Mazus. But, if the Communists were convinced that the Americans would intervene in that case, they would confine their actions, at least at first, to blockade and interdiction. The President, if not everyone else, was determined to limit the American response as much as possible—but seemed to accept that the need to use tactical nuclear weapons might well arise.[7]

The Crisis Begins

On August 23, the Communists began to heavily shell Jinmen. Some 20,000 rounds fell on a densely populated island of 153 square kilometers.

Although John Foster Dulles was to be a bit "harder" in this crisis than the President, his first reaction was "If this seems really serious and critical there is perhaps room for the good offices of some acceptable third power." He also told Undersecretary of State Christian Herter and Walter Robertson, "I do not feel that we have a case that is altogether defensible." It was one thing to contend that the Communists should leave the areas under Nationalist control alone, another to contend that they should when the Nationalists used those areas as a hostile base. But the Secretary issued a public statement warning that it would be "highly hazardous for anyone to assume" that an attack on the offshore islands "could be a limited operation."

The shelling continued, falling off to 8,000 rounds a day, but causing 500 casualties through August 24. That evening, Jinmen was bombed, the only air attack on the island during the crisis. Chiang graciously told the American Ambassador and Admiral Roland Smoot, the head of the Taiwan Defense Command, that he would consult the United States "if at all possible" before using force against the mainland.

What would be the real danger to the Nationalists on Jinmen began to become apparent, as their supply convoys came under attack from shore batteries and motor torpedo boats. One ship was lost. Supplying the islands, which fortunately had considerable stockpiles, was going to be difficult and dangerous.

At a White House meeting on August 25, Eisenhower grumbled that assistance

> would be for one reason and one alone, namely to maintain the morale of the GRC (the Government of the Republic of China) which had deliberately committed major forces to their defense contrary to our 1954 military advice.

He wanted to put off any public commitment to defend the islands, but approved of the United States taking part in the air defense of Taiwan, and taking it over if necessary. He approved sending a fourth carrier to the Taiwan area, and preparing to escort convoys to the offshores.

The orders to the Pacific Theater Commander, Admiral Harry Felt, indicated that, in the event of a major attack seriously endangering the principal offshore islands, Felt was to prepare to assist the Nationalists, including attacking coastal air bases. "It is probable that initially only conventional weapons will be authorized, but prepare to use atomic weapons." A SAC B-47 squadron on Guam could be made available if hostilities broadened to require air attacks on the mainland targets. More supplies would be rushed to the Nationalists. Felt liked the idea of keeping both Chinese sides guessing about what we would do; he noted that "from a pure military point of view, the islands were not worth the risk of getting involved in a war even though it may be possible to keep it limited." Felt estimated that against an all-out effort the offshores could hold out for 5–7 days without American help, but air attacks on enemy airfields were essential to save them. It was "questionable" what success could be achieved with non-nuclear weapons, but planning was taking place for that. His own judgment was that the Chinese Communists were trying to provoke the United States into actions that could be condemned in the world press and the UN, but they could be discouraged by actions short of full-scale war. A Special National Intelligence Estimate issued the next day, August 26, noted the

Communists' interest in arresting any drift toward acceptance of a de facto "two Chinas" solution. It was doubtful the Chinese Communists would assault the offshore islands directly for fear of American intervention, but they might do so if Americans' reactions or the lack of them to lesser pressures convinced them that the Americans would not intervene. The Communists could probably not be deterred from maintaining military pressures without an explicit U.S. guarantee of the offshore islands or a commitment of U.S. forces to at least defend their supply lines.

Confusion and alarm was caused in the West by Chinese Communist Army broadcasts on August 24 and 27, warning that an invasion of Jinmen was imminent, but apparently these statements were unauthorized; there was some blunder or confusion within Mao's government.

On August 27 Chiang requested a clear statement that the United States would intervene to defend Jinmen and the Mazus, and a promise of convoys to the islands. Admiral Smoot recommended the latter step, and also requested authority to let the Nationalists attack selected gun positions in an emergency. Felt concurred on convoy escort only. But Chiang's request was greeted with suspicion in Washington although it was increasingly clear that the Nationalist supply line was the critical factor in the crisis. Eisenhower, that day, publicly declared that the offshore islands were now more important to the defense of Taiwan than in 1955.

The next day, at the Pentagon, Acting Secretary of Defense Quarles thought that the Communists' actions so far had not met the test for an attack on Taiwan; Undersecretary of State Herter and the Chief of Naval Operations Burke both suspected that the Nationalists were holding back their own naval forces precisely in order to draw in the Americans. Burke, however, favored taking over the air defense of Taiwan, and if the Nationalists could not handle the supply problem, we should escort convoys, if necessary, all the way to the Jinmen beaches. Burke noted that the most critical area was near the islands, where the threat of attack by motor torpedo boats was greatest. Only good naval gunfire could counter that, but our ships could deal with it. Burke wanted to initially escort convoys to ten miles from Jinmen, keeping out of shore-based artillery fire. The Nationalists, it was decided, would get twelve eight-inch howitzers as soon as possible. These were capable of counterbattery fire on Communist artillery positions. They could also fire nuclear shells, but those were *not* given to the Nationalists! That capability, however, may have worried the Communists.

At a meeting in the White House, on August 29, planning what to do before any massive attack on the main offshore islands, Eisenhower said that we should hold off using nuclear weapons at the outset, and hoped that it would not be necessary to use them later. His opinion was that a major Communist attack would not be mounted soon. He authorized convoys through international waters, that is, up to the three-mile limit of Chinese territorial waters. There was acid discussion of the fact that Chiang, despite our advice, had put such a large proportion of his strength on the offshore islands and now came "whining" to us, and speculation on his exact motives. Felt was given detailed instructions that atomic weapons would not be used in an early stage of any battle, and not without Eisenhower's direct authority. By August 31, however, Felt concluded that he should be allowed to escort convoys right to Jinmen.

Chiang, typically, was angry that the Americans had rejected his request to let him bomb the mainland. The crisis was sharpening. For the first time, there was a sign of Soviet support for the Chinese, a harsh editorial in *Pravda*. By late August, there were also obscure reports of contacts between the Nationalists and Communists, suggesting that Nationalist elements were considering defecting to the Communists. It was most unlikely that Chiang Kai-shek would do this, but others in his regime, perhaps estimating that the Soviet–Chinese axis was winning in the whole world, might want to strike a deal while one was still possible. Some in the American government feared that Chiang Ching-Kuo, Chiang's son, might lead such a move (which was a total misreading of the man). The defection of the entire Nationalist structure, intact, would have been the absolute worst outcome, short of all-out war. Such an event would have made the worst-case results predicted for the loss of Taiwan most likely—not to mention making the United States look utterly ridiculous.[8]

By September 2, the Taiwan Defense Command was grumbling that the Nationalists were not even trying to help the supply situation, although Smoot was inclined to attribute this to bungling rather than conspiracy. At a conference that day between the State Department and the Joint Chiefs of Staff, the Chief of Naval Operations stressed that shore batteries were the main threat to the Nationalists. General Twining insisted that if the United States became involved, strikes at airfields and shore batteries with small nuclear weapons were the only way to do the job. While the Army Chief of Staff estimated that an initial amphibious landing on Jinmen could be thrown back with conventional weapons, nuclear weapons might be needed if the Communists kept up the attack. Secretary Dulles observed that, in other words, it was not necessary to use nuclear weapons right away, but it would be necessary to do so ultimately against a determined offensive. But, if Nationalist morale threatened to collapse under massive artillery bombardment, only nuclear weapons could knock out the enemy gun emplacements. The same was true if there was heavy and continuing air attack. The military warned that that would require using 7–10 kiloton airburst bombs against airfields—they should produce virtually no fallout. Ground bursts would be more effective, but just too dirty. After hitting five coastal airfields, we would then stop and observe the effect on Communist intentions. Dulles noted that if nuclear weapons were used in defense of the offshore islands, the Japanese government might have to demand that U.S. forces leave Japan, or at least request that the United States stop using facilities in Japan for operations in the Taiwan Strait. General Twining could not understand the "public horror" at the battlefield use of nuclear weapons.

All agreed that the real problem was psychological; as Dulles said, if it were possible to merely let the islands go, no one would mind very much, but it would lead to continued Chinese aggression.

On September 4, Dulles met Eisenhower at Newport, where the President was vacationing. They both assumed the Communist great powers were acting in concert. The Secretary of State noted that a Chinese Communist statement that day, while declaring that China's territorial waters extended out to 12 miles, seemed to him slightly softer in tone than earlier threats—the first, and only comforting sign for some time. Dulles presented a memorandum registering his views, and those of Secretary McElroy, and Chairman Twining, which accepted the assumption that the Chinese were acting with Soviet backing and carrying on a years-old program to liquidate the Nationalists' position by producing a "cumulating rollback effect" to get Taiwan, with serious repercussions in the rest of East and Southeast Asia. Absent our intervention, the Communists could take Jinmen and would do so if they believed the United States would stay out. If they could be convinced otherwise, they probably would not try a direct assault, but they could continue shelling and interdiction, which might lead to a collapse of the defenders. If Jinmen was lost, that might lead to a collapse of the will to resist on Taiwan, the loss of the island, and, over a period of years, disastrous results elsewhere, especially in Southeast Asia. Japan would probably fall into the Soviet orbit. Dulles did emphasize that if the Communists assaulted Jinmen and we did intervene, there might be a period after the start of the attack when prompt and substantial U.S. intervention with conventional weapons might cause the Communists to pull back. Otherwise our intervention would probably not be effective if limited to conventional weapons. If American destroyers escorting Nationalist ships were hit, "at least limited retaliation" might result, and once we were committed to saving the offshore islands we could not abandon the effort. But, he warned,

> if accomplishment of this result required the use of nuclear weapons, there would be a strong popular revulsion against the United States in most of the world. It would be particularly intense in Asia, and particularly harmful to us in Japan. If relatively small detonations were used with only air bursts, so that there would be no appreciable fallout or large civilian casualties and if the matter were quickly closed, the revulsion might not be long-lived, or entail consequences as far reaching and permanent

as the chain of disaster envisaged from the loss of Taiwan. "It is not certain, however, that the operation could be thus limited in scope or time, and the risk of a more extensive use of nuclear weapons, and even a risk of general war, would have to be accepted." Eisenhower agreed with this, and approved a Dulles statement, issued that day, defending the American and Nationalist legal position, and warning that

Any attempt on the part of the Chinese Communists to seize these positions (Jinmen and Mazu) would be a crude violation of the principle upon which world order is based, namely that no country should use armed force to seize new territory.

Dulles noted that the Communists had announced that the purpose of their operations was to take Taiwan as well as the offshore islands, but they might not aim at making an all-out effort, and such efforts might be countered by the Nationalists with American logistical support. The President had not yet made a determination that using American forces was required or appropriate, but he would not hesitate to do so. Dulles declared that the defense of the offshore islands had increasingly become related to that of Taiwan.[9]

Mao and the other Communist leaders were surprised by the American readiness to intervene, their rushing forces to the Taiwan area, and willingness to convoy Nationalist ships. On September 4, by some reports, Mao decided not to take Jinmen, at least by direct assault. The shelling of Jinmen stopped for three days. The Soviets, who had been taken by surprise by the whole crisis, now acted. Worried, they sent Foreign Minister Gromyko to Beijing. Zhou Enlai apparently calmed his fears, at least at first. Then he met Mao, who seemed reckless, if not insane. He seemed to accept the risk of a general war, even perhaps welcome it, telling the Soviet delegation that it might be a good thing if the Americans attacked China. In that event, the Soviets should not act immediately, but let the Chinese handle things, at least at first.

American ground forces should be drawn into the interior of China. Only then, and if the conflict threatened to grow (!) should the Soviets strike. The Soviets were not favorably impressed. Whether Mao was serious—and at least up to the late 1960s, he does seem to have thought of a future Sino–American war as a reenactment of China's war with Japan—or wished only to scare the Soviets, or test their fidelity to the alliance with China, is unclear. His physician, Dr. Li Zhisu, reports that Mao mused in private that it might be a good thing if Chiang got the Americans to drop an A-bomb on Fujian province, and he made similar remarks at party conferences. Mao apparently decided, however, that something had to be done to defuse the crisis, or at least win time for blockade measures to work against Jinmen. On September 6, Zhou Enlai, while attacking U.S. aggression and intervention in China's internal affairs, indicated that his government was ready to resume the ambassadorial talks, as the Americans had proposed on July 28. The Americans were pleased, but little else seemed to go well. On September 7, Khrushchev sent a nasty letter to Eisenhower, defending Mao's actions, warning that there would be no peace until U.S. forces left the Taiwan area, and that an attack on China would be an attack on the Soviet Union. Although later observers sometimes suggested that this letter was a belated effort, which Khrushchev only made after the crisis was subsiding, that point could not have been clear at the time it was dispatched. Mao was, for once, pleased with the "First's" action.[10]

The crisis seemed to get worse, not better. The supply problem had to be solved. On September 7, the Americans escorted Nationalist convoys toward Jinmen, stopping at the three-mile limit. The Communists did not fire on the convoy, but the mission was largely a failure; not much cargo was delivered. The next day, the shelling of Jinmen resumed, while the Nationalists flew an air reconnaissance mission over a mainland airfield, angering the Americans, who had not been informed. Dulles, on September 9, argued that the Taiwan issue was not purely internal, "There is in this situation elements that could lead to international war."

On September 11, another convoy was fired on; although the Communists were careful about avoiding shooting at U.S. ships, a Nationalist ship was lost. Cargo deliveries were small, and many Americans suspected that the Nationalist Navy was "dogging it" as part of Chiang Kai-shek's schemes to get the United States involved. (This, for once, may have been unfair.) The exasperated Secretary of Defense, conferring with Eisenhower on September 11, while the latter prepared a television address to the nation, told the President that the Joint Chiefs thought that from the standpoint of military considerations alone, the offshore islands should be evacuated. Eisenhower agreed; he planned to stress that, while he would not yield them under attack, he was trying not to be intransigent with regard to getting out of them by negotiations. He noted the difficulties involved, and that Dulles tended to take a somewhat stiffer view. McElroy wondered if there was not some way to get rid of Chiang, whose only hope was to "provoke a big fight." In conversation with Dulles later that day, Eisenhower noted that we were committed, indeed "overcommitted" to backing Chiang on the offshore islands, and that the Joint Chiefs now tended to the view that they were neither defensible or necessary for Taiwan's defense. He was quite prepared to see the abandonment of Jinmen, "but of course this could not be said publicly at the present stage." The President's address to the nation presented a somewhat more ferocious face than was really the case. Deeming the bombardment of Jinmen part of an ambitious plan of world conquest, he warned that the United States would not retreat, there would be no appeasement, and he did not believe there would be a war. He did not flatly state that the United States would defend Jinmen, but indicated that a major assault would be countered by U.S. forces, if the Nationalists could not stop it, and warned the Communists against miscalculations.

Chiang complained about the Americans staying beyond the three-mile limit, and American rejection of retaliation against the mainland. Dulles bluntly told the Nationalist Ambassador that it had been "foolish" to put so many troops on the islands, and quoted Eisenhower as saying it was "utterly mad." He warned Ambassador Yeh that the United States was isolated in world opinion on this issue.[11]

That was indeed true. By early September, criticism of the American position was becoming widespread, and in the United States itself, even from people who were emphatically not soft on other Cold War issues. Ex-Secretary of State Acheson, on September 5, complained that "We seem to be drifting, either dazed or indifferent, toward war with China, without friends or allies, and over issues which the Administration has not presented to the people, and which are not worth a single American life." John Knight, Republican head of a big newspaper chain, who had been increasingly critical of the Administration, denounced the idea of defending the offshore islands.

> Who are we to decide for all humanity that the risk of extinction is preferable to letting the Chinese Communists take over two little groups of islands to which we ourselves have not the shred of legal or moral right.

The *New York Times*, a usually pro-Eisenhower Republican paper, endorsed Acheson's views on September 26. That same day, Senator Morse declared that if Eisenhower and Dulles persisted in their policy, they should be impeached. Other Democrats were critical of the Administration. There was no popular support for the American position in Western Europe—the British Conservative government was willing to "agree to disagree"—and little in East Asia, although Dulles believed that there was some in government circles there. He admitted to other senior officials, on September 20, that 90 percent of the representatives at the UN wanted the United States and the Nationalists to disengage. He confessed, "in a sense they are right" but cited the danger of a Nationalist collapse and its results. Eisenhower himself thought, on September 23, that two-thirds of the world and half our own people opposed the course followed.[12] With the possible exception of rearming West Germany, the American position in the second Taiwan Strait crisis must have been the most unpopular policy of the entire Cold War up to the massive intervention in the Second Indochina War in 1965.

Had the Communist great powers agreed on a policy of "neutralizing" the offshore islands, they might well have gotten somewhere. The Norwegian government wished to introduce such a proposal (the British showed some openness to "neutralizing" Taiwan as well) and the Americans would have found it difficult to resist. Conceivably that might have enabled the Chinese Communists to achieve, slowly and piecemeal, the disintegration the Eisenhower Administration feared. But Gromyko, when approached, dismissed, in accordance with Mao's position, any distinction between the offshore islands and Taiwan. The Chinese Communists also turned down the idea when approached indirectly.[13] As on a number of other occasions in the Cold War, the enemy missed an opportunity by demanding just a little too much at one time.

On September 14, the Nationalists began using "LVTs"—American amphibious tractors—to unload the larger amphibious landing ships, greatly improving supply deliveries to Jinmen. Things got better. On September 17, three eight-inch howitzers were brought ashore. The next day, ambassadorial talks resumed in Warsaw. These did not prove productive. The Chinese Communists denounced American actions and rejected offers of a mutual renunciation of force, a guarantee that the offshore islands would not be used for provocative actions against the mainland, and discussions of a planned reduction of forces in the area. Dulles, as he told the British Foreign Secretary on September 18, would not have minded completely demilitarizing the offshore islands so long as the "naked title" to them remained in Nationalist hands. The Nationalists opposed all such ideas and hoped that the Warsaw talks would fail.

The supply situation in Jinmen still seemed bad. The Nationalists there needed 700 tons a day, but from August 23 to September 18, less than one day's worth of supplies had been unloaded. On September 19, Khrushchev sent another long letter to Eisenhower, this so abusive that it was formally returned; Eisenhower declared that it contained "inadmissible threats." The next day, Dulles concluded that nothing was likely to come out of the Warsaw talks. It now looked like there would be no direct assault on Jinmen.

Now the supply situation was beginning to improve and Jinmen should be able to hold out for two more months. There was also reassurance from the fact that the Soviets had not taken any military measures, even of the sort made in the Middle East crisis. By September 23, Dulles doubted that the Chinese would make any new military moves, and began to suspect that the crisis would just gradually subside if the supply problem was solved. On September 29, Twining was able to assure Eisenhower it had been "broken" and it was no longer a matter to worry about. The air fighting over the Taiwan Strait also favored the Nationalists. Their F-86 Sabrejets, now using the Sidewinder missile, outfought the MIGs. Four had been downed on the first day the missiles were fired, and over six weeks of fighting, the Nationalists destroyed thirty-one MIGs for the loss of only two F-86s.

Eisenhower grimly told Twining, on the day he got the good news, that Chiang had to be made "more flexible," and he wanted him out of the offshore islands. That day, Dulles told the Norwegian Foreign Minister and Ambassador that he thought the native Taiwanese wanted to be independent of the mainland; he had also told the British, on September 26, that he did not think that the Chinese Communists could be kept out of the UN forever.

On September 30, the Administration began publicly disassociating itself from Chiang. At a press conference, Dulles termed a Nationalist return to the mainland, Chiang's *raison d'etre*, a "highly hypothetical matter" (the Administration had never thought anything else but had tactfully never said so) and bluntly said that it had been "rather foolish" of Chiang to pile up forces on the offshore islands, a thought Eisenhower publicly endorsed in a milder way the next day. Dulles observed that there could be an arrangement to withdraw the Nationalist forces, and if there was a cease-fire they should certainly be reduced.

Some thought the crisis would drag on for a few more weeks until the Communists were sure that they could not starve out Jinmen, but they acted faster, if in a very strange way. On October 5, they announced that they would suspend shelling for a week, if the United States did not escort convoys. The United States responded by suspending convoys, over Nationalist opposition, of course. On October 12, the Communists extended the ceasefire for two weeks, and began talking about "peacefully" liberating Taiwan. They opened fire again on October 20, however, allegedly because a U.S. destroyer, against orders, had accompanied a landing ship going to Jinmen. The Americans, however, insisted that no U.S. ship had been within 15 miles of Jinmen. Shelling continued for some days. On October 25, the Communists announced that they would not fire on even-numbered days, but might do so on odd-numbered days. Thereafter Nationalists, unaccompanied by Americans, delivered supplies on even days. A bewildered Eisenhower wondered if we were in a Gilbert and Sullivan war. Mao had let it be known, within his government, that he had decided to leave Jinmen in Nationalist hands, as a "noose" around the Americans and Chiang and to prevent a "two Chinas" policy. Whether this was true, partly true, or a fabrication to save face is unclear.[14]

Dulles shared the general disgust with Chiang. He was resolved to pressure Chiang to reduce forces on Jinmen and the Mazus. (The Joint Chiefs of Staff wanted them cut to 25,000 men.) Dulles commented, on October 8 that "we cannot allow this crisis situation to confront us again." Chiang had had a "narrow escape," "we have had to strain our relations with Congress and with foreign governments almost to the breaking point to save him this time." Visiting Taiwan, he extracted a promise from Chiang to reduce the Jinmen garrison. (In November, a formal agreement would be reached to reduce the Jinmen force by at least 5,000 men. Chiang being Chiang, this promise was not carried out.) There were some interesting exchanges between the two men. Chiang remarked, on October 22, that using tactical atomic weapons might be advisable to knock out the Communist guns shelling Jinmen. As in 1955, he was quite ready to use nuclear weapons against fellow Chinese. He did show some unease when Dulles pointed out that such weapons could generate fallout, killing millions. A somewhat belated inquiry into the probable results of using nuclear weapons against the guns around Jinmen, communicated to Dulles on November 17, suggested that very dirty ground bursts would be necessary to damage well-built gun emplacements. Success would require dropping a pair of 25-kiloton weapons per target; lethal fallout would extend for six miles, and cover Jinmen itself except in the right weather conditions. However, eight-inch howitzers firing one- or two-kiloton shells from Jinmen could cause considerable damage to the gun emplacements with negligible fallout.[15]

During the crisis the Americans had assumed that the Soviets and Chinese were acting in concert. It became rapidly apparent that there were significant tensions between them. During the crisis Khrushchev had belated second thoughts about helping the Chinese get nuclear weapons, and he began cutting back on aid to the Chinese nuclear program. On November 16, Eisenhower, talking to a delegation due to negotiate with the Soviets in Geneva, said he would be interested in any evidence of Soviet worry about China. By March 1959, at a National Security Council discussion of policy in the event of war, Eisenhower decided that we would attack China, in the event of general war with the USSR, "only as necessary," and we would not strike China if that country could be isolated from hostilities.[16]

The second Taiwan Strait crisis had gravely strained the Soviet–Chinese alliance and helped split the two partners. That was true, of course, only because the Eisenhower Administration had stood fast in incredibly unfavorable circumstances, following an extremely unpopular policy, with strain on our own alliances.[17] Just how serious the risk of war was is not entirely clear even today, if only because sources for the Chinese side seem unusually unreliable and conflicting. The latter tend to suggest, however, that Mao did not intend a direct clash with the United States and backed down when it seemed a real danger. The Chinese were taken by surprise that the Americans quickly took a strong stance, and then by their escorting convoys. The latter, the solution of the supply problem, and victory in the air over the Strait, prevented the loss of the offshore islands to a blockade. The landing of the nuclear-capable howitzers on Jinmen may also have been particularly impressive.

How close Eisenhower came to using nuclear weapons is also unclear. But, as the crisis sharpened, he seems to have steadily shied farther away from doing so, restricting a decision to do so only to a major direct assault on Jinmen that could not be stopped any other way, emphasizing a pause to try out conventional weapons. If anything, the tone of his and Dulles' remarks seems to suggest that they became steadily more disenchanted with the idea of fighting over the offshore islands at all. That the idea of using nuclear weapons at all may have been a bluff on Eisenhower's part (*not* Dulles') is hinted by the President's remarks to the British Foreign Secretary on September 18. When the latter warned that if the United States used them in the Taiwan area "there would be hell to pay," Eisenhower responded that if they were going to be used, it would be an all-out effort rather than a local conflict. He did not plan to use nuclear weapons in any local conflict at the present time.[18]

It should be noted that Mao would demonstrate that there was considerable moral justification for the risks run to maintain the Nationalists, even if their complete collapse had not had the results feared. Bad as Chiang was, nothing he ever did was as remotely awful as the catastrophes Mao's rule inflicted on the Chinese people, especially over the next decade, in the "Great Leap Forward" and the "Cultural Revolution." The former alone is estimated to have killed 20–45 million people and possibly even more! Keeping the people of Taiwan out of his clutches was as morally justifiable an aim as any that can be imagined.

Notes

1 George Kerr, *Formosa Betrayed* (Boston, MA: Houghton Mifflin, 1965), pp. 23–27, 83–109, 125–142, 254–313, 384–391, 419–421, 426–427, 431; John Garver, *The Sino-American Alliance* (Armonk, NY: M.E. Sharpe, 1997), pp. 11–13, 30–38, 52–55, 61, 73–74, 78; Gordon Chang, *Friends and Enemies* (Stanford, CA: Stanford University Press, 1990), pp. 80, 82–88, 91–96; *FRUS 1952–1954, Vol. XIV, Part 1*, pp. 169, 175–177, 257, 278–306, 307–330, 409–411, 422–465; David Anderson, *Trapped By Success* (New York: Columbia University Press, 1992), p. 22; Douglas MacDonald, *Adventures in Chaos* (Cambridge, MA: Harvard University Press, 1992), pp. 12–18. I have borrowed the term "bolstering" from MacDonald's outstanding work.

2 Chang, *Friends and Enemies*, pp. 117–118; Odd Arne Westad, "The Sino-Soviet Alliance and the United States," in *Brothers in Arms*, ed. Odd Arne Westad (Palo Alto, CA: Stanford University Press, 1998), p. 173; Thomas Christensen, *Useful Adversaries* (Princeton, NJ: Princeton University Press, 1996); *FRUS 1952–1954, Vol. XIV, Part 1*, p. 674. Chang, Chen Jian, *Mao's China and the Cold War* (Chapel Hill, NC: University of North Carolina Press, 2001), Michael Sheng, *Battling Western Imperialism* (Princeton, NJ: Princeton University Press, 1997), and Shu Guang Zhang, *Mao's Military Romanticism* (Lawrence, KS: University of Kansas Press, 1995) are all valuable for the background of Chinese foreign policy.

3 Garver, *The Sino-American Alliance*, pp. 54–59; *FRUS 1952–1954, Vol. XIV, Part 1*, pp. 732, 808, 817–819; Kenneth Condit, *History of the Joint Chiefs of Staff and National Policy 1955–1956* (Historical Office: Joint Staff, 1992), p. 194.

4 Chang, *Friends and Enemies*, pp. 116–141; Garver, *The Sino-American Alliance*, pp. 123–131; Eisenhower, *Mandate for Change*, pp. 549–574; Condit, *History of the Joint Chiefs of Staff and National Policy 1955–1956*, pp. 193–209; *FRUS 1952–1954, Vol. XIV, Part 1*, pp. 516, 560, 563–571, 623–624, 674, 827–839; *FRUS 1955–1957, Vol. II*, pp. 10–11, 17, 30–34, 55–68, 69–82, 86, 89–96, 111, 114–115, 123, 135–138, 147–148, 158, 162–163, 210–212, 231–232, 238–240, 248–250, 259–261, 273–276, 283–285, 292–295, 308, 336–337, 343, 345–350, 353–354, 376–384, 390–391, 405, 408, 445–452, 479–489, 491–493, 512, 519; Karl Lott Rankin, *China Assignment* (Seattle, WA: University of Washington Press, 1964), pp. 218, 223, 235.

5 Li Xiabing, Chen Jian, and David L. Wilson, "Mao Zedong's Handling of the Taiwarn Strait Crisis of 1958," *Cold War International History Project Bulletin* no. 6/7 (Winter 1995), pp. 208–218; Chang, *Friends and Enemies*, pp. 144–149, 155–161, 182–183; Watson, *Into the Missile Age*, p. 220; Chen, *Mao's China and the Cold War*, pp. 64–71, 169–175; Rankin, *China Assignment*, pp. 255, 299–301; Westad, "The Sino-Soviet Alliance and the United States," pp. 22–29; Li Zhisu, *The Private Life of Chairman Mao* (New York: Random House, 1994), pp. 205, 225, 261; Qiang Zhai, *China and the Vietnam Wars* (Chapel Hill, NC: University of North Carolina Press, 2000), p. 81; Alexander V. Pantsov with Steven I. Levine, *Mao: The Real Story* (New York: Simon & Schuster, 2012), pp. 458–461; Fursenko and Naftali, *Khrushchev's Cold War*, p. 179; Lorenz Luthi, *The Sino-Soviet Split* (Princeton, NJ: Princeton University Press, 2008), pp. 41–43, 46–53, 71, 75–85, 93–95, 113.

6 *Foreign Relations of the United States 1958–1960, Volume XIX* (Washington DC: Government Printing Office, 1996), pp. 33–35, 39–43, 174; Watson, *Into the Missile Age*, pp. 223–224; Chen, *Mao's China and the Cold War*, pp. 175–177.

7 Fairchild and Poole, *The Joint Chiefs and National Policy 1957–1960*, p. 209; *FRUS 1958–1960, Vol. XIX*, pp. 39–40, 45–47, 50, 52–60, 67–68; Eisenhower, *Waging Peace*, pp. 293–296.

8 *FRUS 1958–1960, Vol. XIX*, pp. 69–86, 88, 89–102, 107–108; Fairchild and Poole, *The Joint Chiefs and National Policy 1957–1960*, pp. 210–211; Watson, *Into the Missile Age*, pp. 228–231; Chang, *Friends and Enemies*, pp. 184–188; Chen, *Mao's China and*

the Cold War, p. 184; Luthi, *The Sino-Soviet Split*, p. 100; Tang Tsou, *The Embroilment over Quemoy* (Salt Lake City, UT: University of Utah Press, 1959), pp. 11, 13, 27, 30, 42–43.

9 *FRUS 1958–1960, Vol. XIX*, pp. 115–122, 130–136; Watson, *Into the Missile Age*, p. 232; Eisenhower, *Waging Peace*, pp. 299, 691–692.

10 *FRUS 1958–1960, Vol. XIX*, pp. 142–143, 145–153; Luthi, *The Sino-Soviet Split*, pp. 100–101; Chen, *Mao's China and the Cold War*, pp. 184–199; Chang, *Friends and Enemies*, pp. 189–190; Garver, *The Sino-American Alliance*, p. 138.

11 *FRUS 1958–1960, Vol. XIX*, pp. 154–155, 161–163, 172–175, 178–183; Eisenhower, *Waging Peace*, pp. 300–302; Watson, *Into the Missile Age*, pp. 234–237.

12 *FRUS 1958–1960, Vol. XIX*, pp. 245, 267; Stebbins, *United States in World Affairs, 1958*, p. 321; Fleming, *The Cold War and Its Origins, Vol. II*, pp. 93–931, 933–934, 937.

13 *FRUS 1958–1960, Vol. XIX*, pp. 249, 275–278, 339–341.

14 *FRUS 1958–1960, Vol. XIX*, pp. 187, 195–200, 209–217, 221–224, 226–228, 231–238, 241–243, 247–248, 270, 272–273, 285–287, 296–299, 301, 375, 395, 411–413, 433–435, 440; Watson, *Into the Missile Age*, pp. 237–238; Fairchild and Poole, *The Joint Chiefs and National Policy 1957–1960*, p. 214; Eisenhower, *Waging Peace*, pp. 302–304, Kenneth Werrell, *Sabres Over MIG Alley* (Annapolis, MD: Naval Institute Press, 2005), p. 232.

15 *FRUS 1958–1960, Vol. XIX*, pp. 426, 431, 439, 487–488; Chang, *Friends and Enemies*, p. 127.

16 *FRUS 1958–1960, Vol. XIX*, pp. 546–547; *FRUS 1958–1960, Vol. III*, pp. 192–195, 202–203; Chen, *Mao's China and the Cold War*, pp. 78, 189; Chang, *Friends and Enemies*, pp. 195, 198–201, 208; Westad, "The Sino-Soviet Alliance and the United States," pp. 158–159, 175–176.

17 Garver, *The Sino-American Alliance*, pp. 140–142. Cf., however, Chang, *Friends and Enemies*, p. 208; Westad, "The Sino-Soviet Alliance and the United States," pp. 180–181.

18 *FRUS 1958–1960, Vol. XIX*, p. 252.

8

THE BERLIN CRISIS

The Taiwan Strait crisis had hardly subsided when the Western powers, not just the United States, faced the most serious crisis of all—one that sputtered on from 1958 to 1962, the crisis over the Soviet threat to West Berlin. Although it has not been much noted, the Soviet push against Berlin, in 1958, and 1961, was accompanied by efforts to cut down on the autonomy of Finland, crises the worried Finns called "night frosts."

In the clash over Berlin, basic interests of both sides would be in direct collision: the Western powers need to hold on to their position in Berlin, versus the Soviet desire to preserve their East German satellite—and, if possible, split and damage the NATO alliance beyond repair.

West Berlin was another exposed outpost established early in the Cold War—during World War II, in fact—but was vastly more important than the Chinese offshore islands.

If proof were needed that the responsible leaders on the Western side had not envisaged the Cold War, the arrangements for the occupation of Germany, tentatively laid out in early 1944 and finalized at Yalta (when Stalin graciously allowed the Americans and the British to allot parts of their occupation zones to the French) would be proof enough. When the occupation zones were laid out, the German capital was left 110 miles inside the Soviet Zone, and cut into occupation sectors itself. The Western occupiers in Berlin were thus vulnerable to being cut off from ground access, at least, any time the Soviets cared to do so. Stalin exploited that vulnerability in the blockade of 1948–1949, to try to get the Western powers to drop their plans for western Germany, the Soviets halted rail, road, and water transport from the Western zones to the city. (Contrary to what is still widely assumed, getting the West to abandon its part of Berlin was a secondary, fallback position. Stalin, at first, was actually after bigger game.) The Western powers defied the Soviets, going ahead with their plans for a West German government and German participation in the Marshall Plan. They defeated the blockade by the great airlift, which, contrary to what they themselves had expected, flew in enough food and fuel to keep the city going indefinitely. (Originally they had hoped only that the airlift would win time and only delay the city being starved out, during which something might turn up.) The Soviets could not interfere seriously with the airlift—they did harass it—without shooting down Western planes and seriously risking war. And the West imposed a "counterblockade," sharply restricting trade between their occupation zones and the Soviet Zone, making the crisis costly to the Soviets as well; with failure visible and costs mounting, Stalin gave up the blockade as a bad job. It had, in fact, backfired badly, angering public opinion in the West and cementing friendlier relations between the Western occupiers and the Germans.

All attempts to negotiate arrangements to unite Germany failed. In 1955, the Western powers ended the formal occupation of Germany, which was admitted to NATO. West Berlin remained separate, under American, British, and French authority, the Western powers resting their legal position on their rights as occupying powers and refused to deal with the East Germans, as opposed to the Soviets, over Berlin. The Soviets recognized the German Federal Republic, but the West did not recognize East Germany (virtually no non-Communist states did so). The West Germans were anxious to maintain this situation, and while they themselves traded extensively with East Germany, insisted that they would sever relations with any state other than the USSR that recognized East Germany. A less defensible, and troublesome, West German policy was that it refused to recognize the actual post-1945 frontier with Poland, the Oder-Neisse line. The West German leaders did not suppose that the lost areas could ever be regained, but feared the reaction of the large number of "expellees" if they made this explicit, and hoped, too, to use eventual recognition of the eastern frontier as a bargaining counter.

The West Germans, like the Americans, wanted Germany reunited with free elections, and the resulting state—really an enlarged Federal Republic— should be free to stay in NATO. The British and French, pro forma, professed to accept this, although they did not really want German unity, period, and, like any realistic person at that time, did not think it possible in any case in the foreseeable future. That estimate was shared, privately, by the West German chancellor, Konrad Adenauer, although he was careful not to admit this in public. That the Federal Republic would absorb the east in a bit over thirty years would have startled most people in the 1950s.

After 1949, despite occasional harassment, West Berlin shared in the "German miracle" of rapid recovery and prosperity, indeed West Germany subsidized the city to make it an even more impressive showpiece compared to the drab tyranny and poverty of East Germany. There was a continual slow drain of people to West Germany, which, as the zonal boundary became harder to cross elsewhere, increasingly passed through Berlin. The East German leaders would have been delighted to close the sector boundary between East and West Berlin, but Stalin's permission to do this, granted in January 1953 shortly before his death, was reversed by his successors before it was implemented, and for one reason or another they did not agree to such a move until 1961. It should be noted that had stopping the refugee flow been the real issue over Berlin, this could have been done without provoking a major international crisis.

Berlin, not united, but not completely divided until then, was the scene of "little blockades," the center of the East German uprising of June 1953, and of constant intrigue, spying, defections, and kidnappings, although the last were infrequent after Stalin died. The most famous spying incident was perhaps the elaborate CIA effort to tap Soviet communication with a tunnel into the Eastern sector, an effort rendered ineffective by a Western traitor. Despite this failure, Berlin was one of the few pipelines Western intelligence agencies had behind the Iron Curtain before the development of the U-2 and other advanced technical means of intelligence gathering. But the Western position was gradually eroded in the 1950s by a succession of Communist pinpricks.[1]

Origins of the 1958 Crisis

During 1957, a new issue arose, the West German government's interest in obtaining tactical nuclear weapons—or, more exactly, joint custody with the Americans over certain weapons, which some suspected played an important role in Khrushchev's decision to put the squeeze on West Berlin. Strangely, however, it appears that this worried the Soviets little and played at most a slight, and probably no role, in what happened. The Soviets did not regard it as much of a threat, or at most one that could be headed off easily.[2] The idea was unpopular in West Germany itself, and even more so in the rest of NATO. It was forbidden by the Paris Agreements that had arranged West German rearmament and admission to NATO. Any attempt to gain West German control over nuclear weapons would have taken years to negotiate, if possible at all. Soviet complaints about it would have had enormous support in the West.

The flow of refugees to the West and preserving the "German Democratic Republic" was more important, but seems not to have been a prime issue in 1958. The refugee flight was actually decreasing in 1957 and 1958, and, although it was still disproportionately composed of especially valuable professionals and highly skilled workers, more refugees were coming from the lower classes. The refugee flow was increasingly channeled, however, through Berlin; by the end of 1958 over 90 percent left through the city. The long-term threat to the viability of East Germany certainly concerned the Soviets, but this defensive motivation was probably a very secondary issue in 1958. (It would be more important, although not primary, in 1961.) Rather, Khrushchev's aims seem to have been offensive—prying West Berlin out of Western hands and undermining NATO.[3]

Khrushchev thought, not without reason, that his position had been strengthened by the overall missile bluff, which he thought had succeeded at Suez and over Iraq. The Soviets also received a long delayed but real addition to their strength, the highly secret "Operation Atom," the deployment of twelve R5M missiles in East Germany on bases from which they could hit Western European targets with 300-kiloton warheads. They appear to have been aimed at the Thor bases and U.S. bomber bases in Britain. Western intelligence was so bad, in this period, even in relatively accessible East Germany, that even in May 1959, five months after the deployment, the Americans were not certain it had taken place.[4]

Soviet policy in Europe, indeed the world in general, seemed to be hardening in 1958, typified by the announcement in June that Imre Nagy and three other Hungarian leaders had been executed, and harassment of road traffic into Berlin, and movement across the sector boundaries within the city as well. In September, the Soviets proposed a four-power commission to consider a German peace treaty, and a meeting of delegates from both halves of Germany to discuss a "confederation" between the two. The Americans rejected such talks unless a representative government was formed in East Germany. In October, Walter Ulbricht, the East German ruler, declared that the presence of Allied forces in Berlin was illegal, and that Berlin had always been part of the Soviet occupation zone, and therefore really belonged to the German Democratic Republic. In response, Secretary Dulles dismissed this claim, and reiterated the usual commitment to hold the Western position in Berlin, "if need be by force," and as long as we stood firm, there was no danger to West Berlin.[5]

It is sill unclear exactly how and why Khrushchev decided to launch a crisis over Berlin. By some accounts, a move on Berlin had been planned since 1957. Khrushchev's biographers, Fursenko and Naftali, however, maintain that it was a largely personal decision reached only in the fall of 1958. Ulbricht and the Soviet Ambassador to East Germany, Mikhail Pervukhin, pressed for action, but a decision was delayed by Khrushchev's concern with domestic issues, notably the development of the new Seven-Year Plan. And Khrushchev was dissatisfied with the Foreign Ministry's vague proposals of how to proceed. He decided to demand a peace treaty with East Germany that would put access to Berlin under East German control.

Anastas Mikoyan, however, regarded the plan as too dangerous and called for the Presidium, as the Politburo was called from 1952 to 1966, to restrain Khrushchev; but the "First's" supporters backed their patron, although not formally authorizing his program either.

In a speech at a Polish–Soviet friendship meeting in Moscow, Khrushchev attacked Western, and especially West German, "militarism," and stated that Germany should be reunified by the Germans. By violating the Potsdam

Agreements the Western powers had forfeited their legal right to stay in Berlin. A "normal situation" should be established there. The time had come for the occupying powers to give up the remnants of the occupation regime; the USSR would hand its functions over to the German Democratic Republic. Military resistance to this would be regarded as an attack on the Warsaw Pact. Before the speech, Khrushchev assured the Polish leader, Gomulka, that he expected a big crisis, but not war. Afterward, when the Austrian and Swedish Ambassadors asked Khrushchev what would happen if the Western powers refused to deal with the East Germans, he was more ominous: "They won't, our rockets are pointing the right way." The next day, TASS, the Soviet news service, representative in London, replied to a comment that Khrushchev was creating a dangerous situation, with the remark that "if there is going to be a war we had better have it now and get it over with."[6]

Some were alarmed by this blustering. Eisenhower was unimpressed. He, and the Dulles brothers, agreed that war was unlikely. The President deliberately delayed in reacting, possibly mistakenly, afraid to give any impression that the U.S. government was edgy. He overruled NATO commander Norstad and the Joint Chiefs of Staff's recommendation for a strong reaction to the blocking of a convoy to Berlin by sending a "battle group" down the autobahn. On November 21, he finally issued a low-key press release affirming our position in Berlin.

Eisenhower's view was not universally shared in the American government. Ambassador Thompson, in Moscow, deemed Khrushchev to be pursuing a generally hard line, but thought his primary aim was to force recognition of East Germany in some form or other. His view was that Khrushchev feared that, when West German rearmament was completed, there was a danger that West Germany might intervene in the event of a revolt in East Germany, facing the Soviets with a choice of world war or losing East Germany, and then the other satellites. Although stressing a "defensive" motive for Khrushchev, he nevertheless favored a strong public response by the United States, while in private we should stress willingness to take Soviet problems with East Germany into account in any German settlement. Others thought a stronger reaction desirable to calm West Germans and especially the West Berliners, who were upset by Khrushchev's speech and the lack of a proper response, and also by learning the details of Allied standing orders on how to deal with the situation if the East Germans replaced the Soviets in controlling traffic. The reactions of other Western governments differed widely. Surprisingly, at first sight, the French took the strongest line of all, basically holding that the Western powers should sit tight and make no concessions—there was nothing to negotiate about. Even the West Germans were more flexible. The French position was arguably more realistic in other ways than any other Allied country. The French government dismissed the possibility of German reunification on any acceptable terms in the foreseeable future, indeed did not want it, and favored swallowing the Oder-Neisse line without much ado. The British took the softest line, to a point where they seriously alarmed their allies. They estimated that the Soviets aimed to stop West Germany getting its hands on American nuclear weapons, induce the Western powers to negotiate a deal on Germany that would lead to military disengagement in central Europe, and get the West to recognize East Germany in order to consolidate their satellite empire. They were ready to accept recognition rather than risk the use of force, in fact were inclined to think that in the end East Germany would have to be recognized. They accepted dealing with East German representatives rather than refuse to do so and trigger a new blockade of Berlin. They, like the other Western powers, had little faith in the success of a new airlift.

The Americans and the French were disturbed by the Foreign Office's initial statement of the British position, which apparently did not represent the thinking of Secretary Lloyd, and the latter disavowed it. The British government then took a somewhat stronger stand, but the relative "hardness" of the Western allies remained consistent throughout 1958–1962, with the French taking the toughest line, the West Germans slightly softer, followed by the Americans, and the British being the softest.

Secretary Dulles, on November 26, declared that the Americans would not accept the East German regime as a substitute for the Soviets in discharging the latter's obligations, but we might deal with them as "agents" of the Soviets. He minimized the whole crisis as just another characteristic bit of Communist probing, the sort of things that happened from time to time, and one that had been expected.[7]

Ultimatum

The Soviets had encountered much difficulty in formulating the precise line to be followed. Mikoyan, and some of Khrushchev's normal supporters, like Mikhail Suslov and Ekaterina Furtseva, thought his approach too dangerous. The Presidium favored sending a new note to the Western powers, which would allow the alternative of West Berlin becoming a "free city" rather than being immediately absorbed into East Germany. Khrushchev actually liked this idea. He did insist that the time limit in which the West would be expected to come to an agreement be cut from twelve to six months. A secret approach to the West Germans, via the Austrian Ambassador, was also to be made to divide the West. On November 27, a long note along these lines was sent to the Western powers. Although the substantial demands were less harsh than Khruschev's November 10 speech, and not as bad as many in the West had feared, it was nevertheless extremely nasty. It argued that the occupation agreements were now void. Properly, Berlin should just become part of the German Democratic Republic, but the Soviets would generously allow an alternative solution. West Berlin was to become a demilitarized free city independent of both Germanies, guaranteed by the former occupying powers, with unhindered communications, but forbidding "hostile activity" against East Germany. But a settlement must be reached in half a year. In that time, the Soviets would make no change in procedures governing military traffic to West Berlin, but, if that period passed without agreement, the Soviet government would conclude a treaty with the German Democratic Republic putting all traffic, surface and air, under its control. The "free city" proposal was full of booby traps that would let the Soviets and East Germans intervene under almost any pretext to do almost anything they pleased. The substance of the proposal followed a lengthy, bitter attack on the Western democracies' supposed behavior dating back before World War II, accusing them (including the United States) of deliberately turning the Nazis eastward, and then violating the Potsdam Agreements and recreating German militarism. Having issued an ultimatum, Khrushchev promptly denied that it was an ultimatum. But he himself does not seem to have known what to do if the time limit ran out and the West stood fast. He told his son Sergei, "no one would start a war over Berlin," but would not say what would happen if the West was not sufficiently scared.[8]

Allied reactions to the ultimatum followed the usual pattern. The British were the weakest. Prime Minister Macmillan, personally, seems to have genuinely feared that war might break out, much more so than other Western leaders. There was an eruption of hostility to the Germans in the British press, as though West Germany had started the crisis, particularly in Lord Beaverbrook's papers. (Ironically, he had been an obstinate appeaser right up to the outbreak of war in 1939!) De Gaulle, as usual, thought there was nothing to talk about. Adenauer was not unwilling to negotiate, but rejected doing so under a deadline or with an agenda involving recognition of East Germany or unification without free elections. The West Berliners remained staunch; Communist attempts to use the crisis to influence the city elections in December were a total flop. The Americans were more flexible, although in the end inclined to a stronger stand than before. Eisenhower was even ready to contemplate a "free city" arrangement, but only on the conditions that it would include all of Berlin, that the UN would guarantee access routes from West Germany, and that the West Germans agreed. None were likely to be fulfilled. The Socialist Mayor of West Berlin, Willy Brandt, was one of the few Germans ready to contemplate such an arrangement, which was far from anything the Soviets envisaged. Given the far-reaching nature of the Soviet claims, it was decided that the East Germans could not now be accepted as Soviet agents. The Americans wanted a Western foreign ministers meeting to concert policy. Eisenhower was dissatisfied with existing contingency plans for Berlin. At a conference on December 11, he described the whole Berlin issue as a can of worms, and deplored the fact that "We are in the position of using an obsolete agreement with a former occupying power as a basis on which to force our way into Berlin." The real issue, as he saw it, was the defense of the freedom of the Berliners, and backing up our pledge; if we yielded on this no one would trust our word elsewhere. And, as Dulles remarked two days later to the American delegates to the NATO Council, "there is no doubt in anybody's mind that, if we give way, it would be a disaster and we would face the same threat later under even worse conditions." It was at the NATO Foreign Ministers Meeting, on December 17, that he stressed that Khrushchev was more of a gambler than his predecessor, and, precisely because of this, should not be given even a partial success. He was pleased with the results of the meetings; only the Canadians seemed "soft" to him.

American opinion in general was staunch at this point. Senator Humphrey, meeting Khrushchev informally in Moscow on December 1, took a forthright stance, much in contrast to some other liberal Democrats later in the crisis. Khrushchev bluntly spoke to him of Berlin as a "cancer" or a "bone in his throat." Khrushchev rather awkwardly argued that Berlin was a threat to the German Democratic Republic, but that the Western troops there were not really important, and then belittled the matter, taking the line that Berlin was the only issue. There was nothing at stake that could harm the Western powers.

The Western Foreign Ministers agreed, on December 14, not to negotiate under threat, a position endorsed by the NATO Council. Tediously, the Western powers drafted identical replies to the Soviet note of November 27, dispatching them on December 31. They rejected the free city proposal, insisted on Western rights, and that any negotiations be over a broad context dealing with Germany as a whole, and ignored the deadline. The note also refuted the numerous falsehoods in the Soviet note.[9]

What would happen if the crisis played out to the end, and Berlin was blockaded was not yet entirely clear. But Western policy makers generally agreed with the conclusion that the American military had reached as far back as 1955; an airlift of the sort that had saved things in 1948 was no longer possible. The British however, favored at least trying an airlift before any ground move to relieve Berlin was made. A few people disagreed with the generally accepted pessimism, notably General William Tunner, who had run the original Berlin Airlift; but most thought it was now too easy for the Soviets to jam the radio and radar aids necessary in bad weather, and, while it might still be possible to feed the city, the enormous tonnages now needed to keep it economically viable just could not be flown in.[10]

To keep Berlin going, the Western powers would have to reopen ground access. That ran into two major problems. The most obvious was simply that the Soviets were vastly stronger in conventional forces around Berlin, and the whole central European front, than the NATO forces, and that assuming that all the NATO allies went along with any move. Should shooting start, any force the West had available would be stopped, and resorting to tactical nuclear weapons, in Europe, would in all likelihood escalate to full-scale war. It had always been accepted that there could be no such thing as a "limited war," like Korea, in Europe. Less noted, and discussed, during the 1958–1959 crisis, was a point that had discouraged trying to push through a ground convoy in 1948 when the Americans had a nuclear monopoly. Even if the Soviets did not shoot, a ground movement to Berlin could be foiled, or at least made fantastically difficult, by what Eisenhower called "passive force." Demolitions and obstructions could make getting a convoy to Berlin extremely slow and costly. And, as soon as a convoy passed, the Soviets or East Germans could close in behind it and again render the autobahn impassable. Every convoy would become a major engineering operation.

With the West taking a strong stand, the Soviets decided it was necessary to somewhat defuse the situation. Mikoyan, visiting Washington, met Secretary Dulles on January 5, 1959. Both sides tried to be conciliatory, Mikoyan again justifying his reputation as the most reasonable and skillful representative of the Communist world. Dulles expressed some sympathy for the Soviets' professed feelings about Germany; noting that we had twice fought wars with Germany ourselves, and, though they had not been as costly to us as to the Soviet Union, those wars had been costly and unpleasant.

> We understand quite well the desire of the Soviet Union that Germany should not again become a military menace, and share its feelings on the question as to what to do to prevent it becoming that. The danger in the situation arises from the fact that the Soviet Union has one solution and we have another.

Mikoyan slickly justified Soviet policies and again denied that the note of November 27 had been an ultimatum. He delivered an aide-memoire outlining a German peace treaty. On January 10, his government formally replied to the Western notes of December 31, with a draft German peace treaty recognizing two German states, requiring all foreign forces to leave Germany, and recognition of the Oder-Neisse line. It renewed the threat of November 27, but offered to meet with the Western powers before a peace conference. On January 16, Mikoyan met Dulles again. The Secretary of State indicated that the United States was willing to negotiate about all questions, reunification as well as Berlin. Mikoyan now indicated that the "deadline" for a treaty actually meant from the start of negotiations, not necessarily November 27. At a meeting with Eisenhower, Mikoyan talked grandly of "ending the Cold War." Since the Soviets defined the Cold War as not simply an existing state of conflict, but as the aggressive struggle the Western powers waged against them, that phrase always meant less than it seemed to many Westerners unfamiliar with Soviet newspeak. (But Mikoyan was probably the sole Soviet leader who, given the power, would have ended the Cold War in the Western sense.)

Dulles, on January 13, had publicly suggested, to the horror of the West Germans, that reunification in some form might be possible without free elections. Two weeks later, he suggested that some sort of German confederation might be possible.[11]

Khrushchev was satisfied with Mikoyan's performance in the United States. The American government, even while trying to be more conciliatory, was having trouble coordinating with its allies and moreover was under internal pressure. During January and February, concern over the missile gap was reaching a peak, as leaks made the dispute over the validity of the December 1958 National Intelligence Estimate a public issue and generated concern that the Eisenhower Administration dangerously underestimated the threat. It was feared that the Soviets had already finished complete ICBM bases, while the planning and construction of our bases left something to be desired. Some criticized the Minuteman and Polaris projects, while others, notably Albert Wohlstetter, argued that the strategic balance was less stable than generally supposed. Polaris and Atlas suffered discouraging failures, setting back the planned Initial Operational Capability for Atlas by 60 days. Only in April, when the Soviets resumed ICBM testing, did it become apparent that the optimists had been right about the reasons for the earlier test halt, and the Soviets were suffering failures in the new tests, too.[12] Although estimates of what the military balance would be in a few years hence might have no immediate practical relevance to handling the Berlin situation in 1959, they undoubtedly had some psychological impact.

Planning on how to proceed intensified in late January. Dulles concluded that accepting the East Germans as agents would dishearten the West Germans and expose a lack of willpower in the West possibly encouraging the Soviets dangerously. He also noted, however, the danger that Europeans might actually think that the United States wanted a "showdown" in Europe, in which it would not (yet) be seriously hurt. He doubted that many Europeans actually believed that, but noted that Selwyn Lloyd thought that it was widespread.

Dulles planned to seek a foreign ministers conference with the Soviets. At an important meeting on January 29, the President, Secretaries of State, and Defense, General Twining and others, thrashed out some basic differences. Dulles stressed the necessity for starting talks on the whole German problem, as of mid-April, to give the Soviets an opportunity to withdraw without loss of face, a thought Eisenhower seconded enthusiastically. All agreed on a firm stand and in opposing a turnover of control of access to the East Germans. Dulles warned, however, that the British were "wobbling" on the matter. Some military preparations had to start soon, preparations that would be picked up by the Soviets but not cause public alarm.

Eisenhower and Dulles sharply differed from the views of McElroy and the Joint Chiefs on what to do if the Soviets stopped traffic to Berlin. All agreed that in that case, a probing action would be attempted. A small convoy with a platoon-sized armored escort (only scout cars) would set out; if blocked, it would return. The military favored quickly launching a larger force—not more than a reinforced division—along the autobahn. Dulles warned that a considerable lapse of time should be allowed to elapse between the first probe, and using any greater force. It was necessary so that Allied and world opinion could be mobilized in support of any use of force, while further military preparations would be made. Eisenhower concurred; he also thought that a reinforced division would be either too big, or too small. Twining warned that we could not hope to fight the Soviets conventionally on the ground; if we made up our minds to go through we must be prepared to fight a general nuclear war. No one disagreed. Eisenhower remarked that "we do not have sufficient forces in Europe," and

> six equivalent divisions were not enough to do this job conventionally. Our policy must be to force the Soviets to use military force, after which we are in a position to issue an ultimatum prior to the initiation of general war.[13]

The fundamental problem of the Western Allies in Germany, which, despite a great deal of thrashing around and debate in the Kennedy Administration, would persist, was that in a showdown the available conventional forces could, at best, make a demonstration that would frighten the other side into backing down before things got out of control. They could not win a battle with conventional weapons, and the forces with which to do so were never in prospect. While the Eisenhower Administration intended to conduct any confrontation with great care, and without haste, it recognized that adding more "conventional" weapons using steps to the "escalation ladder," as the Kennedy Administration sought to do in 1961, was basically pointless, because in none of them would the West enjoy any advantage. If anything, it might undermine Soviet belief in Western resolve. The point was not to get on the ladder at all, not add more steps to it. Actually, both Administrations were overoptimistic on one point, assuming that the Soviets would not quickly initiate the use of tactical nuclear weapons themselves in the event of serious fighting. That assumption seems to have been erroneous.

As Dulles left for Europe to concert Allied actions and obtain agreement for a foreign ministers conference with the Soviets, the latter stopped a truck convoy on the Berlin autobahn. The Americans reacted much more sharply than to the incident three months earlier. While talking with the French, Dulles learned that Prime Minister Macmillan had unilaterally embarked on a summit conference of his own with Khrushchev. (Macmillan had mentioned to the Americans that he might do this earlier, and had contemplated such a summit as far back as January 1958.) The Americans—and Foreign Secretary Lloyd—were not pleased, though they understood that the Prime Minister was under considerable pressure at home, for British opinion was more fearful, and more obsessed with the alleged virtues of summit meetings, than other Westerners. Dulles secured Allied agreement to a foreign ministers meeting, although the French wished to delay any conference until *after* the May 27, 1959 deadline. They also had no faith in ever going to the UN during a crisis. (Henry Cabot Lodge, the American Ambassador at the UN, was not enthusiastic about this either.)

Dulles returned satisfied with his work. He then entered the hospital for treatment of the cancer that would kill him on May 24. He remained active for a time, but resigned on April 15. He was replaced by Christian Herter, who although reasonably able, lacked his air of authority.

On February 16, the Western powers sent notes inviting the Soviets to a four-power foreign ministers meeting, and vowed to uphold Western rights in Berlin. Oddly, Khrushchev was infuriated! His estimate of how the crisis was going seems to have oscillated violently from the start of 1959. He interpreted the invitation as an attempt to torpedo the "mini-summit" with Macmillan, and wanted a full-scale summit or nothing. He was inclined to demand this, and even make a new threat to use military force, but eventually calmed down. On March 2, the Soviets accepted the proposal. By then he had persuaded himself that he would get a summit in due course, and, over a year perhaps, the West could be induced to give in on Berlin.

At his meeting with Macmillan, he was not very forthcoming, and in some sessions was downright abusive, shouting at Selwyn Lloyd in particular. Macmillan himself was not yielding, although (judging by what he said later) perhaps inwardly shaken. He found no sign that the Soviets were weakening, and concluded that it was of little use to deal with anyone but Khrushchev, so some sort of summit was inevitable and necessary. Some Americans, notably Ambassador Thompson in Moscow, and Ambassador Bruce in Bonn, tended to agree.[14]

On March 30, a meeting was arranged for Geneva. While political planning for the conference went on, contingency planning for military measures continued on the lines Eisenhower and Dulles had envisaged earlier. Eisenhower rejected a long list of military recommendations, which included mobilizing up a million men, adding 30 destroyers from the reserve fleet, activating various bases, alerting SAC, and sending 10,000 Army soldiers and a third of a Marine division/air wing team to Europe. He was also cool to a Stale Department suggestion to counter a blockade of Berlin by a naval blockade of the entrances to the Baltic and Black Seas. (Later, he was ready to hold up Soviet merchant ships in Allied ports in the event of a grave crisis.) He stressed that we could not act in Germany without our allies. As he indicated in a National Security Council meeting on April 23, he and the Secretary of Defense would keep close control of any attempt to break through a blockade of Berlin. Rigid plans could not be depended on past a certain point, in a substantial effort to restore access, "things would have to be played by ear." An additional issue that developed during March was the problem of height limitations in the air corridors to Berlin. Customarily, aircraft flying to the city had not flown over 10,000 feet, but the new C-130 turboprop transport, and jets, had to be able to fly much higher. Over Soviet objections and British and West German reluctance, C-130s made experimental flights to Berlin in late March.[15]

Eisenhower had emphasized the necessity of support by America's allies. But there was no particular reason for optimism about this during March. The Embassy in Paris warned on March 4 that the French government was indeed firm, but warned that in the end the United States might have to go it alone. The French people were not yet very interested or worried.

> If and when threat of nuclear war becomes acute, we are not optimistic that French, or indeed any people in Allied countries, will be inclined to give strong support to their governments in standing up to Soviets. Fear of nuclear holocaust runs deep, and recent opinion polls in Western Europe are not encouraging on this subject.

European opinion was not the only weak point. Although the great majority of Americans, Congress, and the principal leaders of both parties had rallied behind Eisenhower, especially after his television address of March 16, that support was not universal. Already, on February 12, and again later, an important Democratic Senator, Mike Mansfield, had denounced the policy (which Dulles in fact was deemphasizing) of seeking German unity through free elections, while explaining solemnly that Germany would soon unify itself! He later called for a "compromise" on Berlin. He and Senator Fulbright strongly opposed the Administration, and Dulles in particular. Fulbright declared that he saw no virtue in "maintaining the status quo." On both sides of the Atlantic, there was a revival of anti-German feeling, and vile abuse of Chancellor Adenauer, as though it was he rather than the Soviets causing the crisis. When Macmillan visited the United States in mid-March he warned of difficulties with public support. He himself sometimes seemed badly frightened, obsessed with the need to negotiate almost for its own sake, and the need for a summit. Eisenhower repeated the normal American insistence that a summit meeting was not a miracle cure, and any should come only after some earlier progress in negotiations. Macmillan spoke to the American leaders, several times, of trying to get all, or as many as possible, young British children to Canada to "keep their stock alive" in the event of nuclear war. Eight bombs on England, he remarked on March 20, meant 20–30 million English dead. Eisenhower could only stress the danger of surrendering to blackmail, and point out that the latest estimate of American casualties in the event of all-out war was 67 million, and that "we don't escape war by surrendering on the installment plan."[16]

The West Germans were also nervous, although in a different way, which tended to validate American worries. During the preparations for the Geneva meeting, on April 14, Secretary Herter met the German Foreign Minister, Heinrich von Brentano. Herter told him that the German proposals seemed little more than negative. Von Brentano admitted that this was so, but expressed the view that the Americans were mistaken in their belief that West Germany was much stronger than East Germany, and warned that proposals for unifying

Germany by a committee selected by the Laender (provinces or states) could be used by the other side to take over all of Germany over a period of years. That surprised Herter. Von Brentano then remarked that what would follow, he would not say gladly. The "present German leaders had experienced how incapable democracy was of resisting a totalitarian drive to power. It was not the government that was weak, but the people."

> Any attempt to deal with the German problem in isolation would bring more dangers than opportunities. It would be better to preserve the status quo for some time than to change it by entering into risks that were not calculable.

He admitted that it was really out of their reach to change the division of Germany, astonishing Herter. (Adenauer had privately talked in a similar way to Macmillan in 1957.) The rather hard-line West German Defense Minister, Franz Josef Strauss told Herter, on April 16, that the popular concept of disengagement in central Europe (which the British were reluctantly apt to entertain) was extremely dangerous. In the end the Germans would slide out of the alliance if any disengagement scheme were put into effect.[17]

The Geneva Conference

With such attitudes, it was difficult for the Western powers to formulate a common position. The foreign ministers meeting did not go well for the West, even though it maintained a common front. It was as tedious as Cold War negotiations could be, with exhausting sessions going over and over the same old ground. On May 14, the Western powers introduced a "package plan" for Berlin and Germany as a whole, reunifying both halves of Berlin and then Germany through elections, establishment of a new city council, a general assembly, and a new constitution. Gromyko, the Soviet Foreign Minister, turned it down instantly. He denounced the presence of Western garrisons in Berlin as a threat to East Germany. On May 16, he elaborated a Soviet peace treaty proposal, abusing the Federal Republic and arguing that the West was being unrealistic in tying the two problems, Berlin and German unity, together. On May 18 he offered three alternate "solutions" to the Berlin problem, in private conversation with Selwyn Lloyd: (1) all non-German troops should leave Berlin, which would become a free city; (2) soviet troops should join the Western forces in West Berlin; and (3) neutral troops would replace the Western forces in West Berlin. At some point, the Soviets realized that to get the summit they wanted, there had to be some progress at the foreign ministers conference for the West, or at least the Americans, to agree to one. Only on May 21 did Gromyko, after the West complained that the East German government was unrepresentative, and propped up by the

Soviets, complain about atomic arming of the Federal Republic. He seemed unimpressed when Herter and Secretary of Defense McElroy pointed out that all atomic warheads would stay under American custody, as they had to under American law.

In late May, there was a short break in the conference as the Western ministers visited Washington for the funeral of John Foster Dulles. The conference shifted over to smaller, "private" sessions. Gromyko harped on the "unnatural situation" in Berlin, saying that the occupation had outlived itself. On May 30, he slyly observed that from a military point of view and looking at the possibility of a military threat, the more troops the West had in Berlin, the better for the Soviets! Lloyd wryly pointed out that this should end the idea that the Western forces in Berlin were a military threat.

The Western powers rejected a Soviet protocol "guaranteeing" a Free City of West Berlin on the grounds that it extinguished Allied rights, and created a third German state, while excluding East Berlin. On June 5, there seemed to be some progress, as Gromyko appeared to accept that any arrangement on Berlin should continue until Germany was reunited. But on June 8, Gromyko refused to sign any agreement reaffirming Western rights. He declared that the Soviet government intended to withdraw from Berlin, while the Western powers declared that they would not increase their forces in Berlin, and might reduce them.

On June 9, Gromyko made a new proposal, which at first sight might have seemed to mean progress, but in fact was a regression. Instead of the "free city" proposal, which the Western delegations had made clear was unacceptable, the Soviets offered to extend Western occupation rights—for one year. But the Western powers must reduce their forces in Berlin to "symbolic contingents," all "hostile propaganda" against the "socialist" countries must stop, and all organizations involved in spying and subversive activities against them must be liquidated; and the Western powers must agree not to place nuclear or missile installations in West Berlin (which was a pretty silly place for either). During the following year an all-German committee, representing West and East Germany equally, would formulate an agreement on reunification and a peace treaty. If no agreement was reached within the time limit, the Soviets would conclude a separate treaty with East Germany. Having revived the ultimatum, Gromyko denied it was an ultimatum. The initial Western reaction was quite hostile. Herter was inclined to press for a recess.

Under this pressure, and without the stout figure of Dulles, the West weakened somewhat. Macmillan was strongly pressing for a summit, if disguised as an "informal" meeting of heads of government, although Eisenhower held that "a summit meeting based on nothing more than wishful thinking would be a disaster." There had to be some progress at Geneva first. Macmillan argued that in case of a deadlock, which he expected, there should be an informal summit, preferably in the United States, stressing the

pressure of British public opinion. On June 16, the Western powers offered
their own version of a temporary settlement. They would consider reducing the Western forces in Berlin and a four-power commission to eliminate
"subversion and espionage" in both parts of Berlin. Many considered these
proposals extremely dangerous, and the West Germans were upset, estimating that the four-power commission would at least let the Communists
eliminate Western-oriented news media. The Soviets, however, overreached
and rejected it.

Eisenhower had sent a letter to Khrushchev to try to break the deadlock.
Khrushchev's reply on June 17 offered to extend the period of negotiations but
linked them to the problem of Adenauer and his alleged policy of militarizing
West Germany and "the policy of preparation of war." On June 19, the Western
powers offered an even weaker proposal, explicitly limiting the Western garrison to 11,000 men with conventional weapons, with still further reduction to
be considered later, East German control of access routes, and curbs on propaganda and intelligence activities in all of Berlin, in return for recognition of
the right to continued free access to the city. Gromyko professed pleasure with
the progress and offered to extend the time limit for negotiations to eighteen months, but with the changes he had insisted on previously on June 9
to take place during that period. Neither side would accept the other's proposals. The conference recessed until July 13.[18]

On June 23, during the recess, Macmillan suggested seeking an interim
arrangement, because there was no hope of getting the Soviets to accept anything else. He warned Eisenhower that

> it would not be easy to persuade the British people that it was their duty
> to go to war in defence of West Berlin. After all, in my lifetime we have
> been dealt two nearly mortal blows by the Germans. People in this coun-
> try will think it paradoxical, to use a mild term, to have to prepare for an
> even more horrible war in order to defend the liberties of people who
> have tried to destroy us twice in this century.

The British would do it, however, if it had been shown that we had made every
endeavor to make a decent settlement first. On June 25, Khrushchev, meeting
Averell Harriman, a leading Democrat and major figure in the Roosevelt and
Truman Administrations with an exaggerated reputation for knowledge about
the Soviets, said that the Soviets would "never accept Adenauer as a representative of Germany." He harshly turned aside Harriman's arguments that his
threats to terminate the occupation unilaterally, and "end your rights in Berlin"
were dangerous and declared that, "if you want to perpetuate or prolong your
rights this means war." He also broadly hinted that the Soviets had provided
nuclear-armed rockets to China for use against Taiwan, a fib that would have
startled Mao.

But the confusing alternation of "hard" and "friendly" gestures continued. A little later, Eisenhower had a surprisingly friendly meeting with Khrushchev's deputy and likely successor, Frol Kozlov (in the demonology of the period, the prime "Stalinist" allegedly pushing on a pacific First). It was not really productive, but led the President to extend a qualified invitation to Khrushchev to visit the United States, before a summit, *if* there was renewed progress at Geneva. But, by mistake, Robert Murphy omitted the qualification in the invitation, and Khrushchev accepted—much to the embarrassment of the Eisenhower Administration!

During the recess, the American military, and Mayor Brandt, cautioned Secretary Herter that reducing the West Berlin garrison would be a serious mistake. The Joint Chiefs regarded it as a demonstration of weakness that would encourage further Soviet harassment. The American commander in Berlin, strongly argued that the garrison, and the West Berlin cops, were really just enough to block an East German attempt at a coup to seize the city with "civilian" rioters. Herter was convinced, and reducing the garrison was eliminated from Western proposals, for a time.

The resumed talks soon deadlocked again, the Western powers insisting on unrestricted access, the Soviets insisting on all German discussions to precede other parts of a settlement. Gromyko again refused to sign any agreement perpetuating occupation rights. Herter, like the French, wanted to quickly wind up the conference as futile, but the British wished to go on. The Soviets pressed for reducing the Berlin garrison, and rejected reciprocity in relation to the proposed restraints on activities in Berlin. The Western powers made a final offer for an interim agreement lasting five years, restricting the Berlin garrison to 11,000 men, no atomic or missile installations, free and unrestricted access to West Berlin as in effect in April 1959, and a UN office in Berlin to report on propaganda activities and interference in all of Berlin. But again the Soviets overreached.

Some thought that, had they accepted, they might have been able to gradually weaken the Western side further, the five-year term suggesting that the West might leave after that time and demoralize the West Berliners. Khrushchev seems to have supposed that, in the planned meeting with Eisenhower and the following summit that he expected, and did get, he would extract bigger and perhaps quicker-acting concessions. That, however, did not turn out to be the case. Eisenhower, at the end of July, had considered reducing the Western force in Berlin a bit (but nowhere near the degree the Soviets sought)—only in return for assurances on Allied rights and delinking all-German talks from any "moratorium agreement" on Berlin. But things did not turn out as the Soviets expected. When Khrushchev met Eisenhower in September, he found the President more stubborn than he expected. He finally lifted the ultimatum. By the time the full summit conference came in 1960, the Western position had hardened again, and the U-2 incident led to the conference being aborted. Like many other Cold War issues, the first phase of the long Berlin crisis had no dramatic end, and led to no agreement. It simply trailed off, to be revived in 1961.[19]

Notes

1 Donald E. Murphy, Sergei Kondrashev, and George Bailey, *Battleground Berlin* (New Haven, CT: Yale University Press, 1997), Thomas Parrish, *Berlin in the Balance 1945–1949* (Reading, MA: Addison Wesley, 1997), and Ann Tusa, *The Last Division* (New York: Perseus, 1997), esp. pp. 304, 23–26, 34–37, 53, 60, are good on the background of the crisis. Cf. also Hope Harrison, *Driving the Soviets Up the Wall: Soviet-East German Relations 1953–1961* (Princeton, NJ: Princeton University Press, 2003), esp, p. 19. On the "night frosts" see James Billington "Finland" in *Communism and Revolution*, edited by Cyril Black and Thomas Thornton (Princeton, NJ: Princeton University Press, 1964), pp. 133–139.
2 Fursenko and Naftali, *Khrushchev's Cold War*, pp. 189–190; Tusa, *The Last Division*, p. 81. Cf. Haslam, *Russia's Cold War*, p 176.
3 *A Cardboard Castle?* p. 13; Fursenko and Naftali. *Khrushchev's Cold War*, pp. 190–191; Tusa, *The Last Division*, pp. 74–75, 86; Harrison, *Driving the Soviets Up the Wall*, pp. 51–52, 71–74, 99.
4 Fursenko and Naftali, *Khrushchev's Cold War*, pp. 193–207; Matthias Uhl and Vladimir Ivkin, "Operation Atom," *Cold War International History Project Bulletin*, no. 12/13 (Fall/Winter 2001), pp. 299–307; Steve Zaloga, *The Kremlin's Nuclear Sword*, pp. 40–41; *Foreign Relations of the United State 1958–1960, Volume VIII* (Washington DC: Government Printing Office, 1993), p. 764. Curiously, despite "Operation Atom," the U.S. government, before the Cuban Missile crisis, pooh-poohed the idea that the Soviets might base strategic weapons in Cuba on the curious grounds that they had never put any outside Soviet territory before, a classic illogical deduction from a false premise.
5 *FRUS 1958–1960, Vol. VIII*, pp. 36–37; Harrison, *Driving the Soviets Up the Wall*, p. 100; Jean Edward Smith, *The Defense of Berlin* (Baltimore, MD: Johns Hopkins Press, 1963), pp. 156–162; Tusa, *The Last Division*, p. 86.
6 Fursenko and Naftali, *Khrushchev's Cold War*, pp. 192–199; Murphy, Kondrashev, and Bailey, *Battleground Berlin*, p. 305; Tusa, *The Last Division*, pp. 88–97; *FRUS 1958–1960, Vol. VIII*, p. 49.
7 Fursenko and Naftali, *Khrushchev's Cold War*, pp. 203–204; Tusa, *The Last Division*, pp. 97–115; *FRUS 1958–1960, Vol. VIII*, pp. 47–48, 69, 78–84, 86–88, 97, 121–127; Smith, *The Defense of Berlin*, p. 163; Eisenhower, *Waging Peace*, pp. 331–332.
8 Fursenko and Naftali, *Khrushchev's Cold War*, pp. 205–208; Smith, *The Defense of Berlin*, pp. 166–180; Taubman, *Khrushchev*, p. 399.
9 Tusa, *The Last Division*, pp. 117–135; Smith, *The Defense of Berlin*, pp. 181–193; *FRUS 1958–1960, Vol. VIII*, pp. 148–153, 172–177, 188, 193–195, 207.
10 Watson, *Into the Missile Age*, p. 600; Fairchild and Poole, *The Joint Chiefs and National Policy 1957–1960*, p. 125; Tusa, *The Last Division*, pp. 110, 113, 125; *FRUS 1958–1960, Vol. VIII*, p. 226; William Tunner, *Over the Hump* (Washington DC: Office of Air Force History, 1985), p. 224.
11 *FRUS 1958–1960, Vol. VIII*, pp. 233–239, 246–247, 270–274, 276–281; Tusa, *The Last Division*, pp. 138–140; Fursenko and Naftali, *Khrushchev's Cold War*, pp. 212– 216; Smith, *The Defense of Berlin*, p. 195.
12 Levine, *The Missile and Space Race*, pp. 86–87.
13 *FRUS 1958–1960, Vol. VIII*, pp. 292–306; Eisenhower, *Waging Peace*, pp. 340–342; Watson, *Into the Missile Age*, pp. 598–600; Fairchild and Poole, *The Joint Chiefs and*

National Policy 1957–1960, pp. 31, 126–127. It should be pointed out that the dilemma in the Eisenhower era was unusually sharp because the Army was then so completely geared to using tactical nuclear weapons; without them, the "pentomic division," a later Army Chief of Staff remarked, was incapable of fighting its way out of a wet paper bag! Tauschweitzer, *The Cold War US Army*, pp. 81, 94–95.

14 *FRUS 1958–1960, Vol. VIII*, pp. 314, 334, 376–377, 385–392, 396–397, 402–407; Fursenko and Naftali, *Khrushchev's Cold War*, pp. 219–225; Tusa, *The Last Division*, pp. 142–158; Horne, *Harold Macmillan, Vol. II*, p. 196.

15 *FRUS 1958–1960, Vol. VIII*, pp. 419–425, 471–475, 498–500, 625–628; Watson, *Into the Missile Age*, pp. 601–603; Fairchild and Poole, *The Joint Chiefs and National Policy 1957–1960*, pp. 127–129; Smith, *The Defense of Berlin*, p. 201; Tusa, *The Last Division*, pp. 159–160.

16 *FRUS 1958–1960, Vol. VIII*, pp. 390–391, 417, 419, 512–529; Fleming, *The Cold War and Its Origins, Vol. II*, pp. 947–950, 959, 994, 1044; Smith, *The Defense of Berlin*, pp. 202–203; Horne, *Harold Macmillan, Vol. II*, pp. 135–136. Senator Fulbright's later treasonable actions, as detailed by Ambassador Dobrynin in his memoirs (Anatoly Dobrynin, *In Confidence* (New York: Random House, 1995), p. 292) might suggest the worst possible interpretation of his motives in 1959, but there does not seem to be evidence that he had sunk that far by that time.

17 *FRUS 1958–1960, Vol. VIII*, pp. 580–584, 619–620; Horne, *Harold Macmillan, Vol. II*, p. 33.

18 *FRUS 1958–1960, Vol. VIII*, pp. 709, 714, 731, 743, 771, 773, 786, 797, 842, 856–857, 859, 865, 868, 872, 879, 885, 894, 902, 906–908, 914–917, 922–926; Tusa, *The Last Division*, pp. 169–177; Smith, *The Defense of Berlin*, pp. 203–204.

19 *FRUS 1958–1960, Vol. VIII*, pp. 940–943, 955–961, 987, 1000–1001, 1005, 1007–1008, 1009, 1010–1014, 1019, 1022–1023, 1050, 1054–1056, 1082–1083, 1090, 1092; Tusa, *The Last Division*, pp. 175–178; Horelick and Rush, *Strategic Power and Soviet Foreign Policy*, p. 121; Eisenhower, *Waging Peace*, pp. 404–412; Fursenko and Naftali, *Khrushchev's Cold War*, pp. 225–227; Harrison, *Driving the Soviets Up the Wall*, pp. 124, 130–132.

9

THE LAST DOMINO

American Intervention in the Indonesian Civil War

During 1958, the United States faced a major Cold War crisis in Southeast Asia. Contrary to what might be supposed by people obsessed with later disasters in Indochina, this was not on the Southeast Asian mainland at all, but in the largest and most important Southeast Asian country, Indonesia—the biggest and last "domino" of the famous, or infamous, domino theory.

Few, in the 1950s, would have argued that Southeast Asia in general, and Indonesia in particular, were not of great importance in the Cold War. The region, due to its natural resources, historical and economic connections with Europe and Japan, and strategic location between East Asia, India, and Australia was a major theater of the Cold War. It was drawn into the struggle by several factors, namely the disruption caused by Japanese occupation, decolonization, and modernization, the independent initiative of the Vietnamese Communists, and deliberate Soviet action, seconded, later, by Chinese involvement.

The first stage of the post-World War II struggle for Southeast Asia was a complicated three-cornered fight between non-Communist nationalists, the local Communists, and the returning European imperial powers. The latter, or at least the Dutch and French, found out, the hard way, that the critical conflict was not between them and the local peoples. At least, that was not a conflict that they stood much chance of winning. The true struggle was over who would succeed them. In Indonesia and Indochina, local forces seized power at the time of the Japanese surrender—a broad front of non-Communist nationalists in Indonesia, but overwhelmingly Communist-controlled in Vietnam, led by Ho Chi Minh, one of the most able of Communist leaders.

While the British rapidly came to terms with the nationalists in Burma, which became independent in 1948, and were ready to do so in Malaya, where nationalism had not proceeded very far, the French and Dutch tried to reconquer their colonies, only to bog down in favor of overwhelming opposition and American disapproval.

Up to 1949, the United States did nothing about Indochina; a French effort at restoration that was bound to fail was not a viable alternative to local Stalinists. But, disgusted by Dutch actions, and fearing that they would play into Communist hands, it belatedly stepped in, threatening to cut off Marshall Plan aid and forcing the Dutch to come to terms with the Indonesians.

Other local events, and the need to defend the far southern flank of advanced allied countries, and ensure their access to resources that they (not the United States) needed, helped draw the United States into Southeast Asia, as it did in the Middle East. And, in both cases, it was pushed or pulled by its Western European allies.

On top of the existing colonial wars, a series of Communist uprisings occurred in 1948, these instigated by the Soviets, in an attempt to exploit the revolutionary situations that seemed to exist and disrupt exports to Western Europe and disrupt its recovery. This led to an attempted Communist coup in Indonesia, which flopped badly, and long, costly guerrilla wars in Malaya, the Philippines, and Burma.

American Involvement

During 1949, the Truman Administration became more and more concerned with Southeast Asia, which, it recognized, might be economically critical, at least for Japan, and the latter's ability to escape being drawn into the Soviet–Chinese orbit. It was distressed by developments in the region, especially in Indochina and the Philippines. The Americans believed, or hoped, that some changes in French policy would now make it possible to counter the Communists in Indochina. In the Elysee agreements, the French made Vietnam an "associated state," allegedly independent within the French Union. Their old Vietnamese puppet, Emperor Bao Dai, a worthless scoundrel, became "head of state," with the French retaining control of foreign policy and military affairs and a special status. Only a few of the most anti-Communist Vietnamese nationalists would work with this arrangement (later the Communists drove more into doing so), but the French were more successful at coming to terms with the Cambodians and Laotians. The Americans, like the more moderate Vietnamese nationalists, regarded the Elysee agreements just as a starting point, not as the last straw, as most of the French did. Many regarded it as a rather slender hope, but they persuaded themselves that it was necessary to act on it, for they believed that a great deal depended on what happened in that one small part of Southeast Asia.[1] By then, the Chinese Communists had reached the frontiers of Indochina and were in a position to aid the Vietnamese Communists.

The Domino Theory

In February 1950, the National Security Council concluded that if the Communists triumphed in Indochina, they would also gain control of Thailand and Burma. To avoid this, the U.S. government would now support the French effort in Indochina. This was the first appearance in American assessments of the nucleus of what was later called the "domino theory," an idea the Americans picked up from the British, that, if one country in Southeast Asia fell under Communist rule, however it did so, the rest of Southeast Asia would follow, like a row of dominos toppling over. During the early 1950s, belief in the "domino theory" became stronger, and while it came in several versions, it was generally thought that should Indochina fall to Communist control the whole mainland of Southeast Asia, and probably also the islands, would also succumb. There were some doubts about this, especially in the military (in contrast to what would be the case in the 1960s, when the military tended to be the most ardent supporters of the domino theory) and a fair number of people thought that the process might be halted by some timely counteraction. Still, much was thought to depend on what happened in Indochina. This was true, although, paradoxical as it may sound, the Eisenhower Administration, while giving the domino theory its name, did not really believe in it—at least in the way the Kennedy and Johnson Administrations did.

The issue seemed critical as a result of the final crisis of the First Indochina War. On January 8, 1954, Eisenhower had remarked at a National Security Council meeting that he could not see putting U.S. ground forces anywhere in Southeast Asia; and the United States could not "replace" France in Indochina. But the collapse of the French "Navarre Plan," the siege of Dien Bien Phu, and the French call for help, made the issue of American intervention immediate. The Joint Chiefs of Staff, on March 12, warned that the rest of Southeast Asia would fall under Communist control if Indochina did, albeit with the significant qualification "in the absence of effective counteraction." Admiral Radford, and with less enthusiasm, the Air Force Chief of Staff favored intervention, and Dulles at least seemed open to the idea. Radford held that U.S. air and naval support—including the use of tactical atomic weapons—would enable the French to win without the help of American ground forces. Other officers were less confident about that; as Admiral A.C. Davis put it, "you don't go over Niagara Falls in a barrel slightly." The able and respected Army Chief of Staff, Matthew Ridgway, and the Marine Corps commandant believed that large American ground forces would be needed, and opposed intervention. Less than a year after the Korean truce, public and Congressional opinion was far from enthusiastic. Eisenhower would not act without Congressional support. Between them, the Administration and Congress posed a formidable list of prerequisites for American intervention: the support of both European and Asian allies, especially Britain, and French promises to fight on until victory and grant full independence to the Indochina states. It was impossible to fulfill all these requirements before Dien Bien Phu fell in May, which broke the French will to fight. Britain's rejection of "united action" gave the Eisenhower Administration the excuse not to act. It is doubtful that Eisenhower had ever actually intended to intervene, as Sherman Adams and Richard Nixon perceived at the time. Remarks the President made at the April 29, 1954, meeting of the National Security Council suggest this, and that the real purpose of the exercise was to frighten the Communist powers (which it did) and strengthen the Western hand at the upcoming Geneva Conference.

Although, in a National Security Council meeting on April 6, Eisenhower had seemed to reject the idea that all of Southeast Asia would go Communist if Indochina did, in a speech the next day, he launched the famous phase, comparing the effects of the fall of Indochina to that of the fall of the first of a "row of dominoes." But neither he nor Secretary Dulles endorsed the domino theory unconditionally, and within a month, both would repudiate it! As Dien Bien Phu fell, both men, in public and private, hastily backed away from the domino theory. In a speech on May 7, Dulles implied that the theory did not apply, and at a press conference four days later he made clear that he thought that the rest of Southeast Asia could be held without Vietnam, Cambodia and Laos. Eisenhower declared that the domino effect would be offset once a regional system of collective defense was set up.

After the Geneva Conference, the United States invested considerable effort in the hope that a viable South Vietnam could be established. But Vietnam, indeed Indochina, was not of vital importance for the Eisenhower Administration. As Dulles remarked in the National Security Council on November 24, 1954, he was

> not at all optimistic about the future of Free Vietnam. Laos and Cambodia are also vulnerable. Yet, if one looked at the other side of the picture, these countries are not really of great importance to us, other from the point of view of prestige, except that they must be regarded as staging grounds for future forward thrusts by the Communist powers.

Nor did he regard Vietnam as any sort of "model" or test case for what might happen elsewhere. He noted that it was a special case, if only because the "French had messed up the situation so thoroughly." He and others justified involvement in Vietnam by the need to "buy time" elsewhere.[2]

Indonesia

Whatever the fallacies of the domino theory, no one doubted the importance of Indonesia. It, not Indochina, or any place on the mainland, was the heart of

Southeast Asia, a fact the Soviets and Chinese, unlike the Americans, never lost sight of. Sprawling over a sea area the size of the continental United States, it was one of the most populous countries in the world; in fact, it was the largest Muslim nation. The Indonesians had been the second most numerous people under Western rule. Indonesia was well endowed with natural resources. Before World War II, it was one of the world's major oil producers. But this potentially rich nation was not in good shape in the 1950s. The Dutch had left it unevenly developed; Jakarta, one of the world's biggest cities, had no sewer system. (President Sukarno, in November 1958, described it to an American official as "the worst city in the world.") Dutch educational and economic policies had not fostered a native civil service, merchants or a professional class, much less prepared for self-government. The country had never fully recovered from World War II or the subsequent war of independence. Even in the mid-1950s, ships had to carefully maneuver around unswept minefields. The country was badly divided, and poorly run. Even after independence, the economy was dominated by the hated Dutch, and the perhaps even more detested Chinese minority. Like the Jews of medieval Western Europe and modern Eastern Europe, they were religiously and culturally distinct from the people among whom they lived and were economically more dynamic than Indonesians (or other Southeast Asians). They formed a disproportionate part of the city populations and what middle class existed, and were regarded as exploitative aliens. There was tremendous inflation, and Indonesia was even more dependent than before on exporting a few raw materials, especially rubber and tin, whose prices fluctuated wildly. To make things more difficult, most of the country's exports, and revenue, came from the thinly populated outer islands, which were exploited by heavily overpopulated Java. Both Java and the other islands were deeply divided by ethnicity and religion. Javanese did not get along well with the Sundanese of the west end of Java, and similar divisions existed among the Sumatrans. People were bitterly divided over religion, fanatical Muslims dominating the north end of Sumatra and western Java. The Darul Islam movement in western Java, and the Atjehnese of Sumatra, had revolted as late as 1953, and were only gradually subdued; Darul Islam still dominated much of western Java's countryside.

Apart from resentment at the continued economic role of the Dutch, Indonesians were united in insisting that the Dutch half of New Guinea ("West Irian") properly belonged to Indonesia, although its people were not Indonesian, showed no desire for Indonesian rule, and West New Guinea was likely to be a burden on anyone who owned it. The Dutch stubbornly held on to it, and the Australians much preferred a continuation of Dutch control to Indonesian rule of the area. The Communist powers strongly backed the Indonesian claim. The United States was caught between the two sides. Secretary Dulles tended to favor the Dutch and Australian position, although some elements in the Administration, and Admiral Stump, the Pacific Fleet commander, favored appeasing the Indonesians on this issue.

The Dutch attempt to promote and use federalism in the late 1940s had discredited that concept, and an extremely centralized system was imposed on a country that was not suited to it. The government and armed forces were swollen and inefficient. (The armed forces had been too big for the available weapons and supplies even in 1948 at the height of the war with the Dutch.)

At the top, Indonesia was badly led. There were able Indonesian leaders, but they were far overshadowed by President Sukarno, a national hero, Indonesia's "George Washington," an immensely popular but not very capable demagogue. A self-indulgent womanizer, Sukarno, a Javanese nobleman, oozed charisma, but had little knowledge of or even interest in Indonesia's domestic affairs. A human chameleon, he posed, and quite successfully, on different occasions as an ardent collaborator to the Japanese, a Jeffersonian democrat to Americans, a democratic socialist to Europeans, an ardent neutralist to Asian and African neutralists, and a reliable ally to Communists. (Secretary Dulles, however, recognized that the figure he most resembled was Gamal Nasser.) Sukarno, like other Indonesian nationalists, and for that matter many Arab nationalists, profited from the conveniently short memories of many Westerners, who were amazingly willing to overlook their collaboration with the Axis powers.

Although his colleagues, and Indonesian diplomats were, in private, remarkably ready to describe him to foreigners as a somewhat ridiculous figure, Sukarno was untouchable with Indonesian public opinion. Even the military dictatorship that succeeded him in 1965, after several disasters had severely tarnished his reputation, was very cautious about trying to fully discredit him. Under his most usual façade in the 1950s, that of the "progressive democrat," he was, unfortunately, a power-hungry, anti-Western chauvinist with no use for democracy. He seems to have held his long-standing lieutenant as leader of the nationalist struggle, the far more honorable and intelligent Mohammed Hatta, a Sumatran, under a strange spell. Hatta often disagreed with Sukarno, and even broke with him, but was reluctant to openly fight him.

The non-Communist political parties in Indonesia were weak and had a narrow base of support. The PNI (Indonesian National Party), closely associated with Sukarno, was really the party of the government bureaucracy, while the Socialists and the Masjumi (modern, moderate Muslims) were not numerous.[3]

The Communists, by contrast, had recovered remarkably well from the disgrace incurred by their failed coup attempt of 1948. They had taken full advantage of the more flexible policies Stalin had allowed to Communists in South and Southeast Asia from 1951 on. And, instead of competing with and complicating Soviet policies in Southeast Asia, as they sometimes did in the Middle East, the fortunes and aspirations of the Indonesian Communists seemed to flow neatly together with Soviet policies.

As we noted earlier, the Soviets and Chinese never lost sight of the fact that Indonesia, not Indochina, was the truly critical part of Southeast Asia. For it was the great island world, not the mainland, that was the center of gravity of the region. Indonesia, the Philippines, and the British colonies later grouped as Malaysia, were more populous and wealthy than the very different mainland countries. This in fact was one of the problems with the domino theory. The people of the islands normally took little interest in what happened on the mainland with which they had little in common. And the islands would militarily be dominated by Western air and sea power even if the mainland fell into the Soviet–Chinese orbit. While the Western powers and their allies might not be able to prevent those countries going Communist by more or less internal processes, they could certainly stop the Communist powers from bringing critical external pressures to bear. And Indonesia was not a good target for a guerrilla struggle of the sort possible in other parts of Southeast Asia (and those *outside* Indochina had failed by the mid-1950s, another problem with the domino theory). The Communists' base of support lay in Java, a relatively small island tied together by a good transportation system and under the thumb of the government and army. Guerrilla warfare had been possible, on Java, against the relatively small and alien Dutch forces, but it was not a practical way to overthrow an Indonesian government. But, it seemed, the Indonesian Communists might not need an armed struggle to take power.

Whether they did take power in any near future was not, perhaps, of great moment to Khrushchev. His reign marked the peak of the policy, first followed by Lenin himself, of promoting alliances with non-Communist nationalist movements and regimes against the West, an alternative to the more publicized policy of promoting Communist seizures of power in the backward countries. His leaping over the Western alliance system to form alliances with radical but non-Communist anti-Western regimes that had imperial ambitions of their own, for a time, seemed even more successful in Indonesia than in the Middle East. In 1956, again using Czechoslovakia as a cover, the Soviets made an arms deal with Indonesia. In the late 1950s and early 1960s Indonesia would get more Soviet aid and support than any other non-Communist country than Egypt, and more than Ho Chi Minh's North Vietnam, although Khrushchev had nothing against Ho, once gushing that he was a "saint." Unlike Nasser and other Arab leaders, Sukarno had no annoying anti-Communist tendencies.[4] The local Communists were allied with him.

As far back as January 1952, they had proposed an alliance to the PNI, and indirectly, to Sukarno. The Communists' energetic new leader, Aidit, built a large, legal party stressing a broad appeal, Indonesian nationalism, and support of Sukarno. The Communists took over the national labor federation, and gained a strong popular base, especially in central and eastern Java. They appealed particularly to white-collar workers, the intelligentsia, and the "abangan"—the landless element of the Javanese peasantry whose belief in Islam was mixed with animist and Hindu ideas.[5]

The CIA had subsidized Masjumi, but that and aid to Sukarno's government failed to prevent Indonesia from drifting toward the Soviet bloc. American intelligence estimates in 1955 and 1956 were not optimistic about Indonesia's economic development, and noted the growth of Communist strength with disquiet, although there were bursts of optimism as late as August 1956. President Eisenhower, unlike Secretary Dulles, was inclined to take an indulgent view of Sukarno for a time. He thought that Indonesia had little alternative to a "noncapitalist" road of development.[6]

During 1956, however, the situation in Indonesia became more worrisome. Sukarno, in a long series of foreign tours, was particularly impressed by the development of China. On returning home, he swung far to the left, passing democratic socialism without stopping. In November 1956, he spoke of instituting a system of "guided democracy," in which a "national council" would replace the elected parliament as the nominal locus of sovereignty, the role of the non-Communist parties would be ended and Javanese domination intensified. He clearly viewed the Communist party as a counter to the Socialists and Masjumi. The more moderate Hatta was forced to resign in December.

Civil War Begins

All of this was not universally popular. A tepid regional military rebellion began sputtering on Sumatra in December 1956. The central Sumatran command at Padang rebelled, but the southern sector hesitated, while the coup failed in northern Sumatra. Another rebellion, "Permesta," began on Celebes in January 1957. But the rebels were badly divided, and were not fully agreed on their aims—whether to overthrow the central government or merely force it to give the outer regions a better deal and curb the Communists. Neither side took the offensive; the rebels refused obedience, but the government did not attack them. The "Colonels" movement, supported by local elements of the Socialists and Masjumis, was not instigated by the Americans. The latter had contact with the rebels from April on, but refrained from aiding them. The Permesta rebels approached the Chinese Nationalists.

The American government dithered about what to do. It had contemplated, for some time, a "break glass in case of emergency" policy of promoting the breakup of Indonesia should the central government and Java come under the Communists' control, and at least saving the more anti-Communist outer islands. But State Department officials persuasively argued that breaking up Indonesia—which the rebels did not want—was not likely, not wanted by *any* Indonesians, and would not, in the end, benefit the United States. And the United States hoped that an early compromise might well be negotiated between the government and rebels, as was attempted in August and September 1957. But the Communists made great gains in the mid-1957 elections on Java, and Sukarno's speech on Indonesian Independence Day in August indicated his bitterly hostility to the West. Even Ambassador Allison, who was less hostile to Sukarno than officials in Washington, read it as a complete break with democracy and the

West. An interview with Sukarno convinced him that Sukarno's attitude to the Communists was dangerously naïve or he was completely insincere. A National Intelligence Estimate of August 27 was very pessimistic about Indonesia's future and the growth of the Communist party, which was being backed by Sukarno. More and more attention was paid to Indonesia; a special report by the National Security Council on September 3 stressed the seriousness of the Communist threat in Indonesia and supporting the anti-Communist forces in the outer islands. Ambassador Allison, however, reported on September 13, rather more optimistically than before, that "Sukarno was not yet beyond redemption." He believed that the Indonesian Army or much of it might restrain him and the Communists, and should be given aid. The Embassy in Jakarta would steadily maintain, correctly, that the Communists' strength, at least in the short run, was being somewhat overestimated, and that the Army was more anti-Communist, and a more effective counterweight to the Party, than Washington assumed. But the basic inclination in Washington was to back the rebels.

Nevertheless, the Americans were surprisingly friendly when Sukarno, angered by Dutch resistance on the New Guinea issue, or using it as an excuse, confiscated all Dutch property in Indonesia in November 1957. (Dulles, by that time, was even willing to placate a "better" Indonesian government by giving it "West Irian.") Sukarno also expelled all Dutch residents and most Eurasians from the country. This move, badly planned and prepared, proved disastrous. Much property was seized, but many Dutch inter-island steamers, on which Indonesia depended, just sailed off before they could be grabbed, disrupting the economy. The nationalized property was handed over to the army, the only people accustomed to running large organizations. As in Nasser's Egypt, "socialism" meant ineffective military domination of the economy. But Sukarno remained untouchable. Ambassador Allison reported on December 5, that the U.S. public relations position was reeling from the reaction to the Little Rock desegregation crisis and the Sputniks.[7]

Intervention

The American government may have decided in principle to back the rebels in September 1957, but was sluggish in deciding how, and how far, to do so. Starting in October, modest sums had been turned over to the Sumatran rebel leaders. Serious arms deliveries began only in January 1958. The British had decided to support the Americans in December, and let them use supporting facilities in Singapore. An American submarine, and surface craft began delivering small arms and other equipment to the Padang rebels. American objectives at this time were to strengthen the anti-Communist forces in the outer islands as a means to influence the central government on Java, and provide a rallying point if the Communists took over Java. The Defense Department wanted an immediate decision to take military action if that occurred, but the State

Department wished to hold off on anything but planning for such a case. The military, however, began actual preparations for such an operation. Secretary Dulles, at a meeting of State, Defense, and CIA officials on January 2, stipulated that we should not make any deal with Sukarno or the present government, but make it known that a reconstituted government excluding the Communists would get our help. Meanwhile, we would build a "position of strength" in the outer islands. All agreed that Sukarno was "wholly undependable." Dulles remarked that he was "dangerous and untrustworthy and by character susceptible to the Communist way of thinking." Whatever the other limitations of Dulles' estimate of the Indonesian situation, and they were serious, that view of Sukarno would be amply justified over the next decade.

At the end of January, Allen Dulles, reporting "Probable Developments in Indonesia," expected the Padang rebels to offer an ultimatum of sorts; the Jakarta government would not give in, but would try to negotiate further. He expected the rebels to agree to that, and estimated that the chances were "better than even" that Sukarno would agree to the formation of a new government, but would not take real action against the Communists. Such a "fuzzy outcome" would probably result in still further negotiations. If and when a real civil war broke out, he estimated that the Padang group could probably hold the outer islands, but "we are unable to estimate the outcome of an effort by the Padang group to defeat the central government on Java." This report overestimated the rebels' capabilities and understated those of the central government. Some have blamed this on Frank Wisner, head of the CIA's office of Policy Coordination, playing up to the inclination of the Dulles brothers. (The brothers did not by any means always agree, but their thinking in the Indonesian affair seems to have been in tune.) By contrast, the Joint Chiefs of Staff were very skeptical of the outer islands holding out for long should the Communists gain control of Java.[8]

Things came to a head much faster than Washington expected. On February 10, the Padang rebels issued an ultimatum demanding a new central government that would make the Communist party illegal. This was flatly rejected the next day. The government also protested Secretary Dulles' hostile remarks, in a press conference, that "guided democracy was a nice-sounding name" for what would become Communist despotism. On February 15, the rebels proclaimed their own government, the "Revolutionary Government of the Republic of Indonesia" (PRRI in its Indonesian initials). The Permesta group in the Celebes reluctantly went along. Permesta was now getting Chinese Nationalist help; or more, exactly, Chiang was selling it a mix of World War II Japanese rifles and modern 75 mm recoilless guns, and delivering them in Nationalist PBY planes.

But Colonel Barlian, still commanding in South Sumatra, would not back the rebels, although he would not join action against them either. Had he joined the PRRI, South Sumatra's oil resources and strategic location might well have given the rebels the upper hand. Some elements in Java—notably

Hatta, still favored negotiations, but Sukarno, the able Army Chief of Staff, Abdul Nasution, and the Communists all wanted the rebels crushed. The rebels, and their foreign backers, gravely underestimated the strength and loyalty of the central government forces and Nasution's resolution and skill. The latter planned well a counteroffensive whose speed, strength and target took the rebels by surprise.

As Robert Johnson of the National Security Council staff pointed out, the Americans had not really planned for the situation now developing. Previous planning had provided for outright military intervention, in the event of an outright Communist takeover, but not for possible intervention in a civil war in which the Communists "laid low" and had not taken control of Java. Allen Dulles, at a National Security Council meeting on February 27, thought, hopefully, that Sukarno was hesitating to attack; that even those forces loyal to him—estimated at only half the military forces on Java—were not really enthusiastic about an offensive. He thought the dissidents had moved too fast, but still had a reasonable chance of winning. If they did not, however, he and his brother agreed that it was fairly certain that Indonesia would go Communist. Eisenhower stated his belief that "we would have to go in if a Communist takeover really threatened." And Secretary Dulles thought that "our chances for successful intervention were better today, with the assistance of an indigenous government on Sumatra, than they would be later on, when we might have to intervene without such a cover." Just such an intervention was now under consideration.

The Indonesian government was seriously worried about outright American intervention and aware of the covert operations already underway. Foreign Minister Subandrio warned the American Embassy counselor, Sterling Cottrell, that his government had proof of "SEATO interference," and warned against aiding the insurrection; "the Soviets have substantial interests here and they will not desert us." On March 4, the Secretary General of the Foreign Ministry told Cottrell that the government planned to bomb the American-owned petroleum storage depots at Padang and Menado but offered to compensate the owners. Cottrell warned of serious consequences if this occurred. Later, after conferring with the manager for one of the owners, he told the Indonesians that there were only limited supplies of kerosene and gasoline in the depots anyway, which had been unloaded into drums and dispersed by the rebels. The Indonesians tried to placate the Americans. Dulles told Cottrell to inform the Indonesians that the United States would lodge a formal protest if the depots were bombed, and the Indonesians backed off. (In fact, they had almost no planes capable of doing the job, and the whole issue may have been an attempt to probe American intentions.) Dulles pondered using a bombing of American-owned installations as a basis for American intervention. But on March 6, the State Department Legal Advisor warned that in the present situation, the facts did not justify American intervention at this time. At a National Security Council meeting later that day,

Allen Dulles indicated that intelligence now expected a government counteroffensive against the Sumatran rebels. The government had carefully chosen the troops it would use, and among them were some very good fighters. Eisenhower interjected that if the Sumatrans had a few good planes, they should be able to throw back the invasion. Allen Dulles expressed some regret that the Jakarta government had *not* bombed the oil installations.

His brother still thought it possible that we could move in. He explored the possibility of landing two Marine battalions to secure the Sumatran oil fields. (On March 9, he virtually endorsed the rebellion at a press conference.) The Jakarta government insisted on getting foreigners away from the area to remove any excuse for intervention; it had decoded messages between the rebels and the Americans.

Whether Eisenhower would have authorized a Marine landing, on any operations beyond evacuating Americans and other foreigners, and/or securing the oil installations—although that alone would have seriously interfered with the Jakarta government's operations—is unclear. For that matter, it is by no means certain that Secretary Dulles would have favored this in the end. He was, usually, hypercautious about America's legal position, which, as the Legal Advisor had pointed out, was weak; and soon he was to conclude that it had been a bad idea.[9]

The Americans had already been finding it hard to supply the rebels. Polish refugee crews who had worked for the CIA for years now flew C-54s to bring in supplies but were discontented.

On March 12, the central government's counteroffensive got underway. Apparently it was rushed to forestall any American landing. Although the government's air force was largely sidelined by lack of spare parts for its obsolete American-built planes—Soviet jets had not yet been unloaded—it mustered most of its remaining aircraft—ten P-51s, four B-25s, and twenty-six C-47s—for the operation. Five battalions of paratroops and marines were moved to an advance base on Bengkalis island, off eastern Sumatra. Two companies of paratroops dropped onto Pekanbaru airfield, which was lightly held, the rebels having expected a direct attack on Padang in the west. The government forces advanced from the east coast to secure the oil installations and the camps where foreigners were sheltered. Rebel plans for scorched-earth actions against the oil installations, to offer an excuse for foreign intervention, were not executed. The offensive ended any possibility of open American military intervention, and deterred Barlian from going over to the rebels. Things might have been different had the rebels had an air force; as Nasution admitted in 1971, "Air cover was critical. If Sumatra had gotten air cover we would have been finished."

Allen Dulles admitted, on March 13, that the government had acted with unexpected rapidity. The Embassy in Jakarta and the CIA men on the spot quickly observed the disastrous turn of events. The Embassy concluded that the Padang regime was fast losing, and had been, in fact before the counter-offensive. A belated successful rebel coup at Medan in northern Sumatra on March 16 was quickly reversed by the central government. On March 20, Allen Dulles told the National Security Council that there was little "contact fighting" on Sumatra. The focus of American operations now turned to providing the Permesta rebels with an air force. A retired U.S. Air Force officer, Lt. General Barnes, a member of the CIA Board of National Estimates, was to serve as advisor to the rebels. They were supplied with P-51 fighters, with a pair of Filipino pilots, and B-26B bombers from mothballed reserves in the Philippines and Taiwan, Some of the Poles who had been flying supply planes returned to fly them, but were dissatisfied and left after one plane was lost while taking off for a strike on the central government air base at Makassar. Later, Americans were recruited to fly the B-26Bs.

The Dulles brothers were more stubborn about carrying on the struggle than others, but even they were getting cold feet. On April 15, the Secretary of State told Eisenhower that it was unlikely that the Sumatran rebels could win without overt outside support; their willingness to fight hard had to be demonstrated before they got that. He recommended against landing U.S. forces to protect American lives and property on Sumatra. It would trigger a "very adverse reaction." The next day, there was a new reverse. The central government mounted a major amphibious and airborne landing and retook Padang. The rebels had lost their capital on Sumatra; the PRRI hastily moved to the Celebes. By April 24, Allen Dulles was reporting that rebel resistance had practically collapsed in the previous week. In May, the Sumatran rebels fell back on guerrilla warfare, which did go on for three years. On May 4, the Secretary of State told the British that the Sumatran rebellion had "pretty well folded up," it had been a lamentable performance. (Eisenhower had already said much the same thing in a letter to Prime Minister Macmillan on April 24.) In response to a question from Selwyn Lloyd, Dulles sharply rejected open intervention— it would have "the most disastrous consequences for us throughout the Far East." To top off the Administration's troubles, American aid to the rebels was increasingly an open secret.[10]

There seemed, however, another way out. The Java government seemed to want a rapprochement, and the Americans realized that the Communists were by no means as powerful on Java as had been supposed—at least not yet. As early as March 19, Sukarno had met the new American Ambassador, Howard Jones, assuring him that he rejected Communism, although he had been impressed by the economic advance of China, and tried to play up to the Americans. That may have been, and probably was, prompted by fear that the Americans would go farther in helping the rebels, but at least suggested that Sukarno was not totally hostile. Other figures, in and out of the government, like Hatta, stressed to the Ambassador that the Communists were not all that strong; the army would restrain them and they were nowhere near seizing power. Jones, on April 15, informed the hardline Assistant Secretary Walter Robertson that the government was clearly opening the door to a rapprochement, we had to make some gesture of support for the Indonesian army. He argued that the policy of backing the Padang rebels, as a lever to relieve the situation on Java, had in fact worked. He noted that his British and Australian counterparts concurred. The Joint Chiefs of Staff came to a similar conclusion by April 18, the rebels would be defeated without U.S. military help, and absent that, we must seek other means to prevent the Communists taking over all of Indonesia. But the Indonesian army under Nasution would be an anti-Communist force and they recommended an approach to him.

The Indonesian government used its own "stick," embarrassing the Americans and their allies. By May, it was protesting against aid to the rebels, although diplomatically referring, at first, only to the Chinese Nationalists. Prime Minister Djuanda and Foreign Minister Subandrio, on May 6, warned Jones that they knew very well that the United States was involved. They made clear that they realized the Communist danger, but any plan to "save" part of Indonesia by splitting it away from the country would just play into Communist hands. Jones and the military attaché met General Nasution on May 8. They, and later American visitors, were favorably impressed by the General. Jones concluded on May 12 that currently a military stalemate existed. The government could not subdue the rebels if the latter continued to get foreign support, but the rebels could not win without massive foreign backing. If they got that, the government would accept more Communist bloc help, and foreign "volunteers," and a major conflict would develop in which the United States would be regarded as an enemy by most Indonesians, be branded as an aggressor in the UN, and the Soviets would be established as an ally of Indonesia. Jones suggested pressures and inducements for a settlement involving aid to the Indonesian army. Dulles was agreeable, although preferring some sort of cease fire, and government actions against the Communists as a prerequisite. But the Indonesian government flatly rejected that; the rebels must be crushed, and the United States should exercise its influence to stop external support for the rebels. But it offered to reorganize itself.

Although things had clearly not gone well, up to the last part of May, the Secretary of State was willing to keep aid flowing to the rebels, at least to hold them over the head of the Jakarta government.[11] As late as May 8, Allen Dulles reported that the Celebes rebels seemed to be enjoying some success. The latter, having acquired some air strength, planned a drive from Celebes to Java. They would first capture Balikpapan, then Banjermasin, on Borneo, and then take Jakarta. On April 27, they took an important air base on Morotai. They had some success, sinking a government gunboat on April 28 and hitting government air bases. But on May 11, the government launched a successful strike against rebel air force bases. On May 17, in an air strike on an airfield and convoy at Ambon, a B-26 flown by an American, Allen Pope, was shot down. He was captured. Contrary to orders, he had not been flying "sterile" and was readily identified.[12]

This concentrated the Dulles brothers' minds wonderfully. The Secretary told his brother that it was now necessary to prevent air strikes, "they were not a winning course." On May 18, aid to the rebels was terminated. On May 20, the Secretary of State publicly backed Jones' policy in a statement that pleased the Indonesian government. The United States agreed to supply Indonesia with surplus rice. Chiang Kai-shek wished to go on helping the rebels and even send forces to support them, but was dissuaded against this. As Jones and Admiral Stump urged, some military assistance was given to Jakarta after Dulles agreed to this on August 1. The Americans now switched over to supporting the Indonesian government and army, although Soviet armaments vastly outweighed the American contribution. Sukarno himself made friendly gestures toward the Americans and expressed concern with the Communists, which even convinced Ambassador Jones, at least for a time, although not John Foster Dulles. Sukarno told Jones on August 26, that he would send his son to the United States for education. The Indonesian government postponed the elections scheduled for 1959 for a year, an action estimated to be a reverse for the Communists.

At a review of Indonesian matters in the National Security Council on January 29, 1959, Secretary Dulles defended the American policies of first supporting the rebellion and then switching over to the Jakarta government. He thought that we had "played the game pretty well." Not surprisingly, the President, according to the minutes, was "not wholly convinced."[13]

Allen Pope was tried and imprisoned, but quietly given an early release in August 1962. The Indonesian civil war sputtered on for several more years, although the rebels were reduced to guerrilla action on Sumatra and northern Celebes. Although there were attempts at negotiations, despite the Jakarta government's earlier resolve, the government's poor policies, its purging of local officials and replacing them with outsiders or local Communists, and misbehavior by government troops, helped keep the war going. The rebels were able to buy supplies and smuggle them in from Singapore, while the Celebes forces got some aid from Taiwan. Fighting did not entirely end until 1962.[14]

The American and British intervention had been badly handled in several respects. As a State Department review in 1959 noted, the Administration's policies had been based on a misunderstanding of the situation in 1957–1958. It had underestimated the strength of anti-Communist forces on Java, and overestimated the rebels' capabilities and the extent to which they were unified by anti-Communist sentiments.[15] Specifically, the Americans, or most of them, had assumed that the army was less anti-Communist than it was, underrated the strength of residual anti-Communism in Sukarno's government, and Sukarno's flexibility—at least in the short run, as well as the loyalty, however unmerited,

Sukarno still commanded. Later, the Americans had underestimated the speed of action of the rebels, and then of the government's response.

However, although they proved weaker than expected, the rebels may not have been doomed to failure. Had they won over the South Sumatran command, with its control of Indonesia's richest area and strategic location, the rebellion might have ended very differently. Had the Western powers acted faster, with more resolution, they might have provided the rebels air cover, making the government counteroffensive impossible. A limited overt American intervention on Sumatra, which seems to have been all the American government ever contemplated, would have seriously complicated things for the Jakarta government, although also likely enraging Indonesian opinion.

The actual results, despite Jones and Dulles' rationalizations, were quite disastrous. Sukarno had made a zigzag, not a permanent change. Support for the rebellion backfired, helping him discredit the remaining moderates. Since some of their members had taken part in the rebellion, the Socialist and Majumi parties were restricted, then, in 1961, dissolved. Sukarno pushed ahead with "guided democracy," while the Communists and the army were strengthened. Sukarno played them off against each other; but over time he increasingly favored the Communists. In 1961 he announced that he was a "Marxist"—by which he probably meant "Marxist–Leninist"—and the Soviets classed Indonesia as a "national democracy"—their term for a special, transitional, radical anti-Western regime that might be transformed into an orthodox Communist regime by a sort of gradual conversion. The economy continued to decline; it was kept afloat only by Western aid. The American government tried to win Sukarno's friendship, but this was a complete failure, although the Kennedy Administration was to carry this policy to insane lengths. It dropped neutrality in the New Guinea dispute to force the Dutch to give Sukarno West New Guinea, and continued to aid Sukarno even when he launched a war against the new Malaysian Federation in 1963. Indonesia seemed on its way into the Soviet orbit, then, as the Soviets and Chinese fell out, into that of China instead. Sukarno finally made the Communist leader Aidit his political heir. The army showed little resistance until 1965 when an attempted coup by army leftists—possibly not wanted by the Communists—narrowly failed to decapitate the army high command. Then the army, complaisant up to then, defeated the coup. Aidit was killed. As in Hungary in 1919, and Chile in 1973, forces that had done little to stem the tide of leftist totalitarianism earlier now reacted with unrestrained violence. A horrible massacre of real and supposed Communists, and the Chinese minority, began; while the Communists in central Java were able to massacre many of their enemies before they were crushed. Bloody private feuds were fought out amid all this. Several hundred thousand people may have been killed. Sukarno's "guided democracy" was succeeded by a harsh although economically more rational military dictatorship.[16]

Blundering as the Eisenhower Administration's policies had been, Dulles' assessment of Sukarno's basic course and its results had hardly been mistaken. Indonesia would have been spared a great deal of suffering, not to mention a narrow escape from Communist tyranny, had he been overthrown in 1958.

Notes

1 Alan Levine, *The United States and the Struggle for Southeast Asia 1945–1975* (Westport, CT: Praeger, 1995), pp. 1–15, 18–26, 28–29; Gary Hess, *The United States Emergence as a Southeast Asian Power 1940–1950* (New York: Columbia University Press, 1987).
2 Levine, *The United States and the Struggle for Southeast Asia*, pp. 12–14, 32–36; *FRUS 1952–1954, Vol. II*, pp. 833–835, 841; *Foreign Relations of the United States 1953–1954, Volume XIII* (Washington DC: Government Printing Office, 1982), pp. 949, 1220–1223, 1224, 1257, 1265–1266, 1280–1281, 1431–1445, 2268–2269, 2391–2392, 2419; *FRUS 1952–1954, Vol. XIV*, pp. 545–547, 720–726, 772; *Foreign Relations of the United States 1952–1954, Volume XVI* (Washington DC: Government Printing Office, 1981), pp. 474, 485–486, 720–726, 772; John Prados, *The Sky Would Fall* (New York: Dial Press, 1983). The oft-ignored point that the Eisenhower Administration did not in practice believe in the domino theory, or at least in its "pure" undiluted form, was early made by two acute early critics of the Vietnam War: Theodore Draper, *Abuse of Power* (New York: Vintage, 1967), p. 38 and Melvin Gurtov, *The First Vietnam Crisis* (New York: Columbia University Press, 1967), pp. 121–122. It was also noted in the *Pentagon Papers, Senator Gravel Edition, Volume I* (Boston, MA: Beacon, 1971), pp. 106–107.
3 *Foreign Relations of the United States 1958–1960, Volume XVII* (Washington DC: Government Printing Office, 1994), pp. 60–62, 196–197, 237, 307, 334; George M. Kahin, *Nationalism and Revolution in Indonesia* (Ithaca, NY: Cornell University Press, 1952); George M. Kahin and Audrey Kahin, *Subversion as Foreign Policy* (New York: The New Press, 1995), pp. 21–47, 62; Howard P. Jones, *Indonesia: The Possible Dream* (New York: Harcourt Brace & Jovanovich, 1971); Levine, *The United States and the Struggle for Southeast Asia*, pp. 40–46, 66–70.
4 *Khrushchev: The Last Testament*, pp. 353–374; Ra'anan, *The USSR Arms the Third World*, pp. 175–218.
5 Levine, *The United States and the Struggle for Southeast Asia*, pp. 69–70; Leslie Palmier, *Communists in Indonesia* (New York: Anchor, 1974), pp. 155–173.
6 *Foreign Relations of the United States 1955–1957, Volume XXII* (Washington DC: Government Printing Office, 1989), pp. 137, 140–141, 153–162, 204, 214, 290, 322–327.
7 *FRUS 1955–1957, Vol. XXII*, pp. 334–339, 351, 354, 357, 362–364, 368–373, 381–385, 406–407, 411–441, 426–427, 436–440, 527; Kenneth Conboy and James Morrison, *Feet to the Fire: CIA Covert Operations in Indonesia 1957–1958* (Annapolis, MD: Naval Institute Press, 1999), pp. 3–13, 15–23; Kahin and Kahin, *Subversion as Foreign Policy*, pp. 62–120.
8 *FRUS 1958–1960, Vol. XVII*, pp. 1–6, 16–24, 30–34; Conboy and Morrison, *Feet to the Fire*, pp. 36, 181 n. 12; Kahin and Kahin, *Subversion as Foreign Policy*, pp. 85, 120–127. The Kahins seem to predate U.S. aid to the rebels.
9 *FRUS 1958–1960, Vol. XVII*, pp. 35–36, 46–47, 49, 51–55; Kahin and Kahin, *Subversion as Foreign Policy*, pp. 129–151; Conboy and Morrison, *Feet to the Fire*, pp. 37–44, 67.
10 *FRUS 1958–1960, Vol. XVII*, pp. 65, 68, 80–81, 86–87, 97, 99–100, 107, 109–110, 121, 125, 128 n. 2, 138; Conboy and Morrison, *Feet to the Fire*, pp. 68–95, 108; Kahin and Kahin, *Subversion as Foreign Policy*, pp. 150–169.
11 *FRUS 1958–1960, Vol. XVII*, pp. 74–75, 83–84, 92, 95–96, 111–113, 120, 126, 127–137, 139–141, 149–152, 157–165, 167, 176–186.

12 Conboy and Morrison, *Feet to the Fire*, pp. 99–136; Kahin and Kahin, *Subversion as Foreign Policy*, pp. 170–172, 176–178.

13 *FRUS 1958–1960, Vol. XVII*, pp. 185–187, 189–190, 194–195, 204–206, 214–216, 227–228, 232–234, 239, 244–248, 252–256, 271, 274–276, 283, 329; Conboy and Morrison, *Feet to the Fire*, pp. 144–149, 160–162; Kahin and Kahin, *Subversion as Foreign Policy*, pp. 183–187.

14 Kahin and Kahin, *Subversion as Foreign Policy*, pp. 197–214; Conboy and Morrison, *Feet to the Fire*, pp. 148, 153–158.

15 *FRUS 1958–1960, Vol. XVII*, pp. 396–401.

16 Levine, *The United States and the Struggle for Southeast Asia*, pp. 71–77; Arnold C. Brackman, *The Communist Collapse in Indonesia* (New York: Norton, 1969); Palmier, *Communists in Indonesia*, pp. 185–264; J.A.C. Mackie *Konfrontasi* (Kuala Lumpur: Oxford University Press, 1974); John Subritzky, *Confronting Sukarno* (New York: St. Martin's Press, 2000); Matthew Jones, *Conflict and Confrontation in South East Asia 1961–1965* (Cambridge: Cambridge University Press, 2002). Cf. Kahin and Kahin, *Subversion as Foreign Policy*, pp. 217–230, for a whitewash of Sukarno and the Communists, which blames practically everything that went badly in Indonesia on the rebels and the United States.

10

THE RISE OF THE "MAXIMUM LEADER"

The Cuban Revolution, Castro, and Latin America

With seemingly much bigger problems elsewhere, the United States dealt, not too effectively, with the Cuban Revolution—an event that led, unexpected by either side in the Cold War, to the Soviets penetrating America's inner line of defense, and events virtually inconceivable in the 1950s, including the greatest of all Cold War crises, the Cuban Missile crisis. The victory of Fidel Castro, the "Maximum Leader" (*Lider Maximo*) as his hysterical supporters called him, and his movement not only produced a Communist regime in Cuba but set off bloody civil wars in several Latin American countries and shaped developments in post-colonial Africa. Castro, the least typical Communist ruler, was probably also the least tyrannical and bloody of any, but proved a deadly enemy of the United States, and did immense harm, not so much to Americans, although not for lack of trying, as to his own country, and less noted, other Latin Americans and Africans.

Understanding what was going on in 1958, and much later, would be hindered by an ideological fog, partly generated by Castro and his admirers—some of which eventually confused them as well. Apart from a general misunderstanding of Latin America and its relations with the United States, it would often be imagined that Cuba was a typical Latin American country—terribly poor, underdeveloped, and horribly exploited by the United States; that Castro was originally a non-Communist radical, somehow driven into the possibly reluctant arms of the Soviets by the Americans, and that Cuba had experienced a "peasant revolution," in which a handful of rural guerrillas defeated a formidable army steadily backed by the United States.

None of this was true.

The general problems of Latin America were no secret in the 1950s: horrible poverty, exploitation, illiteracy, and an extremely high birthrate that complicated almost all other problems. Most of Latin America was not particularly rich in natural resources, while under 5 percent of its territory was good arable land, compared to 10 percent of the United States and Canada, and 37 percent of Europe. Much of what fertile land existed was misused. Most Latin American countries were extremely hierarchical, dominated by rural elites owning vast estates, dominating hapless tenants, often culturally different Amerinds, or even serf-like peons.

The frequent misleading use of the term "feudalism" to describe Latin America's *latifundia* and peasants was probably overly complimentary; the owners were probably more parasitic, oppressive, and less responsible than the average medieval nobleman. Free spending, they squandered money or invested it overseas, and did little to improve their estates. Farming fumbled on with outdated techniques.

Work was for Amerinds or lower-class trash. Latin American upper classes aimed to hold on to what they had, at all costs. Burke's insight that change was the means of conservation was alien to them. Many seemed almost to prefer being destroyed by revolution than to give up anything for reforms. Their mentality toward such matters, and work was neatly demonstrated in an incident in Peru in the late 1960s. When an American adviser tried to explain the "civic action" aspect of counterinsurgency—aiding peasants by building waterworks, schools, etc. to win them over from guerrillas—a Peruvian general angrily responded, "What does your ambassador think we are—a bunch of Indians?"

Upper classes paid little or evaded tax systems entirely: those systems often taxed necessities more than luxuries. Governments, usually dictatorships, either did little or were kleptocracies, plundering honest businessmen or bought by crooked ones. In Venezuela, the word "politician" had become a synonym for "embezzler of public funds." Governments often functioned as machines to manufacture unneeded administrative jobs for the educated minority—or miseducated minority, since Latin American schools tended to produce lawyers and students of the humanities instead of badly needed technical experts. Latin American armies were usually police forces for, and usually officered by, the upper class. They had, as Castro justly observed, more generals than Prussia for armies the size of Switzerland's.

In contrast to the United States and other overseas English-speaking countries, European (and Japanese) immigrants in Latin America tended to enter society near the top, and provided much of what business and middle classes existed. Economies tended to be dominated by the export of a few primary products, while the concentrations of population and what industry there was were split up into twenty widely separated, poorly connected enclaves. Modern industry was often of the "import-substitution" type, heavily dependent on protection and subsidy. Transportation, except in Argentina, tended to be poor, ports and rail lines built primarily to serve export trades.

Although many Americans, in the 1950s, liked to think that the Catholic Church was a strong bulwark against Communism in Latin America, this was based on a double misunderstanding. As France and Italy, the only Western countries with mass Communist parties, should have shown, Catholic countries were hardly immune to Communism, indeed the opposite argument could easily have been made. And the Church was actually weak in Latin America, as both radicalization in the late 1950s and 1960s, and mass conversion to evangelical Protestantism would show. The ratio of priests to population was very low, many communities had little contact with the Church, and many priests were foreigners (peninsular Spaniards and Italians) not particularly close to their charges. Many Amerinds, in some countries, were really pagans under a thin Catholic veneer. Although Latin America mostly lacked the hard-drawn color bar that still existed in part of the United States in the 1950s, there was a good deal of subtler prejudice and discrimination against people of mixed, Amerind, or African descent in most places.

In reaction to the prevailing conditions, Latin Americans veered toward at least a verbal radicalism, worshipping political solutions, and particularly hypostatizing "revolution." The myth of revolution as the cure for all social ills and the gateway to utopia that has afflicted the West, and much of the rest of the world, peaked in Latin America from the 1950s to the 1970s. The radicals' attitude toward work and wealth was closer to that of the traditional upper class than might seem at first sight, sharing the contempt for work and the "get rich quick" mentality of the conquistadors and the belief that wealth was not created but was the result of exploitation (an idea with some reality in the their societies).[1] The myth of revolution as the quick road to utopia, or just development, was just a new version of traditional thinking. Such people were first-class suckers for the idea, then common even in advanced countries, that Imperial Russia had been an underdeveloped country like those of Latin America, Asia, and Africa, and that the Stalinist pattern of industrialization was the answer to their problems.[2]

Such beliefs deeply affected Latin American attitudes toward the United States. The history of American military intervention in the Caribbean was deeply entangled, in the minds of Latin Americans and not a few North Americans, with the role of American investment. It was often assumed, and still is, that the interventions of the early twentieth century were aimed at protecting American investments. Many Latin Americans convinced themselves that foreign investment was a form of exploitation in which they were "robbed" when profits were exported and that foreign investment encouraged, or even caused, dependence on "monoculture" and the export of primary products. The mentality of all too many Latin Americans was illustrated by the Brazilian intellectual da Fonseca's "explanation" of why the standard of living was so high in the United States and so low in Brazil—it was because the United States robbed and pillaged the whole world.

Of course, if foreign investment was harmful, the United States and Canada should long ago have become deserts. While individual American businesses undoubtedly behaved arrogantly or corruptly, they generally treated their workers better than local employers did, and often reinvested profits locally. Without U.S. and other investment, Latin America would have been even poorer than it was.

American military intervention, although widely resented, had been limited in time and scope to some Caribbean countries between the Spanish–American war and the 1930s. It never extended to South America, and while the United States had a near hegemony in the Caribbean, it was, at most preponderant further south; indeed, it was probably not even that until World War II, Britain being the most influential power, at least in the "southern Cone," before then. Nor were the American interventions of 1900 to 1933 motivated by concerns for investment—which were sizable in Cuba, but insignificant in the rest of the Caribbean. Those interventions were initiated by liberal presidents, Theodore Roosevelt and Woodrow Wilson, for liberal and strategic reasons—to secure the Panama Canal and keep non-American powers, especially Imperial Germany, out; they were about the last people to undertake military operations to benefit big business. They were halted and largely terminated by the conservative, pro-business Republican presidents of the 1920s. Even the coarsely titled "Dollar Diplomacy" of the Taft Administration was designed to promote American political objectives, not benefit financial interests.

But, as Dana Munro has written,

> by 1921 after we had ourselves intervened by force in several Caribbean countries, and were ruling two of them under military occupation, we had aroused a resentment and fear throughout Latin America which still affects our relations with other American states.

He noted that "Few South Americans had any real sympathy for the Haitians and Dominicans, but many often disliked and distrusted the United States and were responsive to propaganda portraying it as a greedy and imperialistic power." And, although the United States did not install the Somoza and Trujillo dictatorships in Nicaragua and the Dominican Republic, those regimes—some of the worst in Latin American history—could plausibly be blamed on the preceding interventions. The seemingly firmly anti-intervention stance of the second Roosevelt's "Good Neighbor Policy" could either be ignored, or interpreted so literally that American actions based on Cold War considerations were misinterpreted as a complete repudiation of FDR's policy and a renewal of traditional imperialism. (In fact, though Roosevelt opposed intervention in most circumstances, he never entirely ruled it out—the first American war plan after the Nazi conquest of Western Europe in 1940 was for an intervention in Brazil, if needed to combat a pro-Nazi coup there.)

With the radicalization proceeding in the 1950s, many Latin Americans, like many in other underdeveloped areas, readily bought into the Leninist theory of imperialism, even if they did not swallow Communist doctrine as a whole; and it often served as a gateway to the latter. Many were convinced that, despite the record of American relations with Mexico since the 1920s, and American responses to the Bolivian revolution of 1952, and the Venezuelan revolution in 1958, that the United States would automatically oppose all revolutions, or even social change, in Latin America, and developed what Ernst Halperin described as a "vampire complex," a bigoted, pathological nationalism of resentment, blaming virtually all their misfortunes and failures on the United States, of an intensity even many Arabs and Iranians might have envied.

Cultural and racial factors complicated this. Old Protestant–Catholic conflicts and the difference in mentality between English and Spanish and Portuguese speakers, already alluded to, were serious sources of conflict. As Frank Tannenbaum put it, "our conflicts with the Latin Americans are not only of an economic or political but also of a moral nature. We treat them as inferiors, and can neither avoid nor disguise this fact." The real problem, of course, was that Latin Americans *were* inferior, and knew this at some level.

The racial contempt of too many Americans was often apparent, especially in the Caribbean, while the middle and upper classes often disliked American manners as too egalitarian! This was often reciprocated and complicated by the Latin Americans' own racial hierarchies, where those with the lightest skins were usually on top, while the prestige attached to a Nordic appearance in the United States both fascinated and offended the usually non-Nordic Hispanic upper classes.[3]

The policies of the Eisenhower Administration, although often caricatured out of recognition by some critics, did not improve relations with Latin America in the mid-1950s. The Administration did not really like the dictators common then, but seemed far too buddy-buddy with them, including some of the worst, notably Rafael Trujillo, a mass murdering tyrant of a sort uncommon even in Latin America, and Perez Jimenez of Venezuela, awarding the latter, and the dictator of Peru, "Legions of Merit." It was often blamed for blindly continuing the military aid programs begun by the Truman Administration (which Dulles actually disliked). Even conservative American observers were disgusted by the Administration's tolerance toward Trujillo.[4] Particular damage was done by the CIA's overthrow of the Arbenz government in Guatemala in 1954; the basic facts of what happened were soon well known in Latin America, and however distorted, were less so than the Eisenhower Administration's "cover story" for the operation. Nor could anyone pretend that the successor regime of Castillo Armas, which undid many badly needed reforms, was a good one. And, although the U.S. government had overthrown Arbenz for Cold War reasons—it believed, rightly, that Arbenz' government, often later whitewashed as a reformist social democratic movement, was a Communist regime—its actions were widely portrayed as being taken in the interests of the United Fruit Corporation. (That the Administration had "rewarded" United Fruit by slapping it with an anti-trust suit was widely ignored.) The Guatemalan episode convinced many Latin Americans that their worst fears of the United States were correct.[5]

All of this explains much of the reaction to the Cuban Revolution—although it did little, perhaps, to explain the revolution itself!

The Cuban Background

President Kennedy, in 1963, said "I think that there is not a country in the world, including the regions of Africa and including any country under colonial domination, where the economic colonization, the humiliation, the exploitation have been worse than those which ravaged Cuba."[6] This ridiculous statement was an extreme version of a widespread misconception. For Cuba's revolution took place in the country that departed furthest from the ills afflicting Latin America. Castro came to power in one of the richest, most developed countries of the region, and one of the best-off lands in the tropical world. The tragedy of Cuba in the 1950s was not that it was an impoverished, exploited, underdeveloped country, but a land that needed only a reasonably honest government and a few modest reforms to become a wealthy, fully advanced country.

Very heavy American investment—in the 1950s Cuba was the site of the second highest American investment in Latin America, estimated to total $776 million in 1958—and a preferred place in the American sugar market, and subsequent diversification away from overdependence on sugar had helped give Cuba the fourth best economy in Latin America. Cuba had an excellent transportation system. Some 80 percent of Cubans were literate, a good level by Latin American standards; most illiterates were in rural areas. By most indices, Cuba's economy and standard of living placed it quite close to the industrial countries; in Latin America only Venezuela (thanks to oil), Argentina and Chile had higher per capita incomes. Cuba's standard of living compared favorably with that of Spain, Poland and Hungary, was almost as high as that of Italy, and much higher than that of Japan in the 1950s. Despite the usual concentration of wealth, the lower classes were better off than those of almost any Latin American country, although, as usual in Latin America, there was a sharp difference between urban and rural living standards, and between Havana, which housed a sixth of Cuba's people, but received three fourths of industrial investment, and the rest of the country. Some 57 percent of Cubans lived in cities, and that proportion was rising. Cuba lacked great landed estates of the traditional sort, it was a land of modern-style plantations run on business lines. Cuba's economy depended not so much on a "monoculture" of sugar as on sugar as an export—sugar still provided a quarter to a third of Cuba's national income. But this was far less than had been the case earlier, and the economy was diversifying, with growing emphasis on other agricultural products and industry. (Republic Steel was about to open the first steel mill in Cuba when Castro came to power.) Moreover, the economy was being "Cubanized" in ownership: wholesale trades, railroads, and more and more of the sugar industry were Cuban-owned. Some 85 percent of the industry was Cuban owned by the late 1950s. By then, Cuba was not a true underdeveloped country at all, rather, it was "semi-developed," or, as some put it, an unevenly or inefficiently developed country.

But, precisely because of America's huge economic and cultural influence, Cubans were more aware of the deficiencies, than the successes of their country. They compared themselves, not to other Latin Americans, but to the United States, compared to which Cuba was indeed a poor country and a mess. (This was accentuated by heavy exposure to American television. Cubans had the second highest per capita ownership of TV sets in the world after the United States.) In reaction, at least some Cubans were highly nationalistic. Some, even after decades in exile in the United States, seethed with resentment at the American role in Cuba, and especially at the "Platt Amendment" attached by the early occupiers to the Cuban Constitution, and abrogated only in 1934, and the military interventions it had legally enabled in Cuba. Although those interventions had ceased by 1920, and objectively speaking did Cuba no harm, the Platt Amendment preyed on Cuban minds long after its death.

The sugar industry and tourism were afflicted by heavy seasonal unemployment. Cuba had few real peasants, but most tenant farmers and agricultural workers lived in poor conditions. Cuba's cattle ranches were not very productive. Rufo Lopez-Fresquet (Treasury Minister in 1959–1960) described Cuba's tax structure as "fantastic and idiotic." There was much tax evasion. Cuba's universities spewed out lawyers and would-be politicians—Fidel Castro was both—and too few managers and technicians. The Cuban government, long before Batista, was a corrupt spoils system. The swollen army was a political praetorian guard. It was not liked, respected, or officered by the upper class, but by lower-class parvenus. Indeed, the upper and middle classes had little control over the politicians. There was an invertebrate quality to Cuban society, indeed the Mexican observer Ramon Eduardo Ruiz suggested that there was no unified Cuban middle class, just a set of "middle sectors," much of which would wind up in Miami wondering what hit them.

Cuba had a color bar somewhat more like that in the United States than most Latin American countries. A quarter or more of the population was black. Although there were blacks in the upper class, and no legal discrimination, there was much informal discrimination. (This was not created by North American influence but was reinforced by it.)

The Catholic Church was very weak, even compared to other Latin American countries. Two-thirds or more of the priests were Spaniards. It has been said that Cubans were not religious, but superstitious. The Church had little hold on the white lower class, and less on blacks; the latter, and even many whites, were more attracted to Santeria.

Cuban politics were dirty, even by Latin American standards. Up to the 1930s, Cuba was ruled by a succession of corrupt civilian politicos, culminating in the tyranny of Machado. Thanks partly to American interference the effective replacement for Machado was a lowly military dictator, Fulgencio Batista, who ruled until 1944.

Batista's *first* regime was not particularly bad; it was not harsh, and even introduced some reforms. The lower classes liked him; he was one of them, and opposed racial discrimination. (He was a mulatto and part Indian.) He permitted the development of a strong labor movement, which came under Communist control until 1947–1948. He introduced a new constitution in 1940, a radical and rather ridiculous document promising reforms that would have been tough to carry out in Sweden. He was a firm ally of the United States; Cuba was one of the few Latin American countries to really contribute to the Allied cause in World War II.

Indeed, the country seemed to go downhill after he retired and was succeeded by men democratically elected. The governments of Grau San Martin (a hero who had been shut out of power by the machinations of the American diplomat Sumner Welles in 1933) and Carlos Prio proved utterly disastrous, crooked even by Cuban standards. It was crucial, to later events, that the democratic political parties were utterly discredited in the 1940s and 1950s. When Batista overthrew Prio on March 10, 1952, his coup was not especially unpopular among Cubans, and pleased American businessmen in Cuba. At first, many thought he could not be much worse than Grau San Martin or Prio.

That turned out to be a mistake. Batista had lost any sense of responsibility or standards. His second regime was unprecedentedly brutal by Cuban standards, even if it was not nearly as bad as that of Trujillo or the other Caribbean tyrants. He never regained legitimacy, at least in the eyes of the upper and middle classes (much of the lower class accepted, or even liked him), and he compensated by relying more and more on pure force. Most senior army officers owed their positions to Batista, who followed the advice of the Roman Emperor Septimus Severus, to enrich the army and let everything else take care of itself. The police lost all restraints; they simply split running drugs, vice, and gambling in Havana with the Mafia, which, Cubans found, was not composed of the upright family men depicted in the movies of Francis Ford Coppola (another reason for Cubans to dislike the United States, and more valid than most). Open opposition was crushed by torture, murder, even castration.

It was not Cuba's poverty, but other things, that produced the conditions from which Fidel Castro profited. As Lopez-Fresquet eloquently put it, "Castro is a freak, but he did not create himself. He is the fruit of Cuban soil. He was produced by immorality, cynicism and irresponsibility, by the corrupt, social, political, economic and spiritual forces within Cuba."[7]

The Castros

Fidel Castro may have been a freak, but he was a remarkable man in many ways. Born in 1927, he was the son of a poor Spanish immigrant who had become a rich landowner. Possessing an eidetic memory, highly intelligent, a man of action with enough vitality for ten men, a womanizer, and a professional class baseball player, he was a superb, if interminable, orator who oozed charisma. In September 1960, he gave a four and a half hour speech at the UN, generating an unprecedented amount of hot air even for that institution; and that was quite normal for him. Back home, in 1959, he once gave a *nine-hour* speech! In the English-speaking world, such performances might have put him in a mental institution, but he was a big hit with Cuban audiences. He proved one of the great demagogues of all time—as well as a superb actor, outstanding at fooling people both individually and en masse. But he differed markedly in personality from most dictators, mixing with people far more; well after gaining power he was highly approachable. Peasants would slap him on the back, and he would venture into fields and villages to work with, talk, and even listen to them. Or, at least, pretend to.

He seems to have picked up a particularly bitter hatred of the United States at an early age, perhaps from his father, but more certainly from his—right-wing!—Jesuit teachers. Trained as a lawyer at the University of Havana, he participated in the gangsterish Cuban student politics of the late 1940s, and became a moderately well-known political figure on the left wing of the Ortodoxo party before Batista's coup in 1952. He *seemed* to be a non-socialist radical populist, with a particular reputation for opposing racial discrimination. On that point, Castro's feelings were strong and sincere (his godparents—a more important relationship in the Hispanic world than elsewhere—were black), and while not important before 1959, proved more so in his later consolidation of power.

But Castro was not the moderate leftist he posed as. He had been converted to Leninism while at the University. He did not join the Cuban Communist Party (called the Partido Socialista or PSP—"Socialist Party" from 1944) for several reasons. Above all, apparently, he saw that it would be a political dead end. There was no chance that the Communists as such could take power in the forseeable future. And he disagreed with the PSP leaders on strategy and tactics, and apparently had no respect for them as individuals, an attitude they reciprocated. He never did get on well with them.

Castro was not a one-man band. Like Napoleon, he was just the most important member of a family to which he owed more than is generally realized. (Luckily, unlike the French Emperor, he was never in a position to reward his siblings with suitable satellite kingdoms.) Although the Castro family is often described as dysfunctional, and Fidel got along badly with his father, the Castro brothers got along well with each other. Fidel's younger brother—possibly only a half-brother—Raul, was a loyal lieutenant, an excellent guerrilla commander, and a better organizer and administrator than Fidel. Raul joined the Communist party in 1953. Unlike Fidel, and Ernesto "Che" Guevara, a romanticized figure whose importance has been generally overestimated, Raul got along well with the old-line PSP leaders. The oldest Castro brother, Ramon, was less important, but was also devoted to Fidel. Looking and sounding remarkably like Fidel, he may have impersonated him when it was convenient for the "Maximum Leader" to be in two places at once.[8]

Almost as soon as Batista seized power, many groups had, if ineffectually, plotted against him. Fidel Castro, and other young activists, dissatisfied with the slow or hesitant actions of the older political groups, favored more violent plans. Castro and others gathered a force for a coup to seize the Army's Moncada barracks at Santiago, Cuba's second biggest city, in Oriente province in the far southeast of the island. If successful, this would establish a base far from Havana, secure against immediate counterattack, from which Castro could operate away from the competition of other political groups, building up strength for a march on Havana if events in Oriente did not trigger a coup there.

The attack, on July 26, 1953, was a disaster. Many of the rebels were captured, and murdered after some had been brutally tortured; the atrocities of the authorities soon became known and enraged many Cubans. Castro, captured later, was spared for a trial, at which he was able to make his most famous speech, later printed, in a revised form, as "History will absolve me." He justified the revolt and put forward the basic program he presented as his aims until 1959—a return to the 1940 constitution (under the "guardianship" of the revolutionary movement), land and other reforms, including a better deal for small sugar plantations and profit sharing in big business. He advocated nationalizing the unpopular American-owned electric and phone companies but otherwise there was nothing "socialist" or even nationalist in his program. The widespread idea that the Cuban Revolution was based primarily on Cuban nationalism has little to recommend it, and the 20–30 Americans who eventually fought in Castro's movement never noticed much anti-Americanism either in it or among Cubans generally.[9]

Sentenced to fifteen years, he was freed in an amnesty in May 1955; by then Batista, feeling more secure, was in a position to placate moderate opposition. Castro contacted survivors of the Moncada attack and other oppositionists, but soon prudently left for Mexico. Negotiations by his representatives back in Cuba finally assembled a "26th of July Movement" under Castro (often abbreviated to M26-7 or just M26). Another anti-Batista organization, formed about the same time, by students, the Directorio Revolucionario (DR) became the most powerful rival/ally of the M26. It favored a different strategy. While the M26 envisaged a prolonged struggle, the DR leaders aimed to quickly decapitate the regime by killing Batista. But the DR and the M26 collaborated in attacks on Battista supporters in 1955–1956. Ex-President Prio formed a third, small organization, OA; Prio also helped finance M26. Trujillo, then feuding with Batista, backed Prio, who planned a landing in Oriente province.

Castro gained financing from many sources both in Cuba and exile. Helped by a Spanish Republican officer, Alberto Bayo, he trained men for a landing in Oriente to coincide with a general uprising there and attacks in cities by the DR. The expeditionary force would join the Oriente rebels to take the city of Manzanillo. If things went awry, Fidel's landing force would retreat to the Sierra Maestra to fight as guerrillas. A spy in Prio's OA tipped Castro off about Prio's plans, and the fact that Trujillo's navy had landed arms in Oriente to be picked up by the OA landing force. Castro planned to appropriate the cache for his own use.

In Mexico, Castro met Ernesto Guevara, an Argentinean trained as a doctor, who had become a convinced Leninist while in Arbenz' Guatemala. They became close friends, Guevara becoming Fidel's most important lieutenant next to Raul. He was a good guerrilla fighter, but his hatred for the United States was so hard to control that he caused the more cautious Castro brothers some problems. The only thing American Guevara could stand was the Garand rifle.

The War Begins

Castro's plans went disastrously, almost fatally awry. The local M26 command in Oriente and OA militants had finally peaceably divided Trujillo's weapons between them, but they were in bad condition. The uprising in Oriente flopped. Castro's voyage to Cuba proved a little less disastrous. Eighty-two men were jammed aboard the wooden motor yacht *Granma*, which was in bad shape. She was delayed by bad weather and a navigational error; those aboard were dreadfully seasick. The landing place proved poorly chosen. It was a swamp, and the men lost part of their equipment getting ashore on December 2, 1956. Batista's forces had been alerted in advance. They missed the initial landing, but soon overtook Castro's force, which fled into the Sierra Maestra after heavy losses. Only twenty survivors finally reached the mountains, one of the most rugged areas of Cuba, inhabited by the worst-off people on the island. All else having failed, Castro and the remnant of his force had to resort to lengthy guerrilla warfare from a rural base—which was anything but what he would have chosen. In fact, the true strength of his M26 movement was not even in the mountains, but the cities. It was from there that Castro's guerrillas would be sustained. Batista was nevertheless now beset on several fronts. He had had to cope with a coup plan by the decent elements in his army, and growing opposition in the cities.[10]

Castro rallied his men and successfully attacked a small army post on the coast, gaining food, arms and ammunition, which had been terribly short. The M26 guerrillas survived despite being betrayal by a local guide, and found the attacks of the Cuban air force nothing to worry about. They rarely hurt Castro's men, although occasionally killing peasants; even napalm bombs usually burned out harmlessly in the treetops. The guerrillas came to terms with the local peasants. The latter did not necessarily like them, at first, but Castro's men, while treating opposition ruthlessly, behaved well normally, while the army, in its rare offensive ventures, treated the "guajiros" brutally, making them into outright enemies. Nevertheless, guerrilla morale fell—Castro was down to eighteen men in February 1957. But he gained worldwide favorable publicity when Herbert Matthews of the *New York Times* editorial board (not its regular Cuban correspondent, the able Ruby Hart Phillips) was guided to the Sierra Maestra by the M26 city underground. Castro duped him into believing that he was much stronger and more successful than he really was. Matthews wrote that the revolt had already reached such proportions that it could not be suppressed. His reports made Castro a hero outside Cuba and, relayed back to Cuba, greatly encouraged all of Batista's enemies. The "llano" (plains) M26 city underground led with growing efficiency by Frank Pais got reinforcements and supplies to Castro. Castro attacked army outposts, then retreated, ambushing any pursuing force. The army was reluctant to go into the mountains.[11]

Meanwhile, the DR tried to kill Batista. On March 13, its carefully prepared attack on the Presidential Palace came very close to success, but was stopped with heavy losses. That tragedy was very lucky for Castro. Had the DR succeeded, he and his followers would probably have had little chance to play a decisive role in post-Batista Cuba. The DR's able leader, Jose Antonio Echevarria, a major rival, was killed, and the DR was weakened in relation to the M26 movement, while the attack's near success shook the Batista regime. And Castro's men inherited much of the DR's arms caches. When Prio's OA tried to land in Oriente in May to set up a second front in the Sierra Cristal range, it too suffered disaster.[12]

Castro continued hit and run attacks out of the Sierra Maestra against an almost inert army, which used poor tactics even when it did engage. Pais continued to get a stream of supplies and reinforcements into the mountains from Santiago, and got wounded men down to the city for treatment. Indeed, it was Pais who was dominating M26 until the government caught and killed him in July 1957—another bit of luck for Castro, at least in the long run, for the popular and anti-Communist Pais might have been a formidable rival. The Batista regime continued to fray. In September, a naval mutiny, supported by M26 and other rebels, briefly took over most of Santiago before army reinforcements arrived. In that month the DR's fortunes revived somewhat; it opened a second guerrilla front of its own in the Escambray mountains in central Cuba. A guerrilla group established a small base, supported by a force from Miami that brought in five tons of ammunition. The Escambray (later the center of anti-Castro guerrilla action in the 1960s) proved a fine base, under firm DR control by the summer of 1958. But the DR, unlike the M26, was badly split. Eventually the Escambray fighters, the "Second Front of the Escambray," broke away from the national organization.

Castro's forces expanded, establishing an armory to repair weapons and make bombs, mines, Molotov cocktails, and improved rifle grenades called "Sputniks." By February 1958 a small radio transmitter regularly broadcast from the mountains. The following month, Raul Castro started a second M26 guerrilla base in the Sierra Cristal in northern Oriente. Both the M26 and the DR, however, still envisaged victory coming not from the rural guerilla war alone, but from combining that with urban attacks, sabotage, and a general strike.[13] Rebel groups within Cuba roughly cooperated with each other, but attempts in 1957 to form a full-scale united front had fallen afoul of Castro. He had advanced a political program in the "Sierra Maestra Manifesto" in July, promising elections within a year of victory (they were never held) and calling for a civic-revolutionary front with a common strategy and tentative provisional government. In November 1957 Batista's foes concluded a "Miami Pact," but Castro soon repudiated the signatures of his representatives, on the grounds that the pact did not reject a possible interim military junta or U.S. intervention to end the civil war. He also claimed a special leading role for the M26, especially in maintaining public order and reorganizing Cuba's armed forces.[14]

American Policies

The U.S. government was beginning to make clear that it no longer backed Batista—if indeed it ever had, as opposed to just ignoring his crimes and failures and mechanically continuing earlier policies. One startling element—never dealt with by Castro's apologists, or indeed his bitterest enemies—was that the CIA, between October or November 1957 and mid-1958, actually helped Castro, providing him with at least $50,000![15] Both Castro and the CIA found it convenient to forget this transaction. Up to 1958, the rest of the U.S. government did practically nothing about the Cuban struggle.

Unfortunately, the American ambassadors in Cuba were not competent representatives of the United States. Both Ambassadors Gardner and Smith were political appointees of low caliber. Rufo Lopez-Fresquet commented,

> The deportment of these gentlemen provided Castro with all the examples he needed to convince the Cuban people of the evil intentions of U.S. policy in Cuba. The statements these former U.S. Ambassadors made before the Senate Internal Security Subcommittee in 1960 after they had time for reflection, constitute ample evidence of their incompetence.

Both liked Batista—Earl Smith was a bit more critical than Gardner—and thought his regime would last. Smith was sure that Castro was a Communist, but offered no proof other than Batista's word. Almost all the Embassy staff disagreed with and disliked Smith. Batista was not popular in the State Department— Undersecretary of State Robert Murphy described him as a "gorilla"—but he did not seem as bad as some other Caribbean tyrants—indeed he was not—and, up to late 1957, there was not great worry about the Cuban situation.

But the American government was disturbed by the growing violence and brutality, noting that Batista's use of American-made tanks, armored cars, and bombers against the naval mutineers violated the military aid agreement, according to which such weapons were to be used only with joint agreement and for "hemispheric defense," but the Defense Department, and Smith, favored continuing deliveries. A stab was made at having the United States act as middleman between Batista and his opponents to arrange a peaceful transition through elections, but the State Department (not Smith) soon concluded that Batista was acting in bad faith, and attempts by Smith to get a restoration of constitutional guarantees and free elections failed.

The State Department increasingly bypassed Smith, depending on the reports, highly unfavorable to Batista, of the new consul at Santiago, Park Woolam. Oscar Guerra, his predecessor, had already estimated that Batista was losing; and Secretary Dulles was worried by the growing indiscriminate violence of the government and its violation of its pledges. The Administration was impressed by the reports of the well-known war correspondent Homer Bigart, who reported Castro's growing strength. Bigart found little sign of anti-Americanism among the Sierra Maestra fighters, although he was suspicious of Guevara. The State Department doubted Batista would survive, and was under increasing pressure to halt arms shipments. An embargo was finally slapped on arms shipments in March 1958.

The State Department did not necessarily like Castro. Its officials did not think that he was a Communist, but feared that he might be or come under Communist influence. They were more concerned by his perceived irresponsibility and greed for power. Most worry about him, in 1958 and for some time after, revolved around the possibility that he would be just another non-Communist dictator, or that M26 would end up fighting rivals for the succession to Batista; the civil war would go on, or Cuba would become as chaotic as Haiti. Some officials favored following up feelers from anti-Batista groups, and pushing for a military coup against Batista to cut short the current civil war, saving lives and perhaps avoiding the dangers they foresaw. But, as the diplomat Wayne Smith concluded later, "we talked a bit about what we ought to do but in fact we did nothing." Given the horrendous difficulties in the rest of the world in 1958, it would have been surprising had the United States followed a vigorous course in Cuba.[16]

To Batista's enemies, it seemed, for a time, that the end was very near. On April 9, they launched the long-planned general strike, which, coupled with large-scale sabotage, would, it was hoped, quickly destroy Batista's regime.

The strike fizzled. Batista's men were ready, while many people were afraid to take part. The urban wing of M26 was devastated. That disaster led to the final concentration of leadership in Castro's hands. His base in the Sierra Maestra became national headquarters. The rural guerrillas, although still supported by vigorous sabotage in the cities, would now spearhead the movement.[17]

Entente with the Communists—and a New War

The Communist party now changed its attitude to the anti-Batista struggle—if anything, it seemed to be chasing Castro. Previously, although Raul Castro had been a PSP member since 1953 and Guevara had joined in 1957, and the party was nominally against Batista, it had opposed everything Castro, and the rest of the anti-Batista opposition did. It had bitterly criticized the Moncada attack, the M26 movement, Castro's expedition to Cuba in 1956, the guerrilla war, and the general strike, as well as the DR attack on Batista's palace.

It had even betrayed DR members to the police. But in February 1958 it began talking of armed struggle.

In the spring of 1958, probably May, Communist delegates visited the Sierra Maestra and came to an agreement with Castro. Some of Castro's biographers, notably Tad Szulc, maintained that it was then that he decided to install a Communist regime after victory. But, he had probably never intended to do anything else; this just marked his coming to terms with the orthodox PSP leaders, who now let individual members join M26, especially Raul's "Second Front" in northern Oriente, and the Party formed a small guerilla group of its own in the Yaguajay area of Las Villas province in central Cuba.

If Castro had ever had any doubts about what he would do after victory, they may well have been removed, not by the PSP leaders, who he continued to regard with contempt, but the world situation, of which he was well aware. From his point of view he was not only joining the right side, but after Sputnik, the winning side. And, whatever Castro himself thought, the general perception of the way the world was going on in the "missile gap" era undoubtedly affected the way other Cubans thought in the late 1950s and the beginning of the 1960s; the tide of world events, at the time, in Cuban eyes, favored the Communist side.

Within the M26 movement, the mask of nominal opposition to Communism was now slipping, disturbing some, notably Mario Llerena, the M26 representative abroad, who left the movement in August 1958. While hiding his deal with the Communists, Castro finally agreed to a unity pact with all other anti-Batista movements, signed in Caracas on July 20, on his terms. The M26 got considerable money from ex-President Prio; it was now the dominant element in the anti-Batista opposition.

Castro seems to have come to an even more momentous decision than just the sort of regime he would impose in Cuba. Fantastic as it seems, he planned war against the United States. In a letter to his close friend, Celia Sanchez, he grumbled about attacks by Batista's American-built B-26 bombers, which he blamed on the Americans (typically, the arms embargo, CIA aid, and his own great and growing popularity in the United States ricocheted off his ideology). He declared

> I have sworn that the Americans will pay very dearly for what they are doing, When this war has ended, a much bigger and greater war will start for me, a war I shall launch against them. I realize that this will be my true destiny.

But how could he wage war against the United States?

Castro may already have been thinking along the lines perceived later by Lopez-Fresquet, the last moderate to leave his government. Lopez-Fresquet thought that Castro believed, when he took power, that the United States would invade Cuba with its own forces; "Most of his moves were made with this idea in mind." He prepared for this by transferring military camps from cities to safe areas in the countryside and caching weapons and supplies in mountain caves. He was anxious to import as many weapons as possible, making a big arms deal with Belgium for rifles, ammunition and grenades. (Many of these weapons wound up being sent to the Venezuelan Communists.) Indeed, his economic policy was dictated by the expectation of early war, and aimed at wringing every possible immediate dividend from Cuba's economy to win the maximum popular support before the Americans came, at the expense of normal, sensible long-range planning. Then he would wage a guerrilla war against the occupiers, which he expected to rouse all Latin America against the gringos, and, eventually, spread Communism, Castro-style, over the whole region. (Che Guevara alluded to these ideas in his famous book on guerrilla warfare: he seems to have expected the Americans to use *Trujillo* as a spearhead for their forces.)[18]

Such a strategy also helps explain the early, clumsy expeditions sent by Castro against the Dominican Republic, Nicaragua, Haiti, and Panama in the spring of 1959. Had they touched off guerrilla wars in those countries, they would, Castro may have thought, have forced a dispersal of American efforts, sparing Cuba from an overwhelming concentration of American forces and hastening the Latin American revolution. There is some evidence that such ideas were already in Castro's mind in 1958. Manuel Ray, the head of the M26 city underground, was disturbed to learn, in September of that year, that Castro planned to maintain a big army after victory.[19]

No one has ever accused Castro of thinking small.

First, however, he had to defeat Batista, and victory did not seem near after the general strike misfired. Raul Castro, having successfully established an effective base in northern Oriente, moved from the Sierra Cristal north to the Guantanamo mountains, where there was more forest cover and game, and he was assisted by Cubans and Americans working for local mining companies and wealthy landowners. It was now Batista, who, after a year and a half, finally launched the government's only major offensive of the war. It came close to finishing off Fidel Castro, and probably would have, had Batista and his commanders shown a grain of common sense. General Eulogio Cantillo, the most able and decent of Batista's generals, urged allotting twenty-four infantry battalions, supported by light tanks, to the offensive—fourteen battalions to penetrate the Sierra Maestra, the rest to remain in reserve for finally crushing the opposition. Batista would only provide fourteen battalions. Cantillo planned to cordon off the mountains to shut off Castro's supply lines, then attack from the north and northeast to force Fidel into relatively open country where he would be crushed. But many of the 12,000 government troops were barely trained, and influenced by anti-Batista sentiment. But Batista insured the plan would fail by dividing the command between Cantillo and the incompetent General Chaviano—the son-in-law of Batista's top army commander, being given a second chance after having been fired previously. He and Cantillo were not even on speaking terms. Castro had just 300 armed guerrillas under his direct command. He planned to let the Army move forward and counter it with hit and run and ambush operations.

It took the Army over a month to get into position; serious operations began on June 28. Castro, supported by more and more actions by the revived llano, made the Army pay heavily for its advance, inflicting several local defeats and capturing much equipment and supplies. His initial plan having flopped, Cantillo cobbled together a new one. He now planned to have his best battalion, the 17th, land at La Plata in the east, then push inland to attack Castro's forces east of the Turquin peaks. A second landing would take place west of the Turquin peaks while Castro was tied down facing the first landing force, and a battalion would strike inland, north, to cut Castro's retreat. Castro would be trapped, or forced to abandon his old Sierra Maestra base. Cantillo was arbitrarily forced to substitute a less prepared unit, the 18th Battalion, for the first landing on July 11. The 18th Battalion pushed inland, where it was ambushed, then encircled. Cantillo went ahead with the second landing, while also sending two companies at La Plata to relieve the 18th Battalion. He now hoped to encircle Castro by using the two landing forces and the 17th Battalion, coming from the north. The first attempt to land a relief force at La Plata on July 15 was driven off by heavy machine guns. Later on, reinforcements did land, but were ambushed as they pushed inland on July 17, and again two days later. The trapped 18th Battalion surrendered on July 21. Castro's men were now very well armed—with captured equipment. Cantillo now designed a new plan, to tempt Castro into pursuing the 17th Battalion, draw him into an ambush, and surround them. Cantillo decided that going into the mountains would be a mistake; apart from the low morale of his men, most of the locals were on Castro's side and his movements would be instantly detected.

The Cuban General Staff, however, insisted on trying to repeat Cantillo's earlier failed plan. But before their scheme could be tried again, Cantillo got an opportunity to try to implement his own. Castro, hoping to trap and destroy another enemy force, tried to catch the 17th Battalion, which was retreating toward Las Mercedes, planning to destroy it, then ambush and trap the 11th Battalion, under one of Batista's better officers. The latter suffered heavy losses in an ambush on July 27, but took a good position atop a hill. There, it beat off Castro attacks, inflicting heavy losses. Fidel's subsequent moves brought him into the trap planned by Cantillo. The 17th Battalion too was ambushed, but this was only the start of a fierce struggle on relatively flat ground. The Army closed in on Fidel, who was saved by relief attacks by Guevara. He was still in a bad position when he called for truce talks with the Army on August 6. Batista was skeptical, but at Cantillo's urging, let the talks go ahead. Castro won time, and divided the Cuban Army, which was less and less enthusiastic about Batista. Cantillo's negotiators proposed to Castro that a military junta be formed, leading to a cease-fire and elections. Castro accepted this (although it contradicted his own program), Batista did not. The guerrillas slowly slipped out of the ring. The Army's offensive had failed disastrously, with heavy losses. This was the beginning of the end for Batista.[20]

Chaviano's forces failed to effectively fight Raul Castro's men; they sometimes attacked villages and killed innocent peasants. Raul, however, exasperated by air attacks, precipitated an incident that greatly angered some in Washington, who were getting a bit irritated at M26 sabotage operations, which some thought seemed to be disproportionately directed against U.S.-owned property, notably the U.S. government-owned and operated Nicaro nickel plant. The only "strategic" installation in Cuba (it was the source of 10 percent of the non-Communist world's nickel), it perhaps was a special target, Raul's gesture of support for the Soviets. Raul might have precipitated outright American intervention had the U.S. government's attitude been anything like what its critics imagined. He was infuriated by a report that the Americans had refueled a Batista plane or planes at their Guantanamo base. Further, despite the arms embargo they had in fact delivered 300 rocket warheads to Batista—on perverse legalistic grounds, as replacements for defective warheads delivered in 1957! In fact, the U.S. military and Ambassador Smith still wanted aid to the government, and actually got approval for the delivery of ten T-28 trainers to the Cuban air force.

On June 26–27, Raul Castro's men kidnapped some fifty Americans and Canadians, mostly civilians working for local mining operations and wealthy landowners and a United Fruit operation, but twenty-four were Navy- and Marine-enlisted men who had been returning on a bus to Guantanamo. Raul announced on June 30 that the captives would go free if the Americans halted all deliveries of equipment to Batista, promised that Batista planes would no longer refuel at Guantanamo, and that the United States would stop Batista using American equipment against the rebels. The latter would have been hard to do, although the American government had noted that Batista had once again violated his military aid agreement with the United States by using an

American-trained and equipped battalion against the rebels. Many in Washington hit the roof. The Chief of Naval Operations, Admiral Burke, who thought all of Batista's opponents were at least allied to Communists, wanted to send a Marine regiment in to help free the hostages, and resume aid to Batista. Secretary Dulles refused to "pay blackmail" (but the T-28 shipment was canceled) and denied that the United States was letting Cuban planes use Guantanamo. (It was later admitted that one bomber had refueled there in an "emergency" and that transports delivering the rocket heads had landed there.) Eisenhower insisted that the hostages be freed "instantly" but it took Consul Woolam two weeks of talks to get all of the captives freed, during which there was an effective cease-fire that greatly aided Raul Castro's command. The prisoners had been well treated, and were favorably impressed by their captors. Some were even inclined to stay and fight alongside them![21]

The episode guaranteed the permanent hostility of American military leaders, but provoked only a short, mild reaction in the American press. Later, American civilians were occasionally kidnapped by rebels and other efforts made to extort money from American businesses, while incidents over the water supply for Guantanamo irritated the Eisenhower Administration, but these things had no effect on American public opinion, which became steadily more pro-Castro.

Batista's regime was visibly cracking. The economy, still good in 1957, was declining. His cruelty and failures had now alienated almost everyone, and the lower classes were more and more rallying to Castro, beginning to supplant his originally largely middle-class base. Neil Macaulay, a U.S. Army veteran who had joined the M26 guerrillas already in the Pinar Del Rio area in western Cuba in the latter part of 1958, found the peasants there almost unanimously in favor of Castro. Most of the fighters were from the lowlands, but by December, so many peasants were eager to join up that there were not enough weapons for them. In contrast to the "nationalist" explanation of the Cuban revolution, he observed no anti-American feeling. (The remarkable career of William Morgan, an American adventurer who became a leader of the "Second Front of the Escambray" is even harder to reconcile with that version of the revolution.)

Castro now started what became his final offensive. While his main forces would gradually encircle and take Santiago, "Column 2" under Camilio Cienfuegos ("columns" numbered 150 men) left the Sierra Maestra on August 20. It was to march west all the way across Cuba to Pinar del Rio and establish a front there. Guevara, starting August 30, was to lead Column 8 to Las Villas and cut Cuba in half. By this time, it was possible for Guevara's force to make the first part of the trip by truck; but afterward the column ran into the tail end of a hurricane, crossing flooded areas and permanent swamps, attacked by hordes of mosquitoes. The Army tracked the guerrilla movement for once, and forced Guevara to retreat. Some of the units he faced were relatively well led, but he evaded encirclement and got into the Forrestal forest. Cienfuegos' column managed to bypass a whole series of attempted ambushes, but Guevara was nearly trapped, and forced to retreat again, into miserable swamps. After a week, his column slipped through the Army lines, reaching Las Villas on October 7 in bad shape. Cienfuegos was ordered to wait for Guevara in Las Villas instead of proceeding west, until Column 8 recovered. Guevara organized a united front of the M26 forces and the DR in November. Column 2 contacted the Communist guerrilla force that had been fighting in Las Villas, but found it too poorly armed to be of use. He soon rearmed them; the Communists accepted the M26–DR agreement on strategy. Local sugar workers and peasants were mobilized to support the guerrillas. In the end, Cienfuegos never did reach Pinar del Rio; Batista's forces collapsed too fast.

Batista nominally had 40,000 troops and 30,000 police against 7,000–8,000 M26 guerrillas and nearly 2,000 belonging to other groups. Many more rebels could have been put into the field had arms been available; Raul Castro alone had 1,000 men waiting for weapons. Sabotage and guerrilla attacks were paralyzing transportation: the Army was drained by steady desertions.

Castro now planned to have Guevara and Cienfuegos take Santa Clara in Las Villas and cut Cuba in half; then he would take Santiago and its important arsenal, and then move on Camaguey province. The Santa Clara battle proved the decisive operation of the last stage of the war. The rebels were now well-armed, having some heavy weapons, although outnumbered by the 6,000 regular Army men defending Santa Clara on the central highway, and four outpost towns around it, supported by tanks and several hundred police. But the Army was utterly demoralized. The rebels planned to take nearby ports on the north and south coasts—Caibarren and Cienfuegos—to prevent reinforcement by sea, then the outpost towns, then Santa Clara itself, Cienfuegos closing from north of the city, Guevara and the DR forces from the south. The rebels were worried about facing tanks—they had just one bazooka, and no rockets for it. Luckily for them, Batista had once again put Chaviano in command! (He changed his mind later, replacing Chaviano but too late to have any effect.) Some of the outer garrisons put up only token resistance before surrendering, while the police often showed more fight than the soldiers. One Army battalion, holding Yaguajay, under an able officer, put up a terrific fight against Cienfuegos that lasted for eleven days, although, for once the rebels outnumbered the Army, with 450 men to 250. The rebels even got the support of a homemade tank assembled by the eager workers of the Narcisa Sugar Mill, a D-8 Caterpillar tractor armored with steel plate and armed with machine guns, but it was damaged by a bazooka hit and forced to retreat. Guevara had to reinforce Cienfuegos. On the evening of December 30, the Army force, almost out of ammunition, surrendered. This showed what might have happened to the rebels had the Army in general fought seriously. More characteristic of Batista's men, the Navy surrendered the ports even before the rebels entered, going right over to them. Cienfuegos' forces were still tied down when Guevara decided to strike Santa Clara without him. He had just 500 men, while Batista had sent an armored train, carrying

18 armored cars and 600 men, with the best available weapons and equipment to repair the damaged transportation system, to reinforce Santa Clara. It was typical of this stage of the war that the train was an element in a military plot—or possibly, two different plots—to get rid of Batista, and that 50 men, and finally the train commander, deserted before it reached Santa Clara. The rebels tore up the tracks with a bulldozer, and captured part of the train; the rest of it surrendered later. As the rebels advanced on December 30, they came under "air attack"—most of the pilots, however, just dumped their bombs in the sea. When the rebels entered the city, the Army mostly gave up. Tanks just drove away before the rebels attacked. Only the police station, defended by cops and a few soldiers, resisted strongly, even counterattacking until their ammunition ran out. The main army force of 3,000 men just surrendered.

Meanwhile, Fidel had kept Santiago under siege. On December 14, the Army tried to get a column out of the city to break the ring, but it was ambushed with heavy losses, while other units refused to fight. In the end, the city fell without a fight.[22] Between rebel victories, his officers scrambling to buy their way out, and American pressure, Batista gave up. Castro's triumph was complete, despite several attempts to frustrate him.

The tone of President Eisenhower's remarks at the National Security Council meeting on October 30 suggests that he was not paying close attention to events in Cuba. The State Department had long regarded Batista as doomed, but as late as November 24, the CIA estimated that the Cuban struggle would go on for several more months. It warned that any military junta replacing Batista would have to make a deal with Castro, otherwise the war would go on.

By December 16, a special National Intelligence Estimate ruefully concluded that things were moving faster than had been expected. In late November, the Administration had belatedly moved to try to get Batista to capitulate to a caretaker government of moderates, which might get U.S. military assistance to keep Castro out of power. Batista would get asylum in Florida. Once again Smith was bypassed (he wished to back Batista's puppet president, Rivo Arguero!) and the originator of the scheme, William Pawley, a businessman and political fixer who Eisenhower liked, was dispatched to persuade Batista, who refused to play. Finally Smith was ordered to just tell Batista to go. The dictator avoided seeing him for some days, but on December 17 Smith gave him the bad news. Coming from his most ardent supporter in the U.S. government, this seems to have registered, and, some time over the next few days, Batista decided to leave, although not without last attempts to pull strings and arrange things in Cuba for after his departure.

The CIA seems to have backed, or at least known and approved of, a plan by Cuban liberals to spring Colonel Ramon Barquin and other Army "puros" purged in 1956 from prison to lead an interim regime. Barquin was also a figure in Army high command schemes to strike a deal with the Maximum Leader. General Cantillo, commanding in Oriente, was told to reach an agreement with Castro, offering a coup, and a junta including Barquin as well as Castro. Castro refused this offer on December 28; instead, he suggested a joint Army-rebel operation to capture Batista before the latter fled Cuba. Cantillo doubted this was workable; in any case he had to consult with his colleagues. Castro alternatively offered to have Cantillo just take over the regular Army forces besieged in Santiago over to the rebel side, Cantillo refused that, and went to Havana. He reported to Batista, who dismissed the whole business. Cantillo was also viewed by the Americans as a possible leader of a junta to include Barquin, but he apparently got the idea of replacing Batista with himself. Batista then informed Cantillo, and his generals, on December 31, that he would leave in a few hours. Batista fled, with a fortune of several hundred million dollars—the equivalent of billions in today's money—and everything fell apart. His sudden departure surprised most Cubans, who had expected him to fight to the end, then kill himself. Cantillo finally brought Barquin from the Isle of Pines prison, he took command of the armed forces, and arrested Cantillo. Barquin pondered trying to "moderate" Castro's victory by threatening a last-minute battle, but ultimately realized that his "command" was meaningless. He peacefully handed the main Army base at Camp Colombia to Camilio Cienfuegos. After a triumphant march, Fidel Castro entered Havana on January 8, 1959.

The Soviets, observing Castro's rise with pleasure—the KGB had long taken a friendly interest in him—had just decided, on December 27, to give him ex-German World War II vintage weapons through Czechoslovakia. Batista had collapsed much faster than anyone, even Castro, had expected.

A rather belated report reached Eisenhower, on December 23, that there had been Communist penetration of Castro's movement. The President was irritated on hearing of this only at such a late date, but, while few in the Administration really wanted to see Castro take over—his behavior in 1958 had not made Washington love him—no one but Admiral Burke thought he was a Communist. Rather, he was suspected of being an incompetent big mouth, likely to run Cuba badly—at worst, a radical Caudillo, another Juan Peron. John Foster Dulles seems to have had even fewer misgivings than most, and approved quick recognition of the new Cuban government. He made it quite clear that Batista and his cronies were not wanted in the United States—they might have been reluctantly tolerated, had Batista given in earlier and more gracefully, but there was no reason to pay him off now. Ambassador Smith was unceremoniously dumped. An able liberal professional diplomat, Philip Bonsal, replaced him. Bonsal, and the Eisenhower Administration, did their best, despite misgivings to get along with Castro for the next year.[23]

During that time, Castro masterfully maneuvered to establish his dictatorship, destroying effective opposition, subordinating the old-line Communists, and remaining remarkably popular while shifting his base of support. While losing much of the middle class, he mobilized the lower class, much of which had been lukewarm until a late stage about the struggle against Batista. Without ever giving his opponents an opportunity to take a serious stand against him, he took a revolution originally aimed at restoring democracy and introducing moderate, long-awaited social reforms, and established a Communist regime. His personal popularity and moral ascendancy was critical. He was the ultimate national hero, sometimes actually compared with Christ, or identified with the saints of Santeria, and was beyond criticism. Even those who feared his brother, Guevara, and others did not, for a long time, let themselves doubt the Maximum Leader himself, or the goddess of "the Revolution." What the goddess was, and where she was going, was defined by Fidel. For many Cubans, the greatest fear was being, or being seen as, "counter-revolutionary." Gradually, to be anti-Communist was identified with being "counter-revolutionary," making it harder and harder to resist the Communist advance. Castro was aided by the quick recovery of the Cuban economy; in 1959, Cuban business did well. Only the American-owned power and phone companies were put under state control. (In Cuba, as in practically all Communist states, nationalization almost entirely followed, rather than preceding, establishment of the party dictatorship. Then, it was extraordinarily fast, faster than the old-line Communist leaders or the Soviets liked.) The wave of prosperity might have lasted even longer had Castro known more about economics, or had he not put Guevara, an even bigger ignoramus, in charge of the economy in November 1959, where he flopped badly. As already noted, Castro followed policies that would ensure prosperity for a time and especially pay off for the poorer people of Cuba, in the short run. The government's first reforms and development efforts genuinely made the poor, especially the rural poor and blacks, better off. A major effort was made against illiteracy. Probably, many adults learned to do little more than write their names, and read signs, but they knew their children, at least, would get a real education. A U.S. State Department study in December 1959 concluded that wage increases, price freezes, and reductions in rents and utilities prices had improved the living standards of most Cubans, although this could not be maintained indefinitely. In the end of course, Cuba's economy would be badly run even by Communist standards. Castro blew the equivalent of *several* Marshall Plans' worth of Soviet aid, while Cuba would be left more underdeveloped and sugar-dependent than in 1958.

Beginning in January 1959, Castro concerted policy in secret meetings with the Communist leaders. They had not been popular, but the Communists had 17,000 members and were much better organized than any other political force on the island. Many supporters who had fallen away in the late 1940s, or after Batista made the party illegal, returned to the fold. All this was covered by a smokescreen, as Castro professed to be just a "humanist" and made anti-Communist remarks for public consumption as late as May 1959. In private, he assured moderates in the government, as late as November, that he would crack down on the Communists at the right moment. He kept a facade of moderates in his government, taking the position of Prime Minister for himself in

February. He had quickly outmaneuvered the chief rival revolutionary group, the DR (its leader eventually joined the Communists) and maintained a monopoly of armed force for the M26. Colonel Barquin, the only potential leader from the old Army, was quickly, quietly exiled to a diplomatic post. Elections were pushed farther and farther into the future. On January 9, Castro decreed that they would be held in fifteen months, then a bit later, in eighteen months. By mid-March, they were to be held in two years, and, by the fall of 1959, were promised in four years.

Castro skillfully fostered and manipulated hostility to the United States. It was now that anti-Americanism, probably latent earlier, but not apparent, became a powerful sentiment. In the first months of his regime, some 550 people were shot for crimes committed during the Batista regime. (Possibly a few more were killed "unofficially.") Probably the vast majority were guilty, but the manner of trial and execution aroused some criticism in the United States and even some Latin American countries, even by some people who had backed Castro earlier. Although the Eisenhower Administration said nothing, Castro exploded, remarking that if the Americans did not like it, they could send in the Marines, and there would be "200,000 dead gringos." He also offensively compared the modest number of his executions to the death toll of Hiroshima and Nagasaki. Less noted, Castro became quite hostile to some of the top democratic leaders in Latin America, Jose Figueres of Costa Rica and Romulo Betancourt of Venezuela.

Castro's first major move to bring the economy, or a major part of it, under control was the agrarian reform law, which was much different from the land reform plans envisaged earlier. It put the whole agrarian sector under state control, and was a preparation for eventual collectivization, not distributing land to peasants or landless rural elements. This involved the first serious potential clash between "reform" and U.S. economic interests, but the American reaction was mild, merely expressing "concern" and insisting on prompt and effective compensation for any nationalized property.

Castro soon moved to smash the remaining moderates in his regime, skillfully turning even acts of resistance in his favor. Diaz Lanz, the head of the Air Force, after opposing Communist infiltration into the armed forces, fled to the United States in June 1959. But Diaz Lanz enraged Cuban opinion, when he testified what was going on before the U.S. Senate Internal Security Subcommittee. (The Eisenhower Administration dissociated itself from the hearings.) Although his remarks were generally accurate, Cubans were doubly angry that he was testifying before an organ concerned with internal American security—as though Cuba were part of the United States!—and one that was chaired by a Senator who was a notorious friend of Trujillo, as well as a segregationist. Diaz Lanz was reviled as a traitor. At about the same time, Castro managed a theatrical ousting of President Manuel Urrutia, partly over the latter's complaints about the Communist advance. He was replaced by Osvaldo Dorticos, who had long been closely connected with the Communists, although he was not a party member.

Castro also profited from the destruction of a real plot against Cuba; Trujillo's plan to invade with 5,000 troops to restore Batista. (The U.S. government's position toward Batista was outlined by Eisenhower, who ordered that if he set foot on American soil he was to be arrested.) Trujillo's scheme was foiled with the help of a "sting" orchestrated by Castro's government, in which William Morgan played an important part, pretending to fall in with the Dominican ruler. (Morgan eventually turned against Castro, and got the usual Communist reward; he was executed in March 1961.) Castro could hardly have asked for better publicity. Trujillo, a sadistic killer, was the most hated man in the Western hemisphere, and then had far more blood on his hands than Castro. The Americans would find out that any action, even gesture, against Castro had to be accompanied by one against Trujillo.

In the fall of 1959, Castro moved against the remaining moderates and many of his old followers. Diaz Lanz again provided a convenient "provocation." In October, flying from the United States, he dropped leaflets on Havana from an old B-25 bomber, defending his record and attacking Castro. Anti-aircraft fire killed two people on the ground. Castro absurdly claimed that Diaz Lanz had dropped bombs, described the affair as worse than the Pearl Harbor attack, and blamed the United States for it. He used it to rouse people against both the Americans and his internal opposition. Anti-Americanism, at its most latent before 1959, now proved a good bet, not only in Cuba itself, but elsewhere. American criticism and hostility just made Castro more popular at home and in the rest of Latin America.

Huber Matos, an M26 hero who governed Camaguey province, had resigned over the Communist issue just before this. Matos was now accused of treason, and he and some of his supporters were court-martialed. Matos spent the next two decades in prison. Castro also reversed the victory of a non-Communist majority in the trade unions congress election and forced through a leadership amenable to the Communists. Reputedly anti-Communist M26 members of the Cabinet were replaced by Communists or their friends. Raul became minister of the armed forces. By the summer of 1960, Castro and the PSP controlled the unions, and had eliminated opposition in the press and on TV. Throughout, Castro maintained his hold over the vast majority of Cubans. Mario Llerena described his fellow countrymen as a "Screaming, frenzied parade of human lemmings, marching on to their political suicide."[24]

Castro had long since moved decisively over to the Soviet side in the Cold War, even though both sides moved cautiously lest they provoke a violent American reaction, apart from any question of mutual distrust, which was not absent. (During 1960, Castro seems to have lost enthusiasm for deliberately seeking an American occupation.) As far back as April 1959, Raul had secured Soviet help, getting them to send Spanish Communist exiles to help develop the army and intelligence organs. By March 1960—over two years before the Soviets put missiles in Cuba—Castro offered them a secret submarine base on the island. But Fidel would never be a simple Soviet puppet. The Soviets did not entirely trust him and were disgusted by the waste of their lavish aid. Sometimes, during the 1960s, Soviet–Cuban relations would be downright bad, and several times the Soviets plotted to replace him with a more amenable leader—Raul, or one of the old-line Communists.[25]

The Eisenhower Administration (unlike much of American public opinion) had not looked forward to Castro's government, but did not react strongly to some early disquieting signs. And, at no time during 1959, did the U.S. government clearly threaten Castro with destruction should he go over to the Soviet side. (American businessmen, by the way, were at first quite happy with the new regime.) Consul Woolam observed growing anti-U.S. sentiment unhappily. Representative Adam Clayton Powell Jr., one of the farthest-left Democrats, who had been pro-Castro earlier, told State Department officials on March 12 that he was very troubled by what he had seen on a visit to Cuba. He believed that Fidel was on the verge of a breakdown, and the Communists were gaining strength; he was sure Raul and Guevara were Communists.

Castro seemed to have little interest in close contact with the United States— Ambassador Bonsal did not even get to see him until March. Allen Dulles warned the National Security Council on March 26 that the Castro regime was becoming a dictatorship but was not "Communist-dominated." Eisenhower was clearly uneasy by this time. Probably mistakenly, he avoided seeing Castro when the latter visited the United States after an invitation extended to the American newspaper editors. (Secretary of State Herter and Vice President Nixon did meet Castro. Nixon, characteristically, claimed later to have detected Castro's real intentions and recommended overthrowing him; this was a lie.) Much was later made of Eisenhower's failure to meet Castro, which did play into his hands, and it was said that Castro had been spurned in an effort to seek aid. In fact, he had not wanted it, and forbade Lopez-Fresquet, who accompanied him, from asking for aid. Actually, Cuba's economy was doing so well, at that time, that there would have been little non-political justification for U.S. aid. Castro used the visit to pose as a moderate and win time. The Agrarian Reform Law triggered consternation in American investors, but only a cautious diplomatic reaction. Bonsal, a particular advocate of caution, made clear that the United States did not contest land reform in principle, while Castro was careful to lead the Americans to expect adequate compensation. The Americans did not react too strongly even to Castro's expeditions to the Dominican Republic and other places; after their quick failure, Castro seemed to disavow them.

The events of October and November, however, convinced everyone in the Administration, even the patient Bonsal, that Castro's regime was hopelessly hostile, although the CIA was curiously reluctant to admit that he had fully gone over to the Communist side. Some pondered cutting Cuba's sugar quota, or some other overt economic sanctions, but Bonsal and others counseled against such actions. (When finally undertaken, in the summer of 1960 and after, they proved self-defeating.) Bonsal was, as he admitted later, wildly overoptimistic, believing that Cubans' alleged love of freedom would turn them against the Castro regime. A new policy was outlined by Secretary Herter on November 5. The United States should quietly encourage opposition to Castro, but undertake no overt hostility or intervention. Eisenhower made one last public attempt to reconcile with Cuba in January. Only in March 1960, did the Americans adopt a policy aimed at just overthrowing Castro.[26]

American policy has often been much criticized, usually for being too unfriendly to Castro, which is ridiculous. But it is hard to see any point, from 1958 to 1960, at which the downward spiral could have been interrupted. Only a more active American policy aimed at toppling Batista in 1958, perhaps by backing a scheme advanced by Venezuela's new democratic government, which was willing to intervene in Cuba militarily if necessary, might have led to a different end. The belated ideas for a caretaker government or third force were based on elements already weak and discredited, while Castro was always too popular and too deft at manipulating other Cubans to be stopped in 1959 or later. Even the *false* appearance of American actions against him seemed to help him. Bonsal, who liked Cubans, gloomily concluded that the Castro-Communist takeover met with a minimum of resistance; "seldom has so much been taken from so many, in terms of both moral and material goods, in so short a time and with so little opposition."[27] It is hard to avoid concluding that, with all due respect to those who fought at the Bay of Pigs and in the Sierra Escambray, Cubans deserve less sympathy than any other people who fell under Communist rule.

Castro and his success roused much enthusiasm on the Latin American left, and even among some earlier moderates. Although the Soviets and old Moscow-line Communists were a bit cautious about whether the Cuban experience could be repeated, many others were less so. As Theodore Draper, an early and able student of the Cuban Revolution wrote in 1962, "It does not seem more far-fetched that Cuba could set off a Latin American revolution than that the tiny group in the Sierra Maestra should have set off a Cuban Revolution."

The distinctive ideas of "Castroism," as it was soon dubbed, were that the Cuban Revolution had been a peasant revolution waged overwhelmingly by rural guerrillas, and that a "revolutionary situation" need not be awaited or prepared for, but could almost be created, and that the "objective conditions" for revolution existed in most if not all of Latin America. A small, armed group could set a revolution in motion without much preparation and defeat a regular army. Even Guevara, the main enthusiast for this doctrine, which actually ignored much of what had really happened in Cuba, at first qualified this, limiting the focus of struggle to the most poorly developed countries and excluded the possibility of applying the Cuban lesson to those countries that enjoyed "bourgeois-democratic" institutions. In his initial writings, such as "Guerrilla Warfare" Guevara even implied that the "Cuban road" might only be practical in the exceptionally vicious and unpopular Caribbean tyrannies. But Castro, and Guevara in particular, eventually dropped those cautions and concluded that their ideas could be applied virtually everywhere; a group of 30–50 armed men could start an armed struggle in almost any Latin American country. Indeed, Castro would initiate a kind of "little Cold War" against democratic Venezuela, and invest more effort supporting the guerrillas there than in those fighting the dictatorships. By June, 1962, Castro told the Soviets that just about all the Central American states, except Mexico, and several in South America—not only Venezuela, but Brazil, Argentina, Peru, and Paraguay were ripe for revolution. Guevara's reckless dogmas led to his death in 1967 and a sort of sainthood, which was a bit strange for a man who declared that "we must follow the road to liberation, even if it costs millions of atomic victims." Luckily, it did not come to that, but Latin America supplied plenty of victims anyway. Some Latin American Communist parties, sometimes in alliance with, sometimes in conflict with, new "Castroite" groups tried to carry out Castro's ideas. The "Castroite" groups, typically named Movimento Izquierda Revolucionario—Movement of the Revolutionary Left or MIR for short—were composed partly of breakaways from the Communists, but mostly from recently radicalized moderates, who were typically dumber and more violent than the Communist old believers. Both types of organization got Cuban training and other help. Civil wars started in no less than seven countries in the 1960s and 1970s—Venezuela, Colombia, Peru, Guatemala, Nicaragua, El Salvador, and Bolivia. In the end, all these Communist ventures failed, save for that in Nicaragua, and that succeeded only after many years of struggle and many ups and downs. As Moscow and some of the older Communists had suspected, the Cuban success could not be reproduced. The later guerillas, despite enjoying Cuban help, were openly Communist and could not duplicate Castro's deception. The governments attacked usually got American aid, although careful scholars have concluded that that was not decisive. The upper and middle classes, and the armed forces, of most of Latin America were not quite as feckless and stupid as their Cuban counterparts. Most countries were badly off, but were not suffering quite as much as those under the Caribbean tyrants. Nor were democratic reform elements as weak or discredited. As in Cuba, but more so, most Latin Americans actually lived in towns and cities, albeit mostly in hideous slums. Rural guerrilla warfare was not the road to power.[28]

The United States learned lessons, although some wrong, from the Cuban experience. Even before Castro won, the famous attack on Richard Nixon in Caracas in May 1958, in which he was nearly killed by hysterical Venezuelans, and the advice of the President's brother Milton, had inspired a degree of liberalization of American policy in Latin America. There was more willingness to extend aid, and dissociate the United States from the Caribbean tyrants. Milton's investigations convinced Ike that we had been making serious errors by *indiscriminate* aid. He concluded, in his memoirs, that, save in exceptional circumstances, foreign aid should be granted mainly to countries that maintained or were moving toward a governmental system and social methods that command the respect and support of a vast majority of its citizens. Otherwise our aid, if it helps to sustain in power regimes which are oppressive, may actually become self-defeating. To be effective, our assistance must be discriminating.

That lesson was not always understood. When the Kennedy Administration came into office, along with ideas of "counterinsurgency" that were often a mirror image of Castroite misconceptions, it seized on the "Operation Pan America" plan for Latin American development that had been advanced by Brazil's great President Kubitschek in 1958, in which the Eisenhower Administration had taken an increasing interest. Making it the "answer" to the Castro-Communist threat, the Kennedy Administration redubbed it the "Alliance for Progress," grabbed the credit for it, and sank considerable sums into it. Like most of Eisenhower's successor's plans, it was poorly executed and largely ineffective. While the number of dictatorships had declined by two-thirds during the Eisenhower Administration, there were no less than six military coups in 1962 and 1963.[29]

Latin American democrats might well have told the Kennedy Administration, "Don't help us!"

Notes

1 Of course, many English settlers went to Virginia to get rich quick, but in North America such people were quickly killed off or adjusted themselves to different expectations.

2 Stanislav Andreski, *Parasitism and Subversion* (London: Weidenfeld & Nicolson, 1966); Boris Goldenberg, *The Cuban Revolution and Latin America* (New York: Praeger, 1965), esp. pp. 15–41, 49, 91; Che Guevara, *Guerrilla Warfare*, 3rd ed. revised and updated by Brian Loveman and Thomas M. Davies (Wilmington, NC: SR Books, 1997), p. 27, Loveman and Davies' commentaries and additions constitute most of this book.

3 Andreski, *Parasitism and Subversion*, pp. 91–102, 104, 205–209; Goldenberg, *The Cuban Revolution and Latin America*, pp. 26–28, 136–138, 325–330; Hugh Thomas, *The Cuban Revolution* (New York: Harper Torchbook, 1977), p. 282; Ruth Leacock, *Requiem for Revolution* (Kent, OH: Kent State University Press, 1990), p. 3; Hugh Seton-Watson, *The Imperialist Revolutionaries* (Stanford, CA: Hoover Institution Press, 1977), pp. 83–84; Timothy P. Wickham-Crowley, *Guerrillas and Revolution in Latin America* (Princeton, NJ: Princeton University Press, 1993), p. 76; Dana Munro, *Intervention and Dollar Diplomacy in the Caribbean 1900–1921* (Princeton, NJ: Princeton University Press, 1964), esp. pp. vii, 6, 16, 28, 161–163; Dana Munro, *The United States and the Caribbean Republics 1921–1933* (Princeton, NJ: Princeton University Press, 1968), pp. 12, 300, 379.

4 Stephen Rabe, *Eisenhower and Latin America: The Foreign Policy of Anti-Communism* (Chapel Hill, NC: University of North Carolina Press, 1988), esp. pp. 22, 30–35, 39–40, 77, 86–88, 97–104; Ruby Hart Phillips, *The Cuban Dilemma* (New York: Obolensky, 1961), pp. 245, 347.

5 Ronald Schneider, "Guatemala," in *The Anatomy of Communist Takeovers*, ed. Thomas T. Hammond (New Haven, CT: Yale University Press, 1977), pp. 563–582; Rabe, *Eisenhower and Latin America*, pp. 42–59; Goldenberg, *The Cuban Revolution and Latin America*, pp. 65–74.

6 The Kennedy quote is from Mario Lazo, *Dagger in the Heart* (New York: Funk & Wagnalls, 1968).
7 Goldenberg, *The Cuban Revolution and Latin America*, pp. 101–102, 120–132; Thomas, *The Cuban Revolution*, pp. 314, 320–327, 338, 344; Ramon Eduardo Ruiz, *Cuba* (New York: Norton, 1970), esp. pp. 13–14, 40–46, 104–106, 109–110, 149–154, 159–160; Theodore Draper, *Castro's Revolution* (New York: Praeger, 1962), pp. 21–23; Theodore Draper, *Castroism: Theory and Practice* (New York: Praeger, 1965), pp. 107–108; Rufo Lopez-Fresquet, *My Fourteen Months with Castro* (Cleveland, OH: World Publishing, 1966), pp. 5–11, 17, 19–24, 116, 185; Wickham-Crowley, *Guerrillas and Revolution in Latin America*, pp. 158–166; Daniel James, *Cuba: First Soviet Satellite in the Americas* (New York: Avon, 1961), pp. 17–21, 30; Phillips, *The Cuban Dilemma*, pp. 20–21, 66; Ramon L. Bonachea and Marta San Martin, *The Cuban Insurrection 1952–1959* (New Brunswick, NJ: Transaction, 1974), pp. 8, 31–34. For a classic statement of the "poor underdeveloped Cuba exploited by the United States" and a "peasant revolution" unwillingly forced into the arms of the Soviets, cf. Maurice Zeitlin and Robert Scheer, *Cuba: Tragedy in Our Hemisphere* (New York: Grove Press, 1963).
8 Tad Szulc, *Fidel* (New York: William Morrow, 1986) is probably the best biography of Castro. Also of interest are James, *Cuba*, pp. 38–41; Lopez-Fresquet, *My Fourteen Months with Castro*, pp. 159–160. 165, 185–186; Lionel Martin, *The Early Fidel* (Secaucus: Lyle Stuart, 1978), esp. 15–16; Goldenberg, *The Cuban Revolution and Latin America*, p. 176; Leycester Colman and Julia Sweig, *The Real Fidel Castro* (New Haven, CT: Yale University Press, 2003), esp. pp. 15, 55, 66, 128; Draper, *Castroism*, 21ff.
    There have been at least five theories of Castro's political development and relations with the Communists:

1) Castro was always a Communist, and the Cuban Revolution was designed and executed by the PSP and Moscow. The classic statement of this theory was Nathaniel Weyl (*Red Star Over Cuba*, New York: Devin Adair, 1960). This was not supported by Soviet records, and was always dubious because the Communists openly and bitterly opposed Castro and his movement up to 1958, and Castro was always visibly on bad terms with the old-line PSP leaders. And, as Lopez-Fresquet pointed out (*My Fourteen Months with Castro*, pp. 159–160), his expedition to Cuba in 1956 was not carried out as if it had been supported by the PSP.
2) Castro was, as he professed to be in the 1950s, a non-Communist, and perhaps not even very radical, until he was pushed into the Communist arms by American hostility. One classic statement of this theory was the manifesto in the *New York Times*, signed by sixty Harvard professors, published on May 10, 1961; another was the Zeitlin and Scheer book cited earlier. This argument is even more absurd than the previous theory, inverting the actual chronology; but it seems to be still widely believed by leftists and even liberals. For recent examples of this, in supposedly scholarly works, cf. Richard Aldrich, *The Hidden Hand* (New York: Overlook Press, 2001), p. 608, and, in a very modulated form, Howard Jones, *The Bay of Pigs* (New York: Oxford University Press, 2005), an otherwise reasonable account.
3) Castro was not a Communist party member or a believer in Marxist–Leninism until 1959, and decided to go over to the Communist side for his own reasons only after taking power. Classic statements of this theory were the accounts by Theodore Draper, Boris Goldenberg, Hugh Thomas, and Ramon Eduardo Ruiz. This thesis, advanced by some of the most able students of the revolution, was more or less orthodox from the 1960s until fairly recently, despite the awkward point that Castro's closest associates—his brother and Guevara—were well known to have been PSP members of long standing.
4) A later theory held that, while Castro was not originally a Leninist, although perhaps "predisposed" in that direction, he decided to cross over to the Communists earlier, in 1958. Supporters of this view included Tad Szulc, *Fidel*, pp. 48–51, 453; Lopez-Fresquet, *My Fourteen Months with Castro*, pp. 159–160; and Mario Llerena,

The Unsuspected Revolution (Ithaca, NY: Cornell University Press, 1978), pp. 200, 235. This theory confused the evidence of Castro's entente or rapprochement with the PSP leadership with his conversion to Communism, which had taken place long before.

5) The theory advanced above—Castro was a Marxist-Leninist, but not a Communist party member, who always intended to create a Communist regime. This theory was tentatively advanced as early as 1961 in one of the first American accounts of the Cuban Revolution, Daniel James' *Cuba*, pp. 38–41, 134, and strongly supported by Lionel Martin in his *The Early Fidel*, and Colman's *The Real Fidel Castro*, and evidence of Castro's early friendly contacts with the KGB. Fursenko and Naftali, *Khrushchev's Cold War*, 285 n. 15, show that, contrary to rather unlikely earlier accounts, Fidel was well aware of his brother's membership in the PSP.

9 Bonachea and San Martin, *The Cuban Insurrection*, pp. 4, 14–28; Szulc, *Fidel*, pp. 214–298; Robert Quirk, *Fidel Castro* (New York: Norton, 1993), pp. 52–58; Martin, *The Early Fidel*, pp. 115–149; Draper, *Castroism*, pp. 5–6.

10 Bonachea and San Martin, *The Cuban Insurrection*, pp. 29–89; Szulc, *Fidel*, pp. 321–323; Draper, *Castroism*, pp. 71–72; Julia Sweig, *Inside the Cuban Revolution* (Cambridge, MA: Harvard University Press, 2002), pp. 7–13; Daniel James, *Che Guevara* (New York: Stein & Day, 1970), esp. pp. 77–89; Ernesto Che Guevara, *Reminiscences of the Cuban Revolutionary War* (New York: Grove Press, n.d.), pp. 40–43.

11 Bonachea and San Martin, *The Cuban Insurrection*, pp. 89–104; 383–413; Sweig, *Inside the Cuban Revolution*, pp. 13–19; Guevara, *Reminiscences of the Cuban Revolutionary War*, pp. 54–91.

12 Bonachea and San Martin, *The Cuban Insurrection*, pp. 109–138; Colman and Sweig, *The Real Fidel Castro*, p. 121.

13 Bonachea and San Martin, *The Cuban Insurrection*, pp. 95–104, 138–187; Sweig, *Inside the Cuban Revolution*, pp. 13–17, 46–47, 61–63, 100–105. Guevara, *Reminiscences of the Cuban Revolutionary War*, pp. 196–205, 240, belittles the efforts and motives of the "llano."

14 Bonachea and San Martin, *The Cuban Insurrection*, pp. 161–167; Szulc, *Fidel*, pp. 426–427; Sweig, *Inside the Cuban Revolution*, pp. 33–36, 67–77, 89–91.

15 Szulc, *Fidel*, pp. 427–428; Sweig, *Inside the Cuban Revolution*, p. 201 n. 1. Virtually no history of the CIA deals with this matter.

16 Lopez-Fresquet, *My Fourteen Months with Castro*, p. 31; Thomas, *The Cuban Revolution*, pp. 163–165, 181–182, 203; Philip Bonsal, *Cuba, Castro and the United States* (Pittsburgh, PA: University of Pittsburgh Press, 1971), pp. 17, 21–22, 31–32; Sweig, *Inside the Cuban Revolution*, pp. 67, 84–87; *Foreign Relations of the United States 1958–1960, Volume VI* (Washington DC: Government Printing Office, 1991), pp. 5–10, 13–14, 30–36, 38, 46–47, 59, 60, 65, 67–70, 90–92; Wayne Smith, *The Closest of Enemies* (New York: Norton, 1987), pp. 20–21; Paul Bethel, *The Losers* (New Rochelle, NY: Arlington, 1969), pp. 61–62, 67.

17 Sweig, *Inside the Cuban Revolution*, pp. 7, 46–47, 104–108, 121–151, 171; Bonachea and San Martin, *The Cuban Insurrection*, pp. 201–222.

18 Szulc, *Fidel*, pp. 48–51, 62, 453; Martin, *The Early Fidel*, pp. 218–219; Thomas, *The Cuban Revolution*, pp. 198–199, 225–226; Llerena, *The Unsuspected Revolution*, pp. 161–173, 198, 200, 225; Lopez-Fresquet, *My Fourteen Months with Castro*, pp. 159–160, 164–167, 177–178; Bonachea and San Martin, *The Cuban Insurrection*, pp. 220–221.

19 Lopez-Fresquet, *My Fourteen Months with Castro*, pp. 81, 164–167, 177–178, 200; Bonsal, *Cuba, Castro and the United States*, pp. 64–67; Thomas, *The Cuban Revolution*, pp. 225–226; Szulc, *Fidel*, p. 51; Guevara, *Guerrilla Warfare*, pp. 140–147. The grandiose strategy here attributed to Castro resembles ideas entertained by other Communist leaders, notably Mao. Some Nicaraguan Sandinista leaders are known to have thought along similar lines in the 1980s, but, as in Cuba, the Americans failed to play along.

20 Bonachea and San Martin, *The Cuban Insurrection*, pp. 187–198, 227–262; Szulc, *Fidel*, pp. 445–446.

21 Bonachea and San Martin, *The Cuban Insurrection*, p. 244; Szulc, *Fidel*, pp. 447–450; *FRUS 1958–1960, Vol. VI*, pp. 90–91, 109–111, 1113–116, 122–132, 140–141, 147–148, 157, 174–179, 180, 183–185, 201, 237–238, 243, 245, 272–273; John Dorschner and Roberto Fabricio, *The Winds of December* (New York: Coward, McCann & Geoghegan, 1980), pp. 92–93; Fairchild and Poole, *The Joint Chiefs and National Policy 1957–1960*, p. 179.

22 Dorschner and Fabricio, *The Winds of December*, pp. 171, 198–204, 207–210, 320–330, 353–354; Bonachea and San Martin, *The Cuban Insurrection*, pp. 263, 267–301; Guevara, *Reminiscences of the Cuban Revolutionary War*, pp. 243ff.; James, *Che Guevara*, pp. 98–99; Neil McCaulay, *A Rebel in Cuba* (Chicago, IL: Quadrangle, 1970). The story of William Morgan is told in Aran Shetterley, *The Americano* (Chapel Hill, NC: Algonquin, 2007).

23 Dorschner and Fabricio, *The Winds of December*, pp. 223, 226, 239, 285–286, 314–318, 323, 342–345, 365, 423–424, 445, 455, 460–461; Bonachea and San Martin, *The Cuban Insurrection*, pp. 303–328; Thomas, *The Cuban Revolution*, pp. 233–235, 237, 241, 244–245; Aleksandr Fursenko and Timothy Naftali, *One Hell of a Gamble* (New York: Norton, 1997), pp. 11–12; Eisenhower, *Waging Peace*, p. 521; Fairchild and Poole, *The Joint Chiefs and National Policy 1957–1960*, p. 180; *FRUS 1958–1960, Vol. VI*, pp. 163–168, 245, 265–268, 271, 279, 281, 302–303, 313, 316, 323–328, 331, 347, 349, 352, 355, 362–363, 390–391; Bonsal, *Cuba, Castro and the United States*, pp. 22–28, 39–41, 59.

24 Goldenberg, *The Cuban Revolution and Latin America*, pp. 179–187, 184, 201, 203, 210–218, 223–226, 293, 311; Thomas, *The Cuban Revolution*, pp. 276, 283, 291–293, 295, 298, 301, 423, 435–455, 464, 473–474; Bonsal, *Cuba, Castro and the United States*, pp. 5–6, 51, 68, 71, 75, 79–80, 97–100, 100, 115; Szulc, *Fidel*, pp. 463–464, 472–477; James, *Cuba*, pp. 104–105, 125–126, 151, 156, 173; Lopez-Fresquet, *My Fourteen Months with Castro*, pp. 135, 169–170; Shetterley, *The Americano*, pp. 164, 170, 181–199; *FRUS 1958–1960, Vol. VI*, pp. 345–346, 380–381, 440–442, 55, 579, 631–632, 702–703; Llerena, *The Unsuspected Revolution*, p. 251.

25 Fursenko and Naftali, *One Hell of a Gamble*, pp. 11–12; Fursenko and Naftali, *Khrushchev's Cold War*, p. 302.

26 Bonsal, *Cuba, Castro and the United States*, pp. 5–7, 28, 36–37, 51, 59, 61, 70–71, 75, 80–81, 93–94, 97–100, 106, 115; *FRUS 1958–1960, Vol. VI*, pp. 347, 356, 362–363, 369, 372–375, 380–381, 383, 395–396, 401–404, 424–428, 431–432, 440–444, 458–466, 468, 475–476, 482–483, 490, 492–493, 509–510, 512, 515–516, 529–530, 553–554, 605–612, 615–620, 627–628, 635–637, 648–650, 658–663.

27 Bonsal, *Cuba, Castro and the United States*, pp. 4, 23.

28 Draper, *Castro's Revolution*, p. 108; Draper, *Castroism*, pp. 40–43, 46–48, 50–55, 60–63, 68–69; Goldenberg, *The Cuban Revolution and Latin America*, pp. 353–355; James, *Che Guevara*, pp. 308–309, 337, 341, 347, 349; Guevara, *Guerrilla Warfare*, pp. x, 7–14, 50–51, 184ff.; William Ratliff, *Castroism and Communism in Latin America 1959–1976* (Washington DC: American Enterprise/Hoover Institution, 1976), esp. pp. 2–4, 18–31, 130–133; Wickham-Crowley, *Guerrillas and Revolution in Latin America*; Robert J. Alexander, *Romulo Betancourt and the Transformation of Venezuela* (New Brunswick, NJ: Transaction, 1982), pp. 481–493, 543–545; Robert J. Alexander, *The Communist Party of Venezuela* (Stanford, CA: Stanford University Press, 1969; "Soviet Report By (sic) Cuban Involvement in Assisting Partisans in Other Latin American Countries," 9 June 1962, Cold War International History Project digital archive. wilsoncenter. org/document A 114518. Wickham-Crowley and Loveman and Davies' accounts in their edition of Che Guevara, *Guerrilla Warfare*, which actually constitute most of the book, are among the few American accounts of the Castro-inspired struggles in Latin America but make up for this with their excellence.

29 Eisenhower, *Waging Peace*, p. 623.

EPILOGUE

As we noted earlier, the problem in the late 1950s for the United States and the West was not winning the Cold War, but surviving it—or put another way, not losing it. Although, in many ways, they were better men than their successors, it was not given to Eisenhower and the other Western leaders to see victory. The major crises and tensions they dealt with were halted short of disaster; they had trailed off or subsided, but would recur.

In the period after Sputnik, the Americans and the other Western powers had sometimes succeeded, sometimes failed in their polices, which sometimes were not wise. With difficulty, the immediate crisis in morale after Sputnik was more or less surmounted. Despite the post-Sputnik fears, the U.S. allies had not collapsed. The Western powers had fended off the Soviet offensive in Berlin, and prevented a complete collapse of their weak allies in the Middle East, and East and Southeast Asia. The courageous but very (and understandably) unpopular American stand over the Taiwan Straits had helped to weaken the Soviet–Chinese alliance. They had failed to overthrow Sukarno, or change the basic unfavorable trends in the Middle East. The overt success of the Lebanon landing, and the failed intervention in the Indonesian Civil War had frightened Nasser, Sukarno and others into veering away from the Soviets for a time. But the basic orientation—and hostility to the West—of many Arabs, and of Sukarno's regime had not changed at all. After a short interval of feigned reasonableness, Nasser and Sukarno reverted to their previous stances. And, thanks to Castro's victory a whole new front in the Cold War had opened up. Khrushchev's offensive would be renewed, and converging with the unexpected triumph in Cuba, would produce the greatest crisis of the Cold War.

INDEX

Adams, Sherman 60, 70
Adenauer, Konrad 141, 146, 152, 155
Advanced Research Projects Agency 68, 86, 88
The Affluent Society 71
Allen, George 96, 114
Alliance for Progress (Operation Pan America) 205
Allison, John 106–107
Alpha Plan for Arab–Israeli settlement 95–96
America—Second Class Power 61
America—Too Young to Die 61
"Arab socialism" 92
"Argus" nuclear tests 84
arms control 27
Army Ballistic Missile Agency 39, 54, 66, 86
Aswan Dam 96–97
Atomic Energy Commission 68–69
"atomic plenty" 24, 36
Aviation Week 60

Baath party 91, 100, 101, 112
baby boom 5
Baghdad Pact 94, 95, 99
Baldwin, Hanson 61
Ballistic Missile Early Warning System 67, 71
Batista, Fulgencio 184, 185, 186–187, 188, 190, 192, 193, 194, 196, 197–198, 199, 201

Beria, Lavrenti 45, 50
Berlin 1, 24, 29, 31, 76, 140–142
Berlin blockade of 1948–1949 24
Berlin crisis of 1958–1959 142–157, 209
Bohlen, Charles 26, 121
"bomber gap" 38
Bonesteel, Charles 35
Bonsal, Philip 198, 202–203
Braun, Wernher von 54, 61, 64, 65, 85
Brentano, Heinrich, von 182–183
Britain 43, 58–59, 66, 78, 80, 152; policy in Berlin crisis 143, 145, 146, 147, 149, 151–153, 155; policy in Indonesian Civil War, 167, 172, 173; policy in Middle East 90, 92–99, 105, 107, 108, 112, 122, 134, 135; policy in Southeast Asia 161
Burke, Arleigh 129, 130, 195, 198

Carney, Robert 37, 120, 122
Castro, Fidel 2, 106, 177, 209; attempts to stir revolution in other countries, 192, 202, 203–204; background, character and views 185–186, 206n8; early program 186, 188; entente with Communist party, 191; landing in Oriente and revolutionary war 187–198; plans for war with US 191–192, 201; rule over Cuba 198–202
"Castroism" 203–205
Castro, Ramon 186

Castro, Raul 185, 189, 191, 191, 192, 194, 195, 201, 202
Causes of World War III 72
Central Intelligence Agency 25, 28, 31, 40, 41, 60, 64, 78, 79, 94, 96, 107, 142, 163, 168, 170, 171, 181, 189, 197
Chamoun, Camille 102–105, 106, 108–109
Chehab, Fuad 103–105, 108–109
Chiang Ching-kuo 130
Chiang Kai-shek (Jiang Jieshi) 3, 35, 118–119, 124, 125–136, 168, 173
China 24, 27, 31, 35, 36–37, 117–137; Geneva and Warsaw contacts with US, 124, 126, 134–135; offshore islands, 117–118
Chinese Nationalists 21, 25, 117–120, 124–131, 133, 134–136, 166, 168, 173
"Chinese Titoism" 31
Christofilos, Nicolas 84
Churchill, Winston 94, 112
Cold War 1–3, 22; United States policy and strategy 24–38
Commentary 72
Concept of the Corporation 7, 48
Cuba: background of revolution and social problems 182–183; Castro's rule 198–203; Communist Party (PSP) 184, 185, 191, 199; economy 182–183, 199, 200; guerrilla war 187–198; legends about 177, 182; Soviet policy toward 198, 199, 201–202; United States intervention 183, 184; United States policy 189–190, 194–195, 197–198
Cuban Missile crisis 75, 77, 177
Cutler, Robert 36
"Czech arms deal" 54, 95, 96

De Gaulle, Charles 146
De Seversky, Alexander 61
de-Stalinization 50–51
Diaz Lanz, Pedro 200, 201
Directorio Revolutinario (DR) 186, 188, 189, 191, 196, 200
Dominican Republic 180, 192, 200, 201, 202
domino theory 120, 159, 161–162, 165, 175n2
Drucker, Peter 7, 48

Dulles, Allen 26, 27, 64, 64, 78, 90, 104, 125, 144, 168, 169, 170, 171, 172, 173, 202
Dulles, John Foster 2, 25–27, 29, 31, 32, 33, 59, 60, 63, 121–122, 124, 126, 130; Berlin crisis 135–137, 143, 144, 145, 147, 148, 149, 150, 151; Cuban revolution 1995 198; on Chiang Kai-shek and
authoritarian allies 118–119; First Indochina War 161–162; "hot negotiations" debate 35–37; intervention in Indonesian Civil War 163, 164, 166, 167–174; intervention in Lebanon 103, 104–105, 106–109, 110; Iran 113; IRBM bases 79; Latin American policies 181; Middle East policies 94, 96, 97, 99, 101; on neutralism 26–27; on problems of underdeveloped world 90; on Sputnik 60, 71; Taiwan Straits crisis 119–137
Dyson, Freeman 88

East Germany 141–142, 143, 146, 147, 152
Eden, Anthony 30, 97, 98, 112
Edsel 71
Egypt and United Arab Republic 91, 92, 94–102, 103, 104, 105, 110
"Eisenhower Doctrine" 99–100, 108
Eisenhower, Dwight D. and Eisenhower Administration 1–8, 11–16, 60, 61, 66, 68; attitude to Chiang and Chinese Nationalists 118–123; Berlin crisis 144, 146–148; 149–150, 151–152, 154, 155, 156; character and ideas 11–14, 18–19; civil rights 14–15; critiques of 11, 16, 37, 60–64; defense reorganization 68; domino theory 161–162, fear of nuclear war 28–29; foreign policy 25–28; intervention in Indonesian civil war 166, 169, 171, 173; intervention in Lebanon 106–109, 116; missile development 38–43; missile gap 77–79; "New Look" strategy 32–33, 37; policies in Latin America 181–182; policy in Cuban revolution 189–190, 194, 197–198; policy toward Cuba under Castro 198, 200–201, 202–203; reaction to incidents on Soviet border 77; reaction to Sputnik 59, 60–73; space program 87–89; Suez crisis

97–99; Taiwan Straits crisis 117–123, 126–137

Eisenhower, Milton 11, 204

Felt, Harry 128, 130
Films 16–17
Finland 53, 140
First Indochina War 159–162
Formosa *see* Taiwan
Formosa Resolution 121, 126
France: in Berlin crisis 144–145, 146, 150; in Indochina 159–162; in Middle East 97, 98
Fulbright, J. William 107, 121, 152, 158n16

Gaither Report 62–64
Galbraith, John Kenneth 71
Gardner, Trevor 39, 41, 60, 61, 65
Geneva Conference on Berlin 151, 153–156,
Geneva Conference on Indochina 162
George Washington 67, 83
German missile team 39, 66
Ghana 54
Grapes of Wrath 48
Great Arms Race 61
Greek Civil War 24
Gromyko, Andrei 132, 134, 153, 154
Guatemala 96, 181–182
Guevara, Ernesto "Che" 186, 187, 192, 194, 195, 195, 196, 199, 203–204
"guided democracy" 166, 168, 174
guilt complexes 21, 30, 93
Guinea 54

"Hardtack" nuclear tests 84
Harriman, Averell 155
Hatta, Mohammed 164, 166
Have Spacesuit, Will Travel 61
Herter, Christian 113, 127, 129, 151, 153, 154, 155, 202
Ho Chi Minh 166
Hook, Sidney 72
"hot negotiations" 34–38, 63
Hughes, H. Stuart 72
Humphrey, Hubert 110, 121, 147
Hungarian revolution 50, 97, 99

Indochina 24, 27, 28, 36, 159–162
Indonesia 54, 90, 159, 160, 162–175; American intervention 167–175; civil

war 166–173; Communist party 160, 164–165, 166, 167, 175; coup and massacres of 1965 174; problems in 1950s and 1960s 163–164
intercontinental ballistic missiles (ICBMs) 38–42, 54–55, 57–58, 59, 63, 64, 67, 68, 75–76, 81–83, 86, 149; *see also* missiles
intermediate-range ballistic missiles (IRBMs) 42, 59, 61, 63, 67, 75, 79–81; *see also* missiles
Iran 92, 93, 94, 96, 109, 110, 112–114
Iraq 54, 91, 92, 94–95, 100, 102, 104, 107, 108, 111–112
Iraqi revolution of 1958 105–106, 107, 109
Israel and Arab–Israeli conflict 90, 91, 95, 96, 97–98, 106, 109, 111

Jackson, Henry 41, 59, 88
Japan 24, 110, 130, 159, 160
Jet Propulsion Laboratory 65, 66, 69, 87
Jinmen (Kinmen, Quemoy) 119–120, 121, 122, 125, 126, 127, 128, 129, 131, 132, 133, 134, 135
Johnson, Lyndon and the Johnson Committee 63, 65
Joint Chiefs of Staff, 25, 30, 34–36, 68, 99, 124, 126, 127, 130, 136, 144, 149, 156, 161, 172
Jones, Howard 171–172, 174
Jordan 91, 94, 96, 100, 102, 104–105, 106, 109

Kassim, Abdul 105, 106, 109, 110, 112
Kennedy, John F. and Kennedy Administration 11, 79, 80–81, 161, 174, 182, 205
Khrushchev, Nikita 2–3, 14, 26, 29, 34, 38, 45–54, 57, 58, 97, 98, 101, 103, 106, 110–111, 132, 135, 136–137, 142, 144, 145–146, 151–155; agricultural policies 39, 47–48, 52; character and views 47, 48–49; decision to launch Berlin crisis 143–144; foreign policy 52–54; Indonesia 165; missile bluff 75–76; views on nuclear war 47, 49
Killian, James and Killian Report 40–41, 64
Kistiakowsky, George 64, 77
Knowland, William 12, 34, 36, 37, 70, 121

Korean War 5, 11, 13, 24, 25, 27, 28, 31, 32, 53, 93–94, 117–118, 121, 147, 161
Korolev, Sergei 57, 76
Kozlov, Frol 49, 156
Kuwait 99, 106

labor movement 4, 8
Latin America: influence of Cuban revolution 203–204; myth of revolution 179; society and problems 93, 177–182; United States' role and intervention 11, 77, 179–182; "vampire complex" 181
Lebanon 92, 99; civil war 102–105, 111; United States' landing and intervention 103, 104–105, 106–109, 111, 112, 209; reaction to 109–111
Li Zhisu 125, 132
"liberation" 25
Libya 91, 96, 99, 104
Life and Time-Life organization 16, 60, 71
Lippman, Walter 61, 110
literature 16
Lloyd, Selwyn 26, 145, 149, 150, 151, 153, 154, 171
The London Times 59
Lopez-Fresquet, Rufo 183, 184, 189, 192, 202, 206n8

M-26 movement 186–189, 190, 191, 192, 194, 195, 200, 201
MacMillan, Harold 29, 59, 146, 150–151, 152, 153, 154, 155, 171
Malenkov, Georgi 47, 50, 51, 53
Malinovsky, Rodion 47, 52, 53
manned spaceflight 86–87
Mansfield, Mike 121, 152
Mao Zedong 2, 31, 37, 53, 17, 119, 124–125, 127, 132, 137–138, 155
Marshall, S.L.A. 108
"massive retaliation" 26, 32
Matthews, Herbert 188
McCarthyism 11, 14, 21, 61
McClintock, Robert 108, 112
McElroy, Neil 66, 78, 126, 131, 149, 153
Medaris, John 66
Middle East 90–114; basic problems and conflicts 91–93; Cold War in 93–101; Communist parties in 92,

100–101, 106, 111, 112; evolution of nationalism 92–93; Western attitudes and illusions 92, 93, 100
Middle East Resolution ("Eisenhower Doctrine") 99–108
Mikoyan, Anastas 50, 51, 143, 145, 148
Mills, C. Wright 72, 74n11
missile gap 38, 57–58, 64, 70, 74n9, 75–79, 82, 90, 111, 149, 191; intelligence on 64, 76–79
missile race 38–43, 54–55, 57–58, 63–64, 67–68, 75–83
missiles: Atlas 38–40, 54, 67–68, 81–82, 84, 149; Jupiter 42, 43, 66, 67, 79–81, 84, 85, 86; Jupiter-S 42; Minuteman 67–68, 81, 82, 149; Navaho 39, 41; R-5, 34, 143; R-7 42, 43, 54, 57–58, 64, 76, 78, 85, 87; R-9 76; R-16 76; Redstone 39, 42, 66, 84, 86; Polaris 42–43, 54, 67, 68, 78, 82–83, 84; Thor 42, 43, 67, 79–81, 84; Thoric 81; Titan 40, 43, 65, 67, 81–82
Missiles and Rockets 60
Molotov, Vyacheslav 51, 52–53, 95
Moon probes and first race to Moon 85–86
Morgan, William 195, 201
Morgenthau, Hans 60
Mossadeh, Mohammed 113
Murphy, Robert 108, 156, 189

NACA 68, 86, 87
NASA 13, 69, 86–87, 88
Nasser, Gamal 2, 90, 91, 94–102, 103, 104, 105, 106, 110–112, 164, 165, 167, 209
Nasution, Abdul 169, 170, 172
National Security Council 11, 28, 29, 32, 33, 35–37, 63, 64, 78, 90, 109, 120, 122, 126, 151, 161, 162, 167, 169, 173, 197, 202
NATO 29, 32, 53, 59, 76, 79, 80, 100, 110, 122, 127, 141, 142, 143, 147
Nation 110
National and Special National Intelligence Estimates 31, 64, 77, 78, 79, 121, 128, 149, 166, 167
"national democracy" 174
National Review 72
Nedelin, Mitrofan 54, 76
Neumann, John von 39, 41
neutralism 26–27, 30, 31, 91–93
"New Look" strategy 32–34, 35

New Republic 60, 69, 78
New Statesman 59
New York Times 61, 134
Nitze, Paul 63
Nixon, Richard 12, 14, 19, 70, 108,
 202, 204
Northern Tier states 94, 104, 110
NSC 162/2 32, 34, 63
NSC 5501 36, 37, 40
nuclear pulse rocket 88–89
nuclear reactor rocket 41, 87–88
nuclear war 5, 28–29, 31, 33–34
Nuri es-Said 105

OA Cuban revolutionary group
 186, 187
Operation Atom 143
Orion (nuclear pulse rocket) 88–89
overflights of Soviet Union 40, 63,
 76, 77

payola 73
Pearson, Drew 61
Philosophy of the Revolution 91, 94
Pope, Allen 170, 171
Presidential Science Advisory
 Committee 64, 69, 79
preventive war 28, 31, 34, 36, 63
Project Control 34
Project Emily 80
Project Orbiter 61, 65
Project Rover, 87–88

Quarles, Donald 43, 129
Quwatly, Shukri 99

Rabi, Isidore 64
Raborn, William 42–43, 82–83
race and race relations 5, 14–15,
 30, 32, 93, 99, 179, 181, 184,
 185, 200
Radford, Arthur 25, 28, 29, 34–37, 120,
 121, 161
Ramo-Wooldridge 39
Rankin, Karl 119
Reagan, Ronald 12, 13
The Reporter 78
Reuther, Walter 59
Ridgway, Matthew 35, 37, 161
rock 'n' roll 18, 73
rockets, satellites and space probes: Able
 upper stage 84; Aerobee 39; Agena
 upper stage 83, 84; Centaur upper

stage 83, 86; Delta space launcher 84,
 85; Discoverer/Corona reconnaissance
 satellites 83; Explorer 65, 66, 83;
 Jupiter C/Juno I 66, 85; Lunas 85;
 Mariner probes 85; Mars and Venus
 probes 87; Mercury 87; Orbiter 85;
 Pioneer probes, 85; Ranger 85; Saturn
 I and IB 86; Saturn V 58, 86; Vanguard
 60, 65–66, 81, 83, 84; Viking 39, 65;
 Vostok 87; *see also* Sputniks
Roosevelt, Eleanor 30
Roosevelt, Franklin D. 12, 19, 180
Royal Air Force 43, 80
Russell, Bertrand 5

satellite programs 43, 55, 60, 65–66,
 83–84, 85, 87
Saudi Arabia 91, 99–100; 104, 112
Schriever, Bernard 39–40, 42, 79, 80
Skunk Works 46
Smith, Walter Bedell 12, 120
Southeast Asia 24, 32, 91, 122, 131,
 159–175
Soviet Union 25, 28, 36–37; agriculture
 47–48, 52; foreign policy 52–55,
 165; Khrushchev's rule 46–55; policy
 in Indonesia 164–165; policy in the
 Middle East 92–112; reforms 46–49,
 50, 52; relations with China 24, 29,
 31–32, 36, 38, 53, 75, 119, 120, 121,
 124–125, 127, 130; relations with
 neutralists 54, 92–93: relations with
 satellites 50, 52–53
Space Age 58
space gap 58
Sprague, Robert 63
Sputniks 1, 34, 52, 55, 57–58, 78, 83
Stalin, Joseph 46, 47, 49, 50, 52, 53,
 117, 124, 140, 141, 142, 164
Stevenson, Adlai 30, 37, 66
Stewart, Homer 65
Strategic Air Command 63, 67, 77, 78,
 80, 107
Suez Canal and base 92, 94, 95
Suez crisis and Suez–Sinai War 27, 30,
 54, 76, 90, 97–99
Sukarno 2, 90, 91, 163, 164, 166–167,
 171, 173–174, 209
Supreme Court 10, 12
Symington, Stuart 59, 78
Syria 54, 91–92, 96, 98, 100–102, 103,
 107, 112
Syrian crisis 100–101

"T-4A" rocket bomber 58
tactical nuclear weapons 32, 120, 122–123, 126, 127, 128, 129, 130, 131, 136, 137, 147, 150, 161
Taft, Robert 12, 13
Taiwan 24, 32, 118, 120
Taiwan Straits crises: American dilemma 117, 122, 130; American and world opinion 133–134; first crisis 119–123; second crisis 125–137
Talbott, Harold 39
Taylor, Theodore 88
Teapot Committee 39
Teller, Edward 59
Thompson, Llewellyn 144, 151
Trujillo, Rafael 180, 181, 186, 187, 192, 200
Truman, Harry and Truman Administration 6, 11, 13, 25, 29, 31, 41, 61, 65, 160
Turkish Jupiter missile bases 79–81, 100–101, 109
Turkish monitoring and radar station 40, 77, 92, 94
Twentieth Party Congress 50–51
Twining, Nathan 106, 108, 120, 122, 126, 130, 131, 135, 149, 150

U-2 40, 63, 76, 77, 156
Ulam, Stanislaw 88
Ulbricht, Walter 143
United Fruit Corporation 182, 194
United Nations 103, 104, 111, 119, 120, 134, 150
Unites States: attitude toward European empires; 29–30; attitudes to Cold War 4–9; changes after the 1950s 20–21; Cold War policy and strategy 24–38; culture and entertainment 16–18; domestic policies 10–15, 78–79; economy and economic policies 6–7, 20, 69; expectations 4–5; failures in 1950s 19–20; fear for alliances 30–31, 59; fear of nuclear war 25, 27, 28, 29, 59; and Latin America 177, 179–183; policy in Cuba 189–190, 194–195, 197–198; policy in Indonesia 162–175; policy in Middle East 93–114; policies to split Soviet–Chinese alliance 32, 35; popular attitudes toward Fidel Castro 188, 192, 195; post-Sputnik policies 67; poverty 8–9; reactions to the Sputniks 57–62, 71–73; recession of 1957–1958 69; revival of radicalism 62; social conditions 4–21; 71–73; social criticism of late 1950s 61–62, 71–73

Van Allen, James 84
Van Allen radiation belts 84, 87
Venezuela 178, 181, 192, 200, 203, 204
Vietnam see Indochina
Virgin Lands 47–48

Warsaw Pact 53
West Germany 110, 141–142, 152–153, 155
Western Development Division 39, 41
Whalen, William 76
What Ivan Knows and Johnny Doesn't 62
White, Thomas 34, 161
Why Johnny Can't Read 62
Wilson, Charles E. ("Engine Charlie") 25, 27–28, 34, 43, 99, 120

X-15 rocket plane and spaceship 68, 87

Yangel, Mikhail 76
Yemen 91, 101, 112

Zahedi, Fazollah 113
Zhou Enlai (Chou En-lai) 132
Zhukov, Georgi 51–52